An Introduction to Feminism

As well as providing a clear and critical introduction to the theory, this refreshing overview focuses on the practice of feminism with coverage of actions and activism, bringing the subject to life for newcomers as well as offering fresh perspectives for advanced students. Explanations of the main strands to feminism, such as liberalism, sit alongside an exploration of a range of approaches, such as radical, anarchist and Marxist feminism, and provide much-needed context against which more familiar historical themes may be understood. The author's broad and inclusive view conveys the diversity and disagreement within feminism with accessible clarity. The analysis of key terms equips readers with a critical understanding of the vocabulary of feminist debates that will be invaluable to undergraduate students.

LORNA FINLAYSON is Lecturer in Philosophy in the School of Philosophy and Art History at the University of Essex. She is the author of *The Political Is Political: Conformity and the Illusion of Dissent in Contemporary Political Philosophy* (2015).

An Introduction to Feminism

LORNA FINLAYSON

CAMBRIDGE
UNIVERSITY PRESS

CAMBRIDGE
UNIVERSITY PRESS

University Printing House, Cambridge CB2 8BS, United Kingdom

One Liberty Plaza, 20th Floor, New York, NY 10006, USA

477 Williamstown Road, Port Melbourne, VIC 3207, Australia

314-321, 3rd Floor, Plot 3, Splendor Forum, Jasola District Centre, New Delhi - 110025, India

79 Anson Road, #06-04/06, Singapore 079906

Cambridge University Press is part of the University of Cambridge.

It furthers the University's mission by disseminating knowledge in the pursuit of education, learning and research at the highest international levels of excellence.

www.cambridge.org
Information on this title: www.cambridge.org/9781107544826

First published 2016

A catalogue record for this publication is available from the British Library

ISBN 978-1-107-12104-1 Hardback
ISBN 978-1-107-54482-6 Paperback

Cambridge University Press has no responsibility for the persistence or accuracy of URLs for external or third-party internet websites referred to in this publication, and does not guarantee that any content on such websites is, or will remain, accurate or appropriate.

Contents

Acknowledgements

First thanks go to Koshka Duff, Katharine Jenkins, Basim Musallam and two referees for Cambridge University Press, all of whom read drafts of this book in their entirety and provided invaluable feedback. I am also grateful to Mezna Qato and Eva von Redecker for comments on parts of the text, and to Natalia Baeza, Nick Bruton, Tim Button, Tessa Frost, Amelia Horgan, Lucy McMahon, Eva Nanopoulos, Remi Oriogun-Williams and a number of seminar participants at the Universities of Cambridge and Sussex for useful discussion of some of the ideas of this book. Finally, my thanks to Hilary Gaskin and Rosemary Crawley at Cambridge University Press for all their help and advice, and to Daisy Hughes for her work on the index.

1   Introduction

There are lots of introductions to feminism, and many of them begin by pointing out that there are lots of introductions to feminism. Then they normally say how the present book is special and different. So I will now try to do that.

Much contemporary feminist political philosophy belongs squarely within a liberal framework. Students unfailingly learn about John Stuart Mill, sometimes with almost the idea that he was feminism's founding father. They learn about 'gender justice', and about the attitudes that liberals should take towards the family, if they are to be good feminists as well as good liberals. They are asked to consider whether the liberal commitment to an attitude of 'tolerance' towards cultural minorities is compatible or incompatible with the liberal feminist commitment to women's autonomy and equality. They also consider whether the liberal commitment to 'freedom of speech' is compatible with feminist critiques of pornography.

I don't want to ignore these familiar debates and questions, but I do aim to provide a different and more distanced take on them, asking about the presuppositions and hidden implications of the way in which these debates and questions are selected, set up and presented. I also want to pay attention to some of the many facets of feminism that are neglected by the standard treatments. For example, I devote a larger portion of the space than is usual, for an introductory text, to the relationship between socialist or Marxist ideas and feminist ones. I also include a chapter dealing with anarchism and 'anarcha-feminism'. If Marxism and socialism are side-lined in mainstream political philosophy, including mainstream feminism, anarchism is often virtually invisible – perhaps because it is thought too obviously stupid or impractical to deserve serious consideration.[1] This can only be 'obvious', however, if

---

[1] As Carol Ehrlich (1977, p. 4) points out: 'Anarchist feminism could provide a meaningful theoretical framework, but all too many feminists have either never heard of it, or else dismiss it as the ladies' auxiliary of male bomb-throwers.'

anarchism is grossly misrepresented (hence, anarchism is grossly misrepresented). I hope to make a small gesture against this misrepresentation and neglect. But perhaps the most important respect in which my discussion differs from the mainstream liberal approach to feminism (and to political philosophy in general) is in the much heavier emphasis I'll place on *practice*: on the actions and activism that make up a crucial part of what feminism is and has been. Feminism is not just a body of theory. Just as socialism was for Marx, it is a real movement to abolish the present state of things.

I should also say something about what this book is not. First, while I hope that the book will give some sense of the diversity and vastness of feminist theory and practice, it is not complete or comprehensive (and in no way intended to be so). There will inevitably be many things that I could or should have talked about (or talked about more), and only some of them will be apparent to me. I have, for example, said relatively little about lesbian and queer feminisms. I have tried to pay heed to the racial dimensions of oppression and to be attentive to the critiques which black feminists have made against a theory and practice in which white women have been dominant. But it is probably only because I am a white woman that I have had to make such a conscious effort – otherwise, it would be difficult *not* to notice these things – and I would be very surprised if the attempt were to be a complete success. The best response to that is not self-flagellation or hand-wringing, however, but just to see it as an affirmation of the importance of black feminist critiques, and of the need for real social transformation that goes beyond the reform of our ways of theorising.

Second, this book is offered neither as an expert guide nor as a guide to the experts: I make no particular claim to expertise, and in fact, that concept often seems to me a dangerously unsuitable one to apply to politics. As should already be apparent, however, this book is an opinionated introduction. It may be more usual, in introductory texts, to affect a position of 'neutrality' – a position which I don't believe to be either possible or desirable. Instead, I have tried simply to write down what I think is relevant, important and true – which I take to be the basic obligation of any writer. I will speak my mind here, and spare readers the usual assurances that they are free to make up their own. Such assurances are bad form, when you think about it. They manage to embody not only the kind of devious appeasement strategy that is often the recourse of subordinates, but to conjure at the same time something of the commanding tone of the patriarch. If I were to marry a man, it wouldn't be a man who assured me that I would be let out of the house whenever I wished.

This book does not represent my settled thoughts. My views on many of the questions and issues covered are still in flux, and even from one day to the next I find myself seeing them in different and contrasting lights. As a result, I cannot expect to agree in the future with everything I have said here. My hope for the book is not that, anyway, but instead that its underlying torn-ness and suspension of ultimate verdict may be in some way instructive.

A final point. This book is not just about women – a reflection of the important fact that feminism is not just about women.[2] Not that it would be such a terrible thing – with women making up over half the population – if a book or even a movement were to be 'just' about them. But all the same, feminism done properly cannot only be about women; and it cannot only be about women for the very simple reason that women are human. For that reason alone, a book about feminism must keep coming back, again and again, to matters and concepts such as *class, race, power*, 'critical theory', 'false consciousness' – things which are not just 'women's issues', but issues for the people that women as well as other kinds of human being are.

---

[2] As the American activist and scholar Angela Davis puts it, 'feminism is not only about women, nor only about gender. It is a broader methodology that can enable us to better conceptualize and fight for progressive change' (2008, p. 25).

2   Feminist theory, feminist practice

There are two main ways of interpreting the question, 'What is feminism?'
The first is to interpret it as asking what the general flavour of the thing
is – what is its *content*? What is it *about*? What does it *stand for*? But another,
equally important, question to ask is the question of what *sort of thing* feminism is, in a more basic sense. All sorts of objects can have 'content', or be
'about' something – books, films, utterances, gestures. What kind of thing is
feminism?

A likely answer to this is that feminism is a form of *theory*: the theory
which identifies and opposes what it calls sexism, misogyny or patriarchy.
But feminism is not just a matter of words; it is also a way of living and
struggling against the status quo. This aspect is often treated as secondary, in
the order of meanings offered in dictionary entries for the word 'feminism',
and also in terms of where political philosophers tend to place emphasis –
feminism may be acknowledged to have a practical aspect, but the focus
of philosophers is on feminist *theory* (with practice regarded as primarily a
matter of the application of theoretical insights). Against this, some feminists
have chosen to emphasise feminism as a practical struggle. bell hooks,[1] for
example, has defined it as 'a movement to end sexism and sexist oppression'
and as a 'liberation movement'.[2] This book sides with hooks in mounting
some resistance to the dominant approach, and emphasising the practical
side of feminism. But in order to see more clearly what it even means to take
sides on the issue of 'theory versus practice', it's useful to say something more
about the notions of *theory* and *practice*, and about the relationship between
them.

---

[1] This is the (intentionally lower-case) pen-name used by the writer Gloria Jean Watkins.
[2] See hooks (2000a, 2000b).

Theory and practice are not two cleanly separate types of feminism, or alternative forms that feminism can take: the protest and the treatise. To expound a theory is also an action, and sometimes an important political intervention – as we'll see, the insight that *to say something is to do something* has been an extremely important one for some feminists. The radical feminist Andrea Dworkin asserts the self-conscious status of her own writing, her theory, *as practice* with unmistakeable force in the opening lines of her first book, *Woman Hating*:

> This book is an action, a political action where revolution is the goal. It has no other purpose. It is not cerebral wisdom, or academic horseshit, or ideas carved in granite or destined for immortality. It is part of a process and its context is change. It is part of a planetary movement to restructure community forms and human consciousness so that people have power over their own lives, participate fully in community, live in dignity and freedom.[3]

Equally, to do something – e.g. to go on strike or to chain oneself to the railings – is not just a dumb physical action; it is also to *say* something, to make a statement or even an argument. As lawyer and feminist theorist Catharine MacKinnon puts it: 'Speech acts. Acts speak.'[4]

In that case, it's not clear that it makes much sense to see theory and practice as two separate classes of thing – or to see 'theory' as a simple and neatly demarcated subclass of 'practice' – where one is dominant over the other. Yet, to dispense altogether with the distinction between theory and practice would be neither good theory nor good practice. Instead, I suggest, the best way to conceive of that distinction is as a distinction between two *aspects* or *ways of looking*, which are both always simultaneously present and available: to look at something as a piece of theory is to look at it with an eye to, for example, its (propositional) content, its argument, scope and presuppositions; to look at the same thing as a piece of practice, perhaps, is to pay more attention to its origin, context, functions or effects.

Of course, the question then immediately arises as to what makes it appropriate or correct to look at something 'as practice' rather than 'as theory'; and it is a question with no short or simple answer. One generally valid thing to say about that, however, is that what is an appropriate way to look at something, an appropriate choice of focus or approach, *must depend on our purposes*.

---

[3] Dworkin (1974, p. 17).   [4] MacKinnon (1994, pp. 20–1).

And it is clear that a central purpose of feminism is that of opposing the system of patriarchy – which means emancipating and improving the lives of women. The ultimate answerability of feminist theory to this objective suggests one powerful reason to keep the practical aspect of feminism firmly in sight.[5]

Having said something about the form, let us now say some more about the content. There is no single, coherent, positive doctrine called feminism. If feminism is to be defined at all, I would suggest, it is better defined negatively, in terms of what it *opposes* – in this respect, feminism is comparable to anti-racism, more akin to anti-capitalism than to socialism. Feminism has two basic components.[6] First, it recognises or posits a fact: the fact of patriarchy. Second, it *opposes* the state of affairs represented by that fact.

'Patriarchy' names a system in which men rule or have power over or oppress women, deriving benefit from doing so, at women's expense. Feminists believe that this system exists, and not as something minor or peripheral or as a hangover from an earlier age, but as central, woven into the fabric of social reality. They may disagree about the nature of patriarchy – what *is* power? What is the benefit that men derive from their collective power over women? – but they all agree that it is real.[7]

It is worth pointing out straight away that in asserting patriarchy as a fact, feminists are *not* committed to the claim that it is *only* women who suffer under that system. Noting the ways in which men suffer is in no way an objection to this basic feminist assertion, but points to something of which most feminists are perfectly aware and which many explicitly acknowledge. In this respect, feminism runs parallel to another much-misunderstood body of thought and practice: Marxism. At least for Marx himself, it is simply not

[5] Of course, most feminists would *say* that the practical aspect of feminism is important. (Mere) sayings are easy. The real question is what we then *do*, where that question includes not just the matter of whether we turn up to protests, but also the matter of *what further things we say*. I cannot make this book turn up to a protest, but I can try to make sure it doesn't just state the importance of talking about feminism as practice *and then forget to talk about feminism as practice*.

[6] Taken on its most general level of understanding, that is. There are many and varied 'feminisms', as we are told at the start of virtually every general introductory article or book on the subject.

[7] This is a *political* claim on my part. There are, of course, people who label themselves 'feminists' but do not believe that patriarchy exists (any longer). They can call themselves what they like, but we do not have to follow suit.

the case that the proletariat are the only ones to suffer under capitalism (for example, to suffer from alienation).[8] From a Marxist point of view, whilst at one level the capitalist clearly benefits from the exploitation of the worker, there is an equally important sense in which the capitalist, too, would be better off in a classless society where human beings would no longer be estranged from one another and would be better able to develop the creative powers that are essential to who and what they are. Marxists can say this whilst simultaneously holding that there is something fundamentally and systematically different about the situations of capitalist and worker.

Any plausible feminist position will say something analogous about the situation of men and women under patriarchy, although it is perhaps helpful to distinguish a stronger and weaker version of the thesis. At the very least, any tenable feminism must make room for the vulnerability and humanity of men, even whilst it regards them as the dominant or oppressor class. It is a short step from this to the recognition that patriarchy is one of the things that might be a cause of suffering for men – the stock example here is the pressure to be conventionally 'masculine' and to suppress emotion. Call this recognition the weaker thesis. But acknowledging patriarchy as one source of men's suffering is not yet to claim that men are overall 'worse off' under patriarchy, or that patriarchy is 'bad for' men. Lots of things which are beneficial for a person or group will also have some downsides for that person or group – e.g. the side-effects of an effective medication, or the higher vulnerability of white people to sunburn – and yet we can still say that people benefit in general from being members of certain groups, and are disadvantaged by the membership of others.

So, to say that men not only suffer some of the downsides of patriarchy, but are actually *worse off* because of it, would be to make a stronger claim. The stronger claim, in turn, admits of two main readings; and it makes sense for a feminist to commit to one reading, whilst disowning the other. To say that men are worse off under patriarchy raises the question: worse off relative to what? What feminists must deny is that men are worse off – or even equally badly off – *relative to women under patriarchy*. To think this would be to abandon the core feminist commitment to the idea of a fact of patriarchy: in what sense is something *patriarchy*, if it damages men more than women, or

---

[8] See 'Estranged labour', in Marx's *Economic and Philosophic Manuscripts* (1967 [1844]).

damages men and women equally?[9] In what sense is something *feminism*, if what it analyses and opposes is analysed and opposed as a system that is not damaging to women in particular? The feminist philosopher Marilyn Frye puts the point by reserving the concept of *oppression* (i.e. patriarchal or 'phallist' oppression) to apply exclusively to the situation of women: 'When the stresses and frustrations of being a man are cited as evidence that oppressors are oppressed by their oppressing, the word "oppression" is being stretched to meaninglessness.'[10] It is worth noting, however, that this does not exclude a second reading of the stronger claim, which restores the parallel with Marxist theory noted above: women are worse off under patriarchy, relative to men; but we may also say that both men and women are worse off under patriarchy, relative to the hypothetical inhabitants of a post-patriarchal world.

Feminists, I've noted, are further united by their *opposition* to the system of patriarchy. The nature of this opposition, like the characterisation of patriarchy, will take different forms depending on the sort of feminist we are talking about. Many feminists have used various moral notions to criticise patriarchy, describing it in terms of 'wrongness' or 'injustice'. Others have sought to avoid 'moralising' language, some aspiring to fight patriarchy through ruthlessly factual analysis of the mechanisms through which it functions, and of the legal and other resources at hand to combat it.[11] Those feminists

---

[9] One rejoinder to this might run along lines analogous to the idea of the 'white man's burden': there is a fact of patriarchy in the sense that men do run the world, but they do not run it in such a way as to benefit themselves relative to women (at least once you factor in the burdens and costs of leadership). I've characterised 'patriarchy' above in such a way as to preclude this – by building into the definition of 'patriarchy' that it is something which serves men's interests and undermines women's – but if we were to adopt a more minimal definition couched only in terms of who *rules* (or leads, has power, etc.), my point would still hold: adopting this version of the stronger thesis might not amount to a denial of the fact of patriarchy, on this understanding of the term 'patriarchy', but it still amounts to a denial of a core feminist commitment, i.e. a commitment to *opposing* patriarchy on the grounds of what it does to women. (In my chosen layout, it was not specified that the feminist opposition to patriarchy had to be on these grounds – as opposed to, for example, being motivated by the need to alleviate the terrible pressures of leadership that the system places on men; but this should be taken as implicit.)

[10] Frye (1983, p. 1).

[11] This is the stance taken most notably by Catharine MacKinnon. Without positively *denying* that women's oppression is wrong – and certainly without judging it to be 'right' – MacKinnon deliberately avoids presenting her thesis as a moral one. She

see their opposition as being stronger rather than weaker for the adoption of this stance and strategy. Once again, then, there is a constant amid the differences: if it doesn't oppose patriarchy, it's not feminism.

There are a number of common ways in which feminism, as just characterised, might be misconstrued, or unfairly dismissed, or both. I will try now to pre-empt two of them.

2.1 Prophylactics

2.1.1 Descriptive and normative: against a gulf

I've described a 'core' of feminism, composed of two main elements: recognition of patriarchy; opposition to patriarchy. In the language currently popular in analytic philosophy, the first element would be classed as 'descriptive' (it says something about what the world is like, namely that it is characterised by the system of patriarchy), and the second element would be classed as 'normative' (it seems to make a claim about how the world *should* be, i.e. that patriarchy should not obtain). This distinction can be a helpful one, so long as we don't mistake its status. For a start, I already noted above that the 'normative' core component of feminism need not necessarily take the form of a commitment to a moral 'should'-claim, e.g. a claim that patriarchy is 'wrong', or 'unjust', or 'should not' exist, or 'should' be swept away. A plain commitment to *resistance* might be what is at issue. We can call such a commitment 'normative' if we like, but it would be an unusual use of that term: *norma* is a rule or standard; and in the context of contemporary analytic ethics and political philosophy, 'normativity' is implicitly understood as being a matter of holding actual or possible practices up against certain rules, standards, or principles, and judging them accordingly. Whether or not that is the right way to think about patriarchy, it should be recognised that it is not an approach that all feminists share. So whilst there is a useful distinction to be drawn between, on the one hand, identifying or analysing patriarchy, and, on the other, opposing it, we shouldn't allow the ubiquitous vocabulary of 'normativity' to push us into a premature narrowing of possibilities as to

says, in the Preface to *Toward a Feminist Theory of the State* (1989, p. xii): 'This book is also not a moral tract. It is not about right and wrong or what I think is good or bad to think or do. It is about what *is*, the meaning of what is, and the way what is, is enforced.'

what *opposition* might mean or what forms it might take. The importance of this will become clearer.

Another mistake to guard against is the idea that there is a simple *dichotomy* between 'descriptive' and 'normative' – i.e. the idea that this distinction delineates two cleanly separate and non-overlapping classes of claims, statements or theories. Take a disagreement between someone who says that women now enjoy 'equality', and someone who denies this. This will most likely not be a straightforward disagreement over empirical matters of fact such as how much women earn, relative to men, for the same work (significantly less, it turns out). The claim that women enjoy 'equality' with men may have the *form* of a descriptive claim, but it will always turn out to carry normative content. To say that there is equality between men and women is not to say that all things are distributed equally between them (what could that even mean? What about the possession of breasts or penises?). It is to say that they are equal in the ways in which it is *right* or *just* that they should be equal: if you think that it is enough that all professions be formally open (where possible) to both men and women, then you may say that 'equality' has (with one or two exceptions) been achieved, even though the women in a given profession will tend to earn less than the men in that same profession; if you don't think this formal equality of opportunity is enough, then you are likely to reject that 'description'. When people say that women and men are equal nowadays, what this means is that they do not think that women and men *should* be equal in the ways in which they are still not equal (or, perhaps, that they don't much care either way).

So, many 'descriptive' statements might also be seen to have a normative dimension: they do describe the world, but they describe the world in a way that can only be fully appreciated if one sees them as containing an implicit evaluation of the world, or at least a supportive or oppositional *reaction* to it. It's worth noting that throughout feminism's history, resistance to feminist ideas has very often presented itself in an at least superficially descriptive form: it would be argued, for example, not that women are innately inferior and deserve their subordinated position – although of course that was often enough argued as well – but that the status quo in fact already displayed a relationship of harmony, reciprocity or even equality between the sexes.[12]

---

[12] The nineteenth-century feminist and economist Charlotte Perkins Gilman was concerned to attack such apologetics for the status quo, arguing vociferously against

Nowadays, certainly, it is much more common to find people taking issue with the idea that society is patriarchal than to find them arguing that patriarchy is acceptable: the 'fact of patriarchy' is the component of feminism that comes in for attack. It is said that women are no longer oppressed, have now achieved equality with men – in some respects are even the dominant sex – and need only to learn to make the most of their liberation. Such 'patriarchy denial' cannot be properly understood as a purely descriptive quarrel with feminism. It is the view that women have already got what the speaker finds it fitting for them to have; and that must involve a view as to *what* and *how much* this is. Of course, that is not to say that it doesn't also have a descriptive aspect: the denial of patriarchy usually rests on fairly crude distortions of reality, or simple obliviousness to certain phenomena. To some extent, therefore, it may be fought with facts. And this brings me to the next point.

2.1.2 'I'll be a post-feminist in the post-patriarchy'

The slogan above has been used by feminists, since at least the 1970s, by way of a retort to any denial of the fact of patriarchy.[13] The slogan links this denial to 'post-feminism', a loose term which represents a contemporary guise of anti-feminism: a position which presents itself as 'pro-woman', 'liberating' or even 'feminist', but which avows a factual disagreement with the gloomy feminist perception of patriarchy as a continuing reality.[14] That is, if we were to think of the core of feminism as consisting of a descriptive and a normative element, 'post-feminism' purports to oppose feminism by rejecting the descriptive component only. As noted already above, this sort of move is

the prevalent idea that marriage represented a fair and equal exchange between men and women. We might also compare this with the use of the phrase 'separate but equal' to justify racial segregation, or 'parity of esteem' to legitimize the deeply divisive 'tripartite' system of secondary education instituted in the UK by the 1944 Butler Act.

[13] Kavka (2002) reports the use of the slogan 'I'll be a post-feminist in the post-patriarchy' as a 1970 New Zealand bumper sticker.

[14] 'Post-feminism' has also been associated with an equation of female 'liberation' with the embrace of previously male-dominated practices, and of so-called 'raunch culture' in particular – i.e. a culture in which women's liberation is identified with their enthusiastic inclusion, both as producers and consumers, in areas traditionally critiqued by feminists under the concept of 'objectification', such as pole-dancing, lap-dancing and stripping (see Levy 2005 for a critical account of this tendency).

by no means new, and in its contemporary guise it rests on the drawing of a particularly sharp division (between 'descriptive' and 'normative') which we would do well to treat with suspicion.

What, beyond that, can the feminist say to the patriarchy-denier? Far, far too many things to attempt to canvas, but it is worth mentioning some of the more basic empirical facts – acknowledged even by mainstream or conservative sources – that may be invoked in reply:

1. Globally, women perform 66 per cent of the world's work, produce 50 per cent of the food, but earn only 10 per cent of the income and own only 1 per cent of the property.[15]
2. Although the Equal Pay Act was passed in the UK in 1970, in 2013 there was still a gap of almost 15 per cent between the full-time earnings of men and those of women; and the fact that women are more likely to work part-time means that the overall gap is considerably bigger.[16]
3. Only 19 per cent of national parliamentarians are female.
4. Despite the disproportionate impact of war and military occupation on women, women make up fewer than 3 per cent of signatories to peace agreements.[17]
5. In the UK, according to the 2009 British Crime Survey, approximately 80,000 women are raped per year. Approximately one in ten rapes is reported, and only 6.5 per cent of these result in a conviction.
6. Forty-five per cent of women have experienced some form of domestic violence, sexual assault or stalking. Around 21 per cent of girls experience some form of childhood sexual abuse.[18]
7. In a survey for Amnesty International, over 1 in 4 respondents thought a women was partially or totally responsible for being raped if she was wearing sexy or revealing clothing, and more than 1 in 5 held the same view if a woman had had many sexual partners.

Now, all this is pretty familiar stuff – although still not as familiar as it should be – and the extent to which it can be expected to alter anyone's view

---

[15] Source: United Nations Development Programme.
[16] Women who worked part-time earned 35 per cent less per hour than men working full-time. Source: *The Guardian*, Staff and agencies (2013).
[17] Source: United Nations Development Programme.
[18] Source: White Ribbon Campaign.

on the feminist assertion of a general fact of patriarchy is limited. Any of the individual points might be fixed upon and disputed, objections (sometimes compelling ones) raised against the underlying observations or the inferences drawn from them – theory is always underdetermined by data, after all.

You either see patriarchy or you don't. If you don't, then you are very unlikely to be convinced by a rehearsal of the sorts of points listed above (try to think of a case where you have witnessed any such conversion . . .). If you do see it, then you don't need any convincing – in any case, the world convinces you every day, in the form of innumerable 'personal' events and interactions ranging from the dramatic and visibly life-shattering to the almost unmentionably banal.

The textbook facts are worth mentioning, nonetheless. One way of putting this is to point out that the disjunction just given ('either you see patriarchy or you don't') is not an exclusive one. There is an important sense in which those who see patriarchy *also* do not see it – in significant respects or a significant part of the time. We don't see it in the same way that we sometimes do not hear a constant humming in the room (only noticing when it stops). The sorts of empirical fact listed above give the feminist something to hold onto, a reminder of some more external or shared evidence that her endless 'personal' pieces of evidence are something other than symptoms of madness. They are sufficiently stark and glaring as to perform this necessary function well – and if they are not so familiar as their starkness might seem to warrant, then this may be the reason why. In media coverage of Middle East politics, there is an eerie absence of maps depicting the share of territory between Israel and Palestine (or the alterations in the respective shares over time). The moment one does look at these maps, it becomes extremely difficult to uphold the position that the Israeli–Palestinian conflict is 'complicated' in the sense often claimed: it is starkly, unmistakably one-sided.

It is also important here, of course, that no Zionist will crumble in the face of such a map, should she be forced to confront it. It will almost invariably make no difference whatsoever. Positions that are in one sense difficult to uphold – that is, almost impossible to square with reality – seem in another sense (i.e. in practice) remarkably easy to cling onto. So with patriarchy, and the denial of patriarchy. Facts are not enough. Indeed, they are surprisingly feeble. Not only is theory always *underdetermined* by data; the sorts of observations made by feminists – no matter how apparently unambiguous or uncontroversial – seem invariably to be *undermined* by something else. That something, I suggest, is best described as 'patriarchal ideology'. The next chapter deals with this idea.

3   Outposts in your head: ideology, patriarchy and critique

The word 'ideology' is one of those words that gets used in a disconcerting number of ways. For example, it may be used to refer simply to a system of beliefs ('my ideology . . . '), or it may be used more pejoratively, to indicate an outlook – usually a political one – which is judged to be dogmatic, inflexible, exaggerated, or in some other way misguided ('your ideology . . . ').

The sense of the term that is most relevant here is neither of the above, but one which I associate with Marx. Marx also used the term 'ideology' in more than one way, so we will need to zoom in further. 'Ideology' in Marx's work can refer to a particular view of history (historical 'idealism', which he dubs 'the German ideology'), and it can also refer in general to the sphere of reality that is composed of ideas (the 'ideal' as opposed to 'material' component of social reality). But there is a further sense of 'ideology' which may be detected in Marx, and which has been extremely important for later theorists. This is the sense of 'ideology' which is bound up with another term Marx uses: 'false consciousness' (*falsches Bewusstsein*). To class something as 'ideology', in this sense, or as 'ideological false consciousness', is to identify it as an instance of a particular kind of *illusion*. I'll say something first about how we should understand the idea of 'false consciousness', before moving onto the 'ideological' bit.

'False consciousness' just means – here, as well as for Marx – 'error' or 'illusion', in the broadest sense: consciousness which is, in whatever way, false or inappropriate.[1] This might be a matter of having a false belief about

---

[1] It is worth bearing in mind that the German *falsch* is not quite the same in meaning as the English 'false'. The English word predominantly connotes *factual or propositional* incorrectness – although there are antiquated usages of 'false' to mean 'unfaithful' or 'bogus' (as in the idioms 'false friend' or 'false economy'). The German *falsch*, on the other hand, retains a greater breadth, and can equally well suggest inappropriateness

the world – e.g. the belief that it is Tuesday when really it is Wednesday. But the 'falsity' might also take other forms. In cases of so-called 'body dysmorphia', a person perceives her body (it is disproportionately often the body of a 'her') as other than it is 'objectively', and other than it is seen by others. To fix on a very common instance:[2] a woman sees her body as bigger and heavier than it really is. She might continue to see herself this way even after any false *belief* she has about her weight or size, in absolute terms or relative to others in her field of view, has been corrected: the illusion persists even when she 'knows' that it is an illusion.

In such cases, although the false consciousness need not take the form of *believing a false proposition*, we might still say that the falseness is a matter of the person's consciousness representing the world in a way that fails to correspond to how the world actually is, just as is the case with false beliefs: the thin woman, confronted with her thin reflection in the mirror, *sees* a fat woman. But the sense of 'false' at play in 'false consciousness' should be understood as being sufficiently broad as to encompass further cases which do not comfortably fit this model – i.e. the model of 'truth' as a matter of representing things as they are – at all. One good example is that of 'Stockholm syndrome', the condition often experienced by people who have been abducted and held captive for long periods: the sufferer develops feelings of deep affection and love for the (often highly abusive) captor. Although we usually think of this as something very rare, it's worth noting that – as with body dysmorphia – 'everyday' versions of this syndrome may actually be pretty common: the feelings many people have for partners or former partners, teachers, bosses or parents often do not seem to be particularly healthy or 'realistic' reactions to the ways in which those figures have behaved. In that sort of case, it seems rather perverse to describe the situation by saying that the victim misrepresents the world, fails to see it as it in fact is, etc. The condition is not necessarily a matter of having any illusions about the deeds done or characteristics possessed by the captor. Rather, it is a matter of having an emotional response which – we say, and the victim might even agree – is

(of the sort conveyed in English by the statement, 'That's the wrong one!') as factual falsehood.

[2] We need not be concerned here only with 'clinical' cases. There is a lower-level, everyday version of this phenomenon, which seems to be almost universal among women.

pathologically inappropriate to the situation and to the relationship. What, exactly, this 'inappropriateness' means here is of course no straightforward matter – when is an emotion 'appropriate'? What makes it appropriate rather than inappropriate? Who gets to judge? – but the present point is just that it is *not* particularly plausible to insist that this inappropriateness, the 'false-ness' of the emotion, must be a matter of the person's failure to represent the world in her consciousness as it in fact is.

Finally, it is important to note that false consciousness might be a matter of *omission* or *lack* rather than (straightforward) illusion – it comes in 'negative' as well as 'positive' forms. Our consciousness may be 'false' by virtue of our failure to notice a relevant truth rather than a belief in a false proposition, or by virtue of our failure to experience a certain emotional state at all – as in cases of pathological absence of empathy or of the capacity for fear – rather than our being in the grip of the 'wrong' emotion.

'False consciousness', then, should be understood as leaving room for more than one way of being false (e.g. inaccurately representing the world – or merely failing to represent it accurately – or else being in some other way inappropriate to the given situation), and also for more than one kind of 'consciousness' (e.g. believing – or failing to believe – a certain proposition; having – or lacking – a certain perception or emotion).[3] False consciousness means, very generally: *something wrong in the head.*

---

[3] The notion of 'false consciousness' should also be understood as being neutral with regard to rival metaphysical theories of truth. That is to say, it's not only the case that this is a term which allows for different senses of 'false' – e.g. what we might call a 'factual' sense of 'falsehood', as well as a quasi-'ethical' sense: a question of what state our consciousness 'should' be in, for some value of 'should' which implies an imperative or duty beyond the imperative to 'get things right' *factually*. Apart from this 'pluralism' about what 'false' might mean in the context of 'false consciousness', it should also be understood that, *even for a given sense of 'false'*, the notion of 'false consciousness' does not in itself imply a commitment to any particular theory of truth, i.e. to any particular *further specification* of what it *means* for something to be 'false' in the relevant sense. For example: if we narrow our attention to the category of 'factual' falsehood, the category of 'false consciousness' doesn't tell us whether we should understand this falsehood along the lines of the 'correspondence' or the 'coherence' theory of truth – i.e. whether we should think that factual falsehood is a matter of believing something which fails to correspond to the way the world is, or whether we should think it a matter of believing something which fails adequately to *cohere* with a relevant set of further propositions.

The notion of 'ideology' that is of interest here is concerned with a particular kind of false consciousness: false consciousness which is 'functionally explained',[4] by reference to its tendency to promote the interests of one social group over another. For Marx, of course, the relevant social groups are classes – under capitalism, the two great hostile camps of *bourgeoisie* and *proletariat*.[5] Not all false consciousness has anything obviously class-related about it. If I misread the clock or forget to turn up to an appointment, this may involve some false consciousness on my part, but there is nothing to suggest that the false consciousness – i.e. the misreading, or the forgetting – serves the interests of any person or group, and *a fortiori* nothing to suggest that it happens *because* it has this function. For Marx, though, there is an important kind of false consciousness which *is* related to class interests in precisely this way. Much of what we call 'morality' or 'religion', in fact, might be seen as a distortion of consciousness, which occurs because it has a certain function, namely the function of maintaining the privilege and dominance of the ruling class.

Social classes are not the only kind of social group, however; and it is not difficult to see how this notion of ideology (as functionally explained false consciousness) might be made use of to respond to purposes and concerns which go beyond specifically Marxist ones. Ruling-class ideology is the distortion of thought which can be explained by its tendency to further the interests of the ruling class. Racist or white supremacist ideology would be the distortion of thought which occurs due to its function of promoting the interests of one racial group, e.g. 'whites', over another, e.g. 'blacks'. We might then use the term '*patriarchal* ideology' to refer to another kind of false consciousness, the occurrence and nature of which we take to be explicable in terms of a tendency to further the interests of a dominant sex (men) over a subordinated one (women).

At this point, it is once again necessary to offer some protection against foreseeable misconceptions. Much of what I'll have to say in this book is best understood as an attempt to unmask and combat various forms of patriarchal ideology. Given this, and given the fact that the notion of ideology (like most

---

[4] The term 'functional explanation' comes from Cohen (1978), who defends this form of explanation as it figures in Marx's theory of history: *X is functionally explained by Y, if X is explained by its tendency to bring about Y.*

[5] This thought has perhaps its clearest expression in *The Communist Manifesto* – see Marx & Engels (1998 [1848], p. 35).

ideas associated with Marx) tends to get a bad press, it's worth trying to pre-empt some of the more predictable objections to it.

3.1 Prophylactics

3.1.1 Not just men . . .

Nothing in the notion of patriarchal ideology implies that this is a phe-nomenon which applies to the consciousness of (all) men, and not to the consciousness of women: the claim is not that men labour under an illusion, of which women are – perhaps through some gift of biology – mercifully (or *unmercifully*) free. Nor is patriarchal ideology supposed to be a matter of some conspiracy of men against women – a crock of lies concocted by men and fed to women in order to keep them in a position of servitude. That is to say: it is a condition that is neither *suffered* nor *perpetuated* by men alone.

To make the first mistake, i.e. to assume that only men are subject to patriarchal false consciousness, would be to make the mirror image of a mis-take made about Marx's view of the relationship between ideology and class. There, a common assumption among commentators is that Marx presents ideological false consciousness as primarily or exclusively a disease of the benighted masses; and this assumption then allows those commentators to wrestle ostentatiously with the worry that the notion of ideology is patro-nising or insulting to the 'common man'.[6] For Marx himself, however, it is perfectly clear that ideological false consciousness is something which applies across the social strata, present not only in the illusions which help to keep the workers from rising up but also in the thought of the leading intellectuals of his day: religion may be described as the 'opium of the masses'; but Marx's withering critiques of Bentham and J. S. Mill as the mouthpieces of bourgeois interests are just as salient (though far less often quoted).

In the present case, this mistake is inverted: it is assumed that the *dominant* class, i.e. men, are the ones accused of labouring under sexist misconceptions, whereas women are often presumed to enjoy an immunity – so that we frequently encounter arguments of the form, 'So-and-so is a woman, and is pro-life / against "positive discrimination" / [insert euphemism for] rape apologist,

---

[6] See e.g. Elster (1986); Rosen (1996); Wolff (2003). See Finlayson (2014b) for a critical discussion of this tendency.

so that position can't be sexist.' [7] In this respect, patriarchal ideology is presented in a way more akin to class 'snobbery' than to what is generally thought of as false consciousness: the upper classes are prone to snobbery, men are prone to sexist or 'chauvinist' attitudes; the lower classes, by contrast, can only really be 'inverted' snobs, just as women may be 'man-haters'. These common misrepresentations of class- and patriarchal ideology are similar, however, insofar as both forms of misrepresentation function so as to aid the ridicule and dismissal of those notions: if Marx's theory of ideology pins false consciousness on the working class, then this can be derided as both naïve and condescending; and if the feminist idea of patriarchal ideology paints men (and only men) as sexists, then it is to that degree simplistic and unappealing.

To make the second mistake, on the other hand – i.e. to assume that patriarchal ideology must be a matter not of illusions under which men labour, but of *lies* they tell about and to women – would be to make a mistake which is straightforwardly *parallel* to one that is commonly made about Marxism. The flipside of the accusation that Marxists portray the working class as especially deluded is the additional suggestion that this is the result of some kind of conscious conspiracy of the ruling class. Similarly, an easy misunderstanding of the notion of patriarchal ideology would portray it as a set of sexist myths propounded by men. But this seems to suggest that *women*, rather than men, are the sole victims of patriarchal false consciousness.

3.1.2 . . . not just women

It seems we are looking at two opposite errors. There is the error of thinking that false consciousness – perhaps equated with 'sexism' – is something which only men are supposed to suffer from. If the notion of patriarchal ideology implies this, then it can be dismissed. But the line which associates this kind of ideology only with men may also take the form of a claim that men are responsible for a cynical patriarchal *lie*, rather than themselves subject to a patriarchal *illusion*. And *that* suggests – if we assume that the lie is to any degree successful – that there must be someone who is taken in: women. Through this perverse logic we move to the opposite error: the thought that patriarchal ideology must be a matter of women being duped by and for men.

---

[7] This is an old phenomenon, of course. A key part of the case against the extension of the franchise to women was always that women themselves didn't want it.

If *that* is the claim to which feminists are committed, then it may be just as easily dismissed as when the illusion is taken to be *men's* alone. It will be pointed out that this claim is both false and insulting. Some will go further – too far – and reaffirm the idea that women are the final and infallible arbiters of the correct social role for, and just societal treatment of, women. Often, the same people may be heard claiming, in other contexts, that it is unfair to suggest that sexism is confined to men, and that women can be their own and each other's worst enemies.

In sum, there are conflicting currents in the discourse surrounding sex, sexism and male dominance. Sometimes the tendency is to associate these with prejudices and misconceptions among men. Sometimes, there is a countervailing tendency to think of men as the deceivers and *women* as the deceived. Both tendencies, however, tend almost magically to arrange themselves so as to protect male dominance – often working in (contradictory) combination. Either women are implicitly blamed for their own subordination – *if only they would raise their aspirations / stop wanting to 'have it all' / stop worrying so much what they look like / have more confidence in themselves* – or they are deemed the non-sexist sex, so that all you have to do is find a woman who excuses or celebrates her own oppression (not difficult) in order to show that this is not oppression after all. And part of this process is the turning of both tendencies *against* the notion of patriarchal ideology (though it may not be called by name): the latter is interpreted as calling women deluded, in which case the retort is that women know what they want; or, it is interpreted as both unfairly stigmatising men and naively exonerating women.

But the notion of patriarchal ideology, properly understood, is specific to neither men nor women. It is no more and no less than the notion of distorted ways of seeing, feeling and relating to the world, which have the function of upholding the system of patriarchy – and exist *because* they have this function. Any remotely plausible account of this, I suggest, will see it as something *shared* between men and women (whilst, no doubt, taking interestingly different forms according to differences of sex, gender, race, class and a whole host of other factors).

We should now be in a position to see why ideology is of such central importance to feminism. It is already well recognised, of course, that feminism is not just about the unequal material conditions of men and women – e.g. the persistent gap in property ownership and income, or the different sorts of work that men and women do – but is also up against a set of ingrained ideas, assumptions, and habits of thought and feeling about the sexes. Most commonly, we think about this under the heading of 'sexism' or 'prejudice'. A large part of the task of feminists is that of criticising those ideas, and – crucially – showing them to be what they are (for the vast majority of instances of sexist consciousness do not take such a crude form as, e.g., the belief that women are less intelligent than men, or otherwise inferior to them).

A first reason why the notion of patriarchal ideology is so important, then, is that it points towards a key task for feminist theorising – a task which we might term *feminist ideology-critique*, or the *critique of patriarchal ideology*. This much may seem obvious, but judging by much of the work that goes on within current feminist philosophy, it is easily forgotten. The main task of feminist political philosophy is often construed as the task of working out what 'gender justice' requires – either as part of an 'ideal' theory (i.e. working out what perfect gender justice would look like) or as the 'non-ideal' project of prescribing appropriate measures to be taken here and now. But these endeavours are blind without some form of feminist ideology-critique: in order to have any real idea of what 'gender justice' might be, we have to understand and see through the distortions of thought surrounding ideas of gender, distortions which have long served to uphold gender *injustice* and oppression; and in order to have any clue how to *realise* a society that better lives up to feminist ideals, we have to have some idea of how to respond to the forms of thought that impede our progress.

This is something which feminists in the late 1960s and early 1970s understood very well. The widespread practice of 'consciousness-raising', in which women met in small groups to discuss and better understand experiences of gender oppression which they often had not previously recognised as such, might be seen as a kind of ideology-critique in action.[8] The guiding thought behind this practice is that systems of oppression have a way of making themselves invisible, and that part of the mechanism through which they do so is by engendering certain 'blind spots' or self-undermining patterns of thought – that is to say, false consciousness – in those who suffer from the oppression, rendering them less able to sustain an accurate view of what is happening to them. As one commentator put it in 1970: 'It's hard to fight an enemy who has outposts in your head.'[9] The practice of consciousness-raising also aims to

---

[8] I owe this thought to Katharine Jenkins.   [9] Kempton (1970, p. 184)

be faithful to the idea of a unity between theory and practice, introduced in the previous chapter: it aims to transform our ways of thinking and our ways of living in a process that is seamlessly theoretical (without being 'academic') and practical. Although consciousness-raising was a matter of controversy, with some regarding it as unserious or insufficiently 'political' (merely 'personal therapy'), for the women involved, the practice could be provocative and galvanising as well as life-changing. As one second-wave radical feminist and civil rights activist, Pam Allen, puts it: 'That women would choose to get together to talk about their lives without any males present was radical. It freaked people out.'[10]

This emphasis on the critique of ideology, on the unity of theory and practice, and on emancipatory self-transformation, is strongly reminiscent of a certain neo-Marxist philosophical tradition not usually associated with feminism. The 'Frankfurt School' – a group of philosophers active in Germany (and later in exile in America) in the 1930s–60s – gave a central place to the critique of ideology, and took this to place an obligation on theory to look at *itself* as well as the world outside itself with a critical eye: the kind of theory which does this, or aspires to do it, has become known as 'critical theory'. A critical theory of society is 'reflexive', which is to say that it sees itself as falling *within the domain of its own enquiry and criticism*.[11]

The important point here is extremely simple: theories, philosophical or otherwise, are made up of ideas; hence, if the theory of ideology has anything to it, we can expect these theories to be subject to all kinds of distortion which serve to benefit the interests of dominant social groups. Applying this to the present case, i.e. that of feminism and patriarchal ideology, what this brings out very clearly is the need to be ever ready to apply ideology-critique (including *feminist* ideology-critique) to theories and approaches within political philosophy (including *feminist* political philosophy). There is no neutral way of telling the history of feminism, for instance. And we should not be surprised to find that dominant ways of telling that history are distorted in ways that are plausibly read as ideological, reflecting and playing into the dominance of some groups over others – including the dominance of men over women. When I begin to look at feminism's history in Chapter 5, therefore, my discussion will maintain a dual focus: on the history of

---

[10] Quoted in Faludi (2013, p. 56).   [11] See Horkheimer (1999 [1937]).

feminism; and on the way in which that history is conventionally mistold. Before that, however, I want to look not at the telling of the history of feminism but at the way in which feminism's subject matter is defined. If feminism is about women, then this means asking the question of what women *are*.

4 (De-)constructing coat-racks: feminism, sex and gender

Usually, we do not stop to ask what women and men *are*, as this is taken to be too obvious a matter to ask about. But it is an issue of some importance for feminists, who have consistently pointed out that the matter of what makes us women (or men) is not nearly as straightforward as we are encouraged, from our first moments, to believe. Is being a woman a matter of biology? If it is, does that mean that it is a matter of a person's physical shape, genitalia, chromosomes, hormones, or some complex calculus of all of these? Or is being a man or woman a matter of adopting certain characteristic styles of dress, sexual preference, bearing and demeanour? Or are women simply those who 'self-identify' as women – that is, who think of themselves as women and expect others to relate to them accordingly (e.g. by using the pronoun 'she' to refer to them and granting them access to women-only spaces such as women's public toilets)?

The line we take on these questions can have important implications for both theory and practice. It will determine the population we are talking about when we say things like 'women are oppressed' or 'women must liberate themselves', and it will have a bearing on questions such as the extent to which being a man or a woman is seen as pre-given and relatively fixed or as something subject to our (individual or collective) voluntary control, or whether we see men and women as fundamentally alike or as fundamentally different.

I will not aim to devise or promote one particular definition of 'women' (I don't think that this is a project which ultimately makes a lot of sense). Instead, I hope to clarify what it might mean for feminists to ask for or to offer an account of what women are, and in the process, I'll try to help locate more precisely some of the worse pitfalls into which feminists might be in danger of falling.

* * *

A distinction which has been extremely important to many feminists – but which (as we'll see) has also come in for strong criticism from among their own ranks – is the distinction between 'sex' and 'gender'. According to the by now traditional model, 'sex' refers to traits or differences that are seen as biological, universal, natural and fixed: e.g. (so it is thought) the chromosomal make-up XX (for women) and XY (for men). 'Gender' refers to those traits which are *related to* or at least *correlated with* sex traits, but which are seen as socialised, culturally and historically variable, and hence changeable: e.g. clothing, conformity to certain norms of appearance, career choice and so on. Faced with the claim that it is 'just natural' that women should be the main carers of children, for example, some feminists have argued that this fails to distinguish sex from gender: that women give birth to the children, and are the only ones able to breastfeed (etc.), may be natural and inevitable; but if women tend to do more of the childcare than men long after they have ceased breastfeeding, are more likely to report a desire to do so or to experience feelings of guilt or inadequacy for not doing so, then this might be put down to social factors.

Being able to make this distinction has clearly been very useful for feminists, enabling them to cast seemingly unchangeable 'facts of life' in a new light: as contingent, constructed, and as potential objects of conscious social change. Many of the things once almost unanimously regarded as belonging to a 'natural' division or difference between the sexes have come to be seen either as false or as products of contingent processes of socialisation: for example, the belief – almost universal in Europe and America prior to the nineteenth century – that women were inherently unsuited to rational thought and unfit for professions such as law, medicine or academia. There can be an important function in shifting certain phenomena from the 'natural'/'sex' category into the 'socially constructed'/'gender' category – a process which sometimes may contribute towards changing social reality so that claims such as 'girls are less academically successful' go from being claims about nature, to being claims about the socialised condition of females in a certain kind of society, (sometimes) to being acknowledged as simply and demonstrably false.

So one question we might want to ask is whether feminists, when they identify and oppose the oppression of 'women', are concerned with the oppression of a sex or of a gender. As noted above, however, the traditional contrast has come in for heavy criticism,[1] not just from those who want to reassert the importance of biological sex and to put back into the 'nature' box the phenomena which feminists argue are socially constructed, but from feminists themselves, many of whom believe that the sex/gender model is insufficiently radical, that it concedes too much to biological 'essentialism' and to the idea of a purely 'natural' category of 'sex'.

The kind of critique I have in mind here holds that the innovation which merely introduces an extra category of 'gender', on top of 'sex', leaves the latter intact and unscrutinised (and ends up with an inadequate understanding of both categories). The problem is not just that things belonging to gender have been mistakenly attributed to sex, so that we need to sort more things into the 'gender' category (and out of the 'sex' one) than we thought. The problem is with holding onto the category of 'sex' itself, and the contrast between this and a distinct category of 'gender' – at least, as this category and contrast have traditionally been understood.

This is one of the areas of feminism which attracts the most notoriety, both within and outside academia, and what some feminists have to say here can strike as either self-evidently contrary to common sense or, at least, highly confusing. I want now to lay out some of the main points which are raised by feminist critiques of the sex/gender distinction, and to show why they deserve to be taken seriously.

As noted already, feminist critics of the sex/gender model tend to take issue with the 'sex' part: they argue that this model is too uncritical of the category of sex, understood as the natural and biological basis which underlies gender. In so doing, they are attacking what is sometimes referred to as the 'coat-rack view':[2] a person's sex is depicted as a structure on which various possible gender identities may be hung. Whilst this image has some built-in flexibility – you can hang more than one thing on any given structure, and you can hang the same thing on more than one structure – it preserves the idea of sex as both *fixed* and *clearly distinct from gender*. Moreover, although a structure may not strictly dictate what thing is to be hung off it, there are usually certain things that 'fit' better than others (just as some clothes will fit a person better than others, and some may not fit at all). So although the two are pictured as clearly distinct ('coat' and 'rack'), in another sense, it follows that sex *extends*

---

[1] See e.g. Butler (1990); Fausto-Sterling (2000a, 2003).   [2] Nicholson (1994, p. 81).

into gender: if, for example, the role of caring for children fits the female sex better than the male, then although it may belong to 'gender' – in the sense that it is possible for society to be arranged so that this role is undertaken by men rather than women – we might still think of a pattern whereby women rather than men tend to do the work of childcare as an extended *sex difference* (in both a normative sense – i.e. 'it's better that way'– and a causal one – i.e. 'that's why it happens'). It would be misleading to suggest that this is the sort of thing which most feminists who use the sex/gender distinction would want to say, but nothing about the distinction itself precludes their doing so.

The sex/gender model is, in fact, quite compatible with many of the traditional patriarchal views which feminists have wanted to criticise. Nineteenth-century Victorians would have been well aware that not *all* differences between men and women were simply natural ones, in the sense of being unalterable and invariant between different social contexts – otherwise they would not have had to put so much energy into arguing that women would be corrupted or 'masculinised' if given access to forms of education traditionally reserved for men (worrying, in effect, about the danger of one set of socially conditioned differences being weakened and replaced with another). The irony of their making these arguments by recourse to an idea of 'nature' has often been remarked upon – for why should so much anxiety and social pressure be necessary in order to get people to live in a way that is already in their natures? But there is nothing strictly incoherent about these traditional patriarchal arguments: unless the word 'natural' is to become meaningless, it must be possible to be in an *un*natural state; and it can take care and effort to make sure that this calamity does not occur.[3]

So although the sex/gender distinction is often presented as a great conceptual breakthrough and a keystone of modern feminism, this presentation is actually quite misleading. There is nothing necessarily feminist about the idea that there is a social dimension to differences between men and women. Nor is the practice of explicitly acknowledging this social dimension particularly modern, for that matter. It is often claimed that the sex/gender distinction originates in the work of psychologists of the 1960s, who introduced it in order to describe the phenomenon of transsexuality: transsexuals are those whose gender identity does not 'match' their biological sex.[4] This may be true

---

[3] As an adage attributed to Calvin Klein has it: 'The best thing is to look natural, but it takes makeup to look natural.'

[4] Mikkola (2012); Nicholson (1998).

of the English term 'gender' (which earlier was used interchangeably with 'sex'), but it hardly follows that there was no acknowledgement or under-standing of the specifically social aspects of man- and womanhood before the 1960s. It doesn't follow, and is also fairly clearly false. For example, the fourteenth-century Sunni Muslim scholar Ibn Qayyim (1292–1350) discusses 'unutha (أنوثة), or 'femininity'/'femaleness', as a quality and set of skills that women are *taught* (since this quality and set of skills is thought appropriate to their sex).[5]

As noted, the feminist potential of the sex/gender distinction lies in the possibility of moving things from the 'sex' to the 'gender' category: if it is gender, the thinking goes, it can be criticised and maybe changed – whereas there is as little point in criticising bona fide sex differences as there is in criticising the law of gravity. The question then becomes: how much can we get away with putting into the 'gender' category? Naturally, many feminists would like to be able to criticise and change more of the social world rather than less. But there comes a point where the 'Oh c'mon!' reaction is inevitable. We may or may not agree that men are just as suited to raising children as women are, but many will have a hard time accepting that having a penis or breasts is just another matter of socialisation.

According to critics of the sex/gender distinction, however, this is just the wrong way to look at things. The point is not to preserve one half of the traditional dichotomy ('gender') and ditch the other ('sex'), but to change the way in which we look at both so that the traditional dichotomy is overcome. What does this mean, though? How, exactly, is it different from pretending that whether or not a person grows breasts is merely a matter of societal influence?

There is no simple answer to this – and of course the answer varies from one feminist thinker to another – but there are a few things we can say. First, feminists have urged that we should change the way we see the category of sex by ridding ourselves of the idea that it is something *unitary* or *simple*. When we put pressure on the issue of what it means to be one sex or the

---

[5] The context for this is a discussion of rights to the custody of children in the event of parental separation. Ibn Qayyim discusses the argument that the woman has priority in a dispute over the custody of children because of her 'unutha, and elaborates on this argument by referring to the skills that are taught to young girls, designed to equip them to care for young children (Ibn Qayyim 1998, vol. 5, pp. 387–437; see especially pp. 392–5).

other, we actually come up with not one criterion but a whole list: males have XY chromosomes, testosterone, a penis and testes; females have XX chromosomes, oestrogen, a vagina and ovaries. Already, sex has emerged as a cluster of properties.[6] And what is more, these properties can come apart. In certain people categorised as 'intersex', a pair of XY chromosomes may coincide with a body type and genitalia that are female in appearance.[7] Internal sex organs may also fail to 'match' outward appearance. In such cases, a person may find out their intersex identity only late in life (or never). The fact that these criteria of male- and femaleness can come apart from one another not only shows that sex is complex rather than simple, but also challenges the idea of a strict binary division between male and female. For when a person fulfils some (but not all) of the criteria for both sexes, such a person seems to be neither male nor female, or both.

Since the conventional understanding of the sexes is that there are two of them, and that they are mutually exclusive (either/or) and opposite, the phenomenon of intersexuality forces us to revise that understanding: either 'male' and 'female' are not the only categories, or we have to come to see these two categories as overlapping. Note that intersexuality does not have to be particularly common in order for the consideration of it to provoke this shift in thinking – in fact, even if it *never* happened, just the conceptual possibility of it might force a partial revision of traditional ways of conceiving of sex differences. As many have pointed out, however, intersexuality is actually much more common than is generally acknowledged. Intersex individuals include not only those whose external appearance is 'normal' – not all of whom will be aware of their atypical status – but also those whose appearance at birth is sufficiently ambiguous that doctors are unable to classify them as either boys or girls. The figure usually given for this latter category is around one in 2,000 births, which makes it less rare than, say, cystic fibrosis, which

---

[6] Stone (2007, p. 44) argues that sex should be treated as a 'cluster concept': to count as male, or female, it is only necessary to satisfy *enough* (but not all) of a set of features that tend (albeit fallibly) to cluster together. Stoljar (2000, p. 27) makes the same claim about the category 'women'.

[7] This is known as 'androgen insensitivity syndrome' (AIS), as it is thought that in such cases the (XY) person's body does not respond to the androgens which usually trigger the development of male sex organs. In those with AIS, external genitalia are female or ambiguous in appearance, and testes usually remain inside the body.

affects roughly one in 2,500 newborn babies (and which is almost certainly more widely known).[8]

It is almost impossible to say with confidence how rare or common intersexuality is: first, because not all cases are externally visible and hence easily detectable; and second, because it depends on how 'intersexuality' is defined – and this is a matter of considerable controversy.[9] Some theorists, such as the psychologist Anne Fausto-Sterling, have argued that as much as 1.7 per cent of the population is intersex,[10] while others have countered that such claims rest on too broad a definition of intersexuality to be useful.[11] Even Fausto-Sterling's allegedly inflated figure might seem to testify to the relative rarity of intersexuality, which, it may be thought, is nowhere near high enough to warrant the suggestion made by some feminists[12] that sex difference should be understood as a spectrum or 'continuum' rather than as a binary split.

[8] This comparison is not meant to suggest that intersexuality is a disease or disorder, by the way. As many intersex activists have pointed out, there are few if any medical problems associated with intersexuality per se (but many socially produced problems, including the complications and damage arising from medical interventions to 'correct' intersex bodies).

[9] According to the Intersex Society of North America: '"Intersex" is a general term used for a variety of conditions in which a person is born with a reproductive or sexual anatomy that doesn't seem to fit the typical definitions of female or male' (ISNA 1993–2008). The British National Health Service (NHS) uses the term 'disorders of sexual development' (DSD) in place of 'intersex', and defines DSD in terms of having 'a mix of male and female sexual characteristics' (see 'Disorders of sex development', online at www.nhs.uk/conditions/disorders-sex-development/Pages/Introduction.aspx). Many intersex people have objected to the term 'disorder', on the grounds that this carries the false and stigmatising implication that their conditions are medically problematic or unhealthy.

[10] Fausto-Sterling (2000b, p. 20).

[11] For instance, Sax argues that Fausto-Sterling's widely publicised views about the incidence of intersexuality are highly misleading: 'If the term intersex is to retain any meaning, the term should be restricted to those conditions in which chromosomal sex is inconsistent with phenotypic sex, or in which the phenotype is not classifiable as either male or female. Applying this more precise definition, the true prevalence of intersex is seen to be about 0.018%, almost 100 times lower than Fausto-Sterling's estimate of 1.7%' (Sax 2002).

[12] E.g. Fausto-Sterling (2000a); Frye (1983); Stone (2007). The image of a spectrum arguably still concedes too much to traditional castings of sex, with 'male' and 'female' construed as opposite poles. The more you think about it, the more unclear it becomes that this way of thinking makes sense. Hippies and hipsters might represent two very different types, but it would be artificial at best to present them as

Arguably, however, this misunderstands the point that those who empha-sise the phenomenon of intersexuality are trying to make. Intersexuality could be seen as of interest not just in itself, but also as a particularly clear illustration of a much broader truth about sex and sex difference. Even where we do not see fit to apply the label 'intersex', there are certainly a great many people who do not completely conform to the usual expectations for the cate-gories of male and female – for example, in terms of their levels of hormones, body shapes, or patterns of hair growth. It is this variety which, as Marilyn Frye has pointed out, makes it necessary for us to engage in perpetual and near-obsessive 'sex-marking' practices in order to uphold a clear and strict division between male and female. Frye argues:

> if you strip humans of most of their cultural trappings, it is not always easy to tell without close inspection which are female, which are male. The tangible and visible physical differences between the sexes are not particularly sharp or numerous and in the physical dimensions we associate with 'sex differences', the range of individual variation is very great. The differences between the sexes could easily be, and sometimes are, obscured by bodily decoration, hair removal, and the like. So the requirement of knowing everyone's sex in every situation and under almost all observational conditions generates a requirement that we let others know our sex in every situation. And we do. We announce our sexes in a thousand ways.[13]

What Frye is emphasising is that sex differences – and she seems happy to use the category of 'sex' in roughly the conventional way here to connote the biological and the physical – are not particularly obvious and salient *in themselves,* and are often less salient than the differences that exist between individuals of the same sex. They are *made* visible and salient by our constant efforts to signal our sex to one another (so much so that, when sex is not unambiguously signalled, everyday interactions in a gendered society are made disconcertingly difficult):

> We deck ourselves from head to toe with garments and decorations which serve like badges and buttons to announce our sexes ... most of the time most of us choose, use, wear or bear the paraphernalia associated with our sex. It goes below the skin as well. There are different styles of gait, gesture, posture,

opposite 'poles', with or without the acknowledgement of a continuum stretching between them.

[13] Frye (1983, p. 23).

speech, humor, taste and even of perception, interest and attention that we learn as we grow up to be women or to be men and that label and announce us as women or as men. It begins early in life: even infants in arms are color coded.[14]

At least on the face of it, though, there are two separate issues here. There is the conventional way of drawing the distinction between male and female – which is being challenged by the considerations discussed above. And then there is the distinction between sex and gender. The two distinctions are often criticised in the same breath, through a general problematisation of what is attacked as 'binary thinking'. But in principle at least, they are independent questions, two different 'binaries'. You could buy all the stuff about sex differences forming a spectrum – or you could judge that there are not two but three sexes, or five[15] – without seeing this as a reason to abandon the sex/gender model. You would just say that the underlying substratum that is sex difference is more complex or gradated than is traditionally acknowledged. Instead of two coat-racks, there are three, five, or however many you like – a whole spectrum of subtly different designs. But we could in principle still think of this as the fundamental, biological or physical, aspect of sex difference (with gender resting on top of it). Almost invariably, however, critiques of the 'binary' distinction between male and female are accompanied by a critical attitude towards the category of 'sex' itself (and of the categories of 'male' and 'female') – where this critical attitude goes beyond the demand for a recognition of a more nuanced set of sex differences.

What, then, is the further problem that feminists have had with the sex/gender distinction, and with the idea of sex in particular? A large part of the answer has to do with the concept of *naturalness*. 'Sex', as we've seen, refers to a cluster of distinct things or ideas. Among them are the concepts of the physical, biological and bodily. And closely connected with these ideas is the thought that sex differences are – whereas gender differences need not be – *natural* differences. The category of 'nature' is usually contrasted with that of 'environment' or 'nurture': natural phenomena are those which are pre-given, obtaining independently of environmental factors; the environment then interacts with this raw material so as to produce the world as we know it.

---

[14] Frye (1983, pp. 23–4).   [15] Fausto-Sterling (1993, 2000b).

Without delving too deeply into the can of worms that is the nature/nurture debate, there are a few things that it is useful to say here. First, many people (and many feminists among them) have argued that there is something wrong with the category of 'nature' as it has traditionally been understood – i.e. as something (a) sharply distinct from environmental factors, and (b) fixed and unalterable. Those making this argument have pointed out that there seems to be *literally nothing* we can point to that is completely independent of its environment. To stick to the case of sex differences, we might say that it is natural for girls to begin menstruating and to develop breasts as they mature. But even that can only happen if they receive appropriate nourishment: this environmental factor is clearly necessary, not only for 'normal' puberty to occur, but for biological survival (which is also a necessary condition for reaching puberty). 'Natural', therefore, cannot mean 'strictly independent of all things environmental' – or else nothing is natural. Another suggestion might be that it means 'that which is fixed and cannot be changed'. But it is not clear that this suggestion really differs from the first: if everything depends in some way on environment, then it is *not* fixed and unalterable – for what it means to 'depend' on something is to be *conditional upon* that something's being in place (which means that if you take that something away, the first thing will be different or absent).

It might be felt that these points are all too academic, and that there is a perfectly workable everyday sense in which the fact that women have breasts is natural and relatively fixed, whereas the fact that many of them wear high heels (for example) is a contingent and variable product of historical and social conditions. And in some sense this must be right – though working out exactly *what* it is that is right here is not a straightforward matter. We'll come back to this shortly. But it is worth just noting, first, that those things generally categorised as sex characteristics (and as 'natural') often seem *not* to be fixed, but to be alterable by (deliberate or non-deliberate) human intervention. Hormones can be altered by medical treatments; genitals can be altered by surgery (such as has been performed on many intersex children and adults as well as others undergoing processes of transition); hair can be removed by waxing, shaving or electrolysis; and bodies in general are not fixed, but constantly changing and change-able in any number of ways – by means ranging from exercise and diet to piercing, tattooing and surgery.

Perhaps when we say that something is 'natural', then, we do not mean that it is strictly unalterable or unavoidable (by any possible intervention or environmental condition), but something more like the following: what is 'natural' is what obtains, or *should* obtain, 'in the normal run of things'. So we class the capacity of women (but not men) to breastfeed and bear children as a sex difference, and a feature of 'nature', because we believe that this is true of women (and not men) across all known human societies, and because there is, as far as we can see, little reason to expect this to change.

This concept of naturalness is also, inevitably, a *value* judgement: the natural is fixed only in the sense of remaining constant across the range of possibilities deemed permissible or appropriate to consider in a given context. For example, we might think, as Marx did, that human beings are naturally social creatures. Or we might say that it is natural for children to want to play. Unlike in the case of the differential ability of the sexes to breastfeed, the claim does not seem to be that these are things which are constant across all social contexts. For Marx, for example, human beings may be naturally social, but when placed under the conditions of labour characteristic of the capitalist mode of production they become alienated from one another in a way that is incompatible with true sociality. So in an important way, humans under the present economic system may *not* be social animals. But the claim that Marx is making is that sociality is the condition that is appropriate to human beings, *whether or not this condition is realised or fulfilled*. And this, though not exactly a moral claim, is clearly not a value-free one.

When it is judged that having certain bodily features (e.g. a penis rather than a vagina) is natural for those with XY chromosomes, only part of what is meant is the descriptive claim that most of those with XY chromosomes have those bodily features (a descriptive generalisation like this could also be true for things that are clearly cultural products, like men tending to have short hair). We say that something is natural only when we take something else to be the case – for instance that it is good for the generalisation to hold, or that the kinds of conditions required in order to stop the generalisation from holding would be fairly drastic, traumatic, or detrimental in their side-effects. In this case, note, the claim does not need to be that it is intrinsically *good* that XY individuals should have penises (why would you think that?). The implicit judgement might be, more comprehensibly, that the steps needed in order to remove a penis or to turn it into a vagina (or something else) are *costly* in some significant way – physically, emotionally, financially, or however else. It follows that what is 'natural' must be relative to context: our range of experience, imagination, technological capacity, and so on.

In addition to pointing out the value-ladenness and context-sensitivity of judgements of naturalness – which, note, is not necessarily to say that we should never make such judgements, just that we should understand the kind of judgement that we are making when we do so – some feminists have also made a further, related point, about what is often termed 'social construction'. This term, in the sense at issue here, is not simply equivalent to the term 'socialisation' (i.e. the influence of social factors on a person). The point is not just that the social environment we live in contributes to making us the way we are. Rather, it is to say that the world is shaped by our ways of understanding and describing it. This is not a simple causal claim: e.g. it is not the claim that our ways of describing and understanding have their own effects (as, for example, in the self-fulfilling effect of labelling a child as 'delinquent'). Instead, we are dealing with a claim about the correct *status* to attribute to the things we say and believe about the world. Crudely put, there are two opposing approaches here. The first, call it 'realism', says that the world is such-and-such, and that our beliefs aim to map the way the world is. The other approach says that it makes no sense to think about the world as it exists prior to certain human ways of understanding it; rather, the world 'for us' is always structured by our concepts.

It's not immediately clear what this could mean. If it means that we understand the world through words and concepts, then that just seems obvious. If it means that there is nothing more to 'reality' than our perceptions of it, then that seems to raise unattractive spectres of idealism and relativism: reality consists of no more than our lonely thoughts, with nothing to attach themselves to; and no way of thinking or perceiving is 'truer' than any other. I've already said that the claim is not an ordinary causal one about the *effects*, on the world, of our ways of relating to it. So what else can it be?

In fact, the idea here is not particularly mysterious – as an example, drawing again on the phenomenon of intersexuality, helps to show. The intersex writer and activist Riki Wilchins emphasises the arbitrariness of the way in which gender is decided at birth:

[T]he overwhelming majority of infants diagnosed as 'intersex' are otherwise unremarkable children whose clitorises happen to be larger than two standard deviations from the mean – an arbitrary measure equal to about three eighths of an inch...If your organ is less than three eighths of an inch long, it's a clitoris and you're a baby girl. If it's longer than an inch, it's a penis and you're a baby boy... But if it's in between, you're a baby herm: The organ is an enlarged clit and it gets cut off.[16]

Wilchins reflects:

It's a startling example of the power of language, knowledge, and science to create bodies to realize that, if pediatricians agreed to increase this rule to, say, three standard deviations from the mean, thousands of intersex infants would be instantly 'cured'.

On the other hand, if they decided to decrease it to one-and-a-half standard deviations, one third to half of the female readers of this book would suddenly find themselves intersexed, and therefore candidates for genital surgery.[17]

Clearly, the claim being made here is not that certain material facts about the physical size and shape of people's organs are affected just by the standards we impose on them. A child's sexual organ would be the same length however we chose to define the cut-off point at which a 'clitoris' becomes a 'penis': what Wilchins is concerned to impress on us is that *without anything about us changing*, between a third and half of women could 'become' intersex overnight. That is because whether we are male or female or intersex is a product of the way in which humans have decided to carve up the world – in this case, literally.[18] If we think of there being a certain range of matter 'out there', we can then impose different categorisation systems or taxonomic schemes on that matter, and the scheme we choose will determine the identities and correct descriptions of various things or portions of matter. Depending on where you draw the line – and we are talking about fractions of inches here – you 'make' some individuals female, some male, and others ambiguous or intersex; draw the line slightly differently, and you can end up with a very different spread.

The same point can also be found in (for example) Foucault's work on the production of social identities such as that of the 'homosexual'. For Foucault, homosexuality may be considered a social construct, not in the sense that social rather than biological processes cause people to be attracted to the same sex (a claim usually associated with the homophobic Right), but in that it only makes sense to speak about 'homosexuals' once society has decided

---

[16] Wilchins (2004, pp. 79–80).   [17] Wilchins (2004, p. 80).

[18] Cf. Preves (2008, p. 33): 'The criteria for what counts as male or female, or as sexually ambiguous for that matter, are human standards.'

to make an *identity* out of the phenomenon of men sleeping with men – in the ancient world, for example, there was plenty of same-sex romantic and sexual activity, but nothing corresponding to the modern category of 'the homosexual', any more than we now have a particular social identity for those who eat a lot of cheese (we just think of cheese eating as an *activity*, rather than as a type of person). So when feminists say that sex differences are 'socially constructed', they don't mean that the differences between those we call male and those we call female are imaginary ones, and they don't *just* mean that the differences are partly generated by social processes, although this point is often made as well (for example, some have argued that the superior physical strength of men and boys is at least partly a product of differences in the ways in which boys and girls are encouraged to use their bodies).[19] The point is about a choice as to which differences we highlight, and what significance we attribute to them: those who invoke social construction are saying that this is at least partly a social matter, not a simple consequence of the nature of the world (i.e. the world independent of human conceptual activity).

It might still seem unclear exactly what is being said here. *Of course* the way in which we carve up the world will be at least partly due to social factors: human beings are the products of social contexts; and different social contexts will make different ways of analysing the world possible or likely or appealing for them – for instance, the explanation of why, prior to Linnaeus's discovery in the late eighteenth century, people considered that whales and dolphins were fish, must be a partly social one. That doesn't seem to mean that the differences and types we recognise are mere human inventions, corresponding to nothing real in the world. We believe, after all, that dolphins really are mammals, that mammals really are different from fish and reptiles – and that a taxonomic scheme based on evolutionary lineage, and on 'deeper' properties such as the way in which an animal reproduces, is in some sense *better* than one based on the more superficial difference between things that swim in water and things that walk on land.

So it's not just that there is a partly social explanation for the human behaviour of drawing up a certain taxonomy – as there will be for *any* given piece of human behaviour. Feminists who talk about the social construction

---

[19] See Young (2005).

of sex differences certainly take themselves to be making a more interesting and more critical claim than that. This more radical claim might hold that there is a fundamental mistake involved in assuming that there can be an independent 'fact of the matter' – even a complex, shifting and malleable fact of the matter – about what sexual types exist in the world. This suggestion takes us to the heart of one of the big debates within the philosophy of science: 'realists' about so-called 'natural kinds' often characterise scientific taxonomy as a project of trying to 'carve nature at the joints'; while critics of realism – such as those who advocate 'pragmatic' or 'interest-relative' accounts – argue that it makes no sense to think of these 'kinds' as already existing in the mind-independent external world, and propose that we should instead assess taxonomies according to the function they serve for us, in a given context and relative to a set of purposes.

Without going into the large and complex debate over the relative merits of realist and interest-relative accounts here, it is important just to note that when feminists talk about the social construction of gender categories, they are not saying anything which would be thought crazy or obviously false in another context. Connecting their critique to a broader movement in the philosophy of science also helps guard against an easy but mistaken way in which social constructionist critiques of sex difference might be dismissed. These critiques need not imply that every taxonomic scheme is as good as any other – they just require us to think in a different way about what makes a taxonomy a good or a bad one: instead of asking whether it correctly traces the dividing lines that already exist in the world, we should ask what the function of our system of sex classification is, how well and in what sense it 'works' for us.

We have already seen some of the reasons why many would say that the binary division between male and female *doesn't* 'work'. For one thing, there are a significant number of cases – the cases of intersex individuals – for which it seems to have no place. The situation of intersex people is important not only because intersex people are human beings who matter and who suffer under deeply hostile social structures, but also because their situation raises the question: what is it about our form of social life that cannot cope with the idea that someone might have both a testis and an ovary, or a set of XXY chromosomes? Why can't we tolerate grey areas (in this area)? Why do we need sex to be simple, so badly that we try literally to cut out of existence those who violate a neat binary system? As one intersex activist, Sarah Graham, puts it: 'We must be given the space to exist.'[20]

* * *

To sum up what has been said so far:

The feminist critique of the sex/gender distinction begins by noting that sex is a complex category, a cluster of distinct criteria rather than something single or simple. It is further noted that these criteria can come apart, as illustrated by the phenomenon of intersexuality, which is in turn a particularly clear illustration of a broader fact, namely that the bodily differences between human individuals do not constitute a clear-cut binary division – it is partly thanks to this that the maintenance and communication of male- or femaleness requires continual attention and effort (through grooming, posture, dress, and various other factors traditionally grouped under the heading of 'gender'). Thus far, the point seems to be just that we need to be more subtle and fine-grained about our categories; but the critique of the idea of sex implicit within the sex/gender model goes further than this.

First, there is an attempt to problematise the idea of naturalness, or rather, to problematise a widespread way of understanding naturalness – as simply equivalent to the fixed and unalterable – and to demonstrate that judgements of naturalness are always value-laden and indexed to a certain context. We may still judge that there are 'natural' differences which (more or less) reliably separate a 'male' category of humans from a 'female' one, of course, but the important thing is that we will have broken with the unreflective understanding of naturalness that many associate with the traditional sex/gender distinction.

The second point is that whatever natural features and differences we take to exist, it will always remain an open question whether these features and differences represent *appropriate points to draw the dividing lines of a taxonomy*. We might very plausibly say that it is a natural difference between cows, on the one hand, and fish and dolphins, on the other, that cows walk on land and fish and dolphins do not: nobody has yet trained a fish to walk. But at least in some scientific contexts, we now think that this natural difference between cows and dolphins is less salient than their common status as mammals. In the same way, we might well acknowledge certain natural differences

---

[20] Quoted in Morrison (2013).

between the sexes, just as we acknowledge that the difference between natural redheads and others is a *natural* difference, without necessarily taking this as being of great taxonomic significance – still less as having the particular, perhaps unparalleled significance that is generally attributed to the division between male and female.[21]

In general, what seems to be most troubling for many feminists is not the binary system of sex classification itself, but the spirit in which it is held and imposed. We act as if sex is a simple category, when on the most cursory inspection it reveals itself as a cluster of distinct things. We talk about sex difference as something 'natural', without acknowledging the ways in which naturalness is a value-laden and context-sensitive notion. And perhaps most striking of all is the sense that the system of sex classification and a person's place within it are (very, very) *important* matters – so important that it is necessary for us to *enforce* the system into holding true when 'nature' fails to co-operate (for instance, by producing a baby with genitals that are not obviously either male or female). Even for those who are able and willing to conform without medical 'assistance', it is necessary constantly to invest energy and attention in order to do so, and in order to signal to others the position which the system has accorded us.

But where does all this leave the present discussion? We set out from the question: what are women – which is to say, what is the subject matter of feminism?

The initially promising-seeming suggestion was then raised that we might either be talking about a sex or about a gender (most likely the gender: the term 'women' is usually regarded as a gender-term, with 'female' denoting the corresponding sex). What I've tried to show so far in this chapter, however, is that the feminist critique of the sex/gender model is a compelling one – and this complicates things.

In any case, the kinds of markers that are conventionally counted as belonging to 'sex' (e.g. chromosomes) fail to pick out 'women' in a way adequate to feminists' purposes. If we insist on meaning, by 'women', 'all and only those with XX chromosomes' (for instance), we will end up arbitrarily leaving out people who seem to have a perfectly good claim to be within the scope of

---

[21] Cf. Frye's extended thought experiment in which society is structured around an energetically cultivated and policed distinction between the owners of curly and straight pubic hair (Frye 1983, p. 30).

feminist concern: people such as some intersex and trans women, who are classed as women or girls in their everyday lives, who identify themselves as women, and who are oppressed as women. Nor is it obviously adequate to define 'women' in terms of gender, whilst retaining the traditional distinction between the latter and sex, for the sorts of reasons we have now seen.[22]

One radical response to this, and to the kinds of problems raised by the critique of the sex/gender distinction, might be to ditch the offending terms altogether: 'sex', 'gender' and also 'women'. Instead of arguing for the liberation of women, we just refuse to acknowledge that category (or the category of men). Whether this is appealing or not will partly depend on the extent to which you think that it makes sense to recognise two basic groupings of human: men and women. On what is probably the most radical possible reading of the social constructionist critique considered above, drawing a division between males and females is no more necessary or sensible than dividing the population up into 'X's – 'people with brown hair and blue eyes who were raised by a single parent' – and 'Y's –'people with dark hair and eyes who were born in London'. Like the categories of male and female, these categories will fail to cover everyone, and there will be some people who have elements of both – e.g. blue-eyed people who were born in London. We may also imagine that, by some energy-intense and often highly traumatic process, some society has managed partially to impose this preferred scheme – by transporting dark-eyed people to London, dying the hair of blond children of single parents, and so on.

In such a situation, there might be some grounds for people who opposed this scheme to simply stop talking about X's and Y's, to point out that these are perverse categories, and to use language in such a way as to acknowledge and concentrate on other, more pertinent features. But even then, it might not be possible or wise. At least in order to talk about social history, it would be necessary to talk about X and Y (and for this to have some meaning for people). And practices of thought, language and action might have shaped themselves around the X/Y division so profoundly as to make it very difficult

---

[22] Moreover, delineating those whose *gender* is female as the subject matter of feminism (and its object of concern) poses the problem that the way in which 'gender' is defined is in danger of resulting in the exclusion of those who fail to exhibit the stock traits and characteristics designated as 'feminine'. 'Masculine' women would then not count as women for the purposes of feminism.

to describe and critique the X/Y-divided status quo without recourse to its own categories.

In the chapters that follow, I will use all of the following three terms without apology: 'sex', 'gender', 'women'. But my usage should not be understood as endorsing the sorts of conflations and false dichotomies detected by critics of the sex/gender distinction. I will use the terms 'sex' and 'gender' loosely, and *more or less* interchangeably (a policy which I take to be in line with ordinary non-academic usage): the term 'sex' may be used where I wish to place emphasis on those features which are – or are generally taken to be – bodily or biological; but I make no suggestion that the bodily and biological are the same as the natural or unalterable; and I do not assume that 'sex' is opposed to 'gender' – i.e. that what is one is not also the other. For instance, I would be inclined to talk about beauty norms as 'gendered', rather than as 'sexed', because *norms* are generally understood as something social or cultural – even though beauty norms obviously apply to the *body* and are applied partly on the basis of (an assumption about) what genitalia you possess. By contrast, I would tend to talk about the inequality 'of the sexes' in the context of (e.g.) voting rights, because I take it that legal restrictions on voting were, in principle at least, intended to follow a biological fault-line, rather than to exclude all those with feminine appearance or mannerisms from voting. I have no idea whether there are any documented examples of this, but I imagine that whipping your cock out would have been sufficient evidence of eligibility to vote in 1900,[23] no matter how smooth and hairless your skin and no matter what you were wearing.

The reason why most feminists still talk about the category of 'women', even those who also profess not to believe in it – and why certain critical race theorists also talk about 'black people' – is similar. It is generally acknowledged – something that cannot currently be said in the case of sex – that race is *not* a scientifically bona fide category, and that terms like 'black' fail to pick out any 'natural kinds'. But there is *also* a sense in which categories such as 'black' and 'white' are painfully real: clearly, real people have used and continue to use these terms to refer to and distinguish between real populations, in order to do real things to them – whether to subordinate, abuse and marginalise, to privilege, or to resist. Because race is not only a fiction, but a

---

[23] As long as you also fulfilled the property requirement, of course. Universal male suffrage wasn't introduced until 1918.

harmful fiction, some have suggested that those people 'racialised as black' should refuse to identify themselves in racial terms – and that we should all stop talking in terms of 'black' and 'white'. In reply, however, others such as Charles Mills have argued that this policy is escapist and self-undermining, and that (for the time being) we have no real option but to continue to use racial terms, whilst taking pains to avoid reifying or endorsing them.[24]

The line I'll take on the language of sex and gender in this book runs parallel to that taken by Mills on race. Sex and gender terms such as 'woman' – whatever we think they refer to in the world – are bound up with a system of practices which degrade and subordinate the people they are used to designate so that, to the extent to which sex or gender is a fiction, it is (like race) a harmful one. At the same time, these social practices are sufficient to make womanhood something real – something which feminists, in particular, need to be able to talk about. The refusal to use any gender and sex terms would make it virtually impossible for us to talk about what we want to talk about. Assuming that patriarchy is not going to dissolve just through our boycotting (whether spontaneously or systematically and gradually) the language of sex and sex difference, feminists have little choice but to deal with and in these terms.[25]

What, though, *are* we talking about? We may have found reason to keep using these terms, but that is not the same as giving an account of what the terms actually mean and what they refer to in the world. The task of giving such an account, as we've already seen, is highly problematic. Doing it in terms of either sex or gender differences didn't seem adequate for feminists' purposes. One other suggestion that might be made is that we understand what it means to be a woman in terms of a shared set of *experiences* that unites an otherwise diverse and disparate group. But this idea has been criticised by feminists who point out that differences of race, social class and sexuality among women may be so profound that there is no single experience or set of experiences which all women share.[26] Any attempt to locate a 'golden nugget

---

[24] Mills (1998).

[25] This does not necessarily mean, however, that there is no place for performative experiments in the elimination of gendered language. These might have a value. The point is only that this *alone* cannot adequately serve feminist ends, and so it would be a mistake to think of this linguistic boycott as something to be imposed on all feminists at all times.

[26] Spelman (1988). This is known as her 'particularity argument'.

of womanness'[27] will only end up committing the old mistake of passing off the characteristics and situation of the relatively privileged as if they applied to everybody – as in what Elizabeth Spelman calls 'white solipsism', where white women generalise from their own privileged experiences of womanhood.[28]

My instinct is that our best course would be to stand back from the 'What are women?' question at this point. It is important to say something against various familiar, flawed and damaging ways of answering that question – as certain critics of the sex/gender distinction, as well as (in a different way) people like Spelman have done. Not only is there no 'golden nugget', but perhaps there is no *generally* useful answer at all to the question of what women are (though there may be locally useful answers, applicable in specific contexts). And perhaps we don't need such a general account. We may not know *what* women are – and perhaps this is no surprise, if the category of 'women' is as problematic as many feminists have suggested. But that doesn't mean we don't know *who* they are.

This may sound like a glib distinction, but I think it is important. There are familiar contexts in which there is a big difference between the 'what' and the 'who' question. Every schoolchild knows who is cool, but they do not necessarily know *what* is cool – i.e. what it is that makes the cool people cool – and that may be because there is no real answer to that question, only a loose and ever-shifting collection of things. The only general thing we can say about coolness is perhaps that it involves the granting and enjoyment of a certain kind of social recognition and esteem. Everything else is up for negotiation, or subject to the arbitrary whim of whoever (if anyone) gets to decide such things.

In a similar spirit, some feminists have argued that if there is anything general which may be said about what women are, it is something about their position in society, the respect and esteem which they are (or rather, are not) accorded.[29] The view of some radical feminists, for example, has been that

---

[27] Ibid., p. 159.   [28] Ibid.

[29] For Catharine MacKinnon, for instance, genders are *by definition* hierarchical, and this hierarchy is tied to sexualised power relations: the meaning of the terms 'masculine' and 'men' is bound up with sexual and social dominance; 'feminine' and 'women' with subordination and submission. It follows that talking about 'gender equality' is at best odd, and that the liberation of women would spell the end of gender categories as we know them. See MacKinnon (1989).

being a woman is to belong to a subordinate social caste. Of course, there are other subordinate castes and groups than women, and so this won't do as a definition, but it is a promising suggestion as to the *kind of category* that 'woman' is. We could do worse, I suggest, than to understand by 'women': *those who are oppressed as women*[30] (*and oppressed also by dominant biologistic and essentialist usages of the term 'woman'*). Of course, this raises the further question of what it means to be oppressed 'as a woman', and might trigger accusations of circularity: how can we define 'women' as those who are oppressed 'as women', when the whole point was that we were trying to work out what women are?[31] But we shouldn't be too intimidated by this kind of fancy analytic footwork, I think. We have a pretty good idea, as a society and as individuals, *who* women are. After all, how else would we know who to subordinate?

* * *

The point of this chapter has not just been to offer a long-winded justification of my own terminological policy. As I observed at the start, the way in which we think about sex and gender makes a difference to the way in which we might think and act as feminists. According to the critique that I've tried to reconstruct above, the sex/gender model adopted by many feminists preserves a key ingredient of the patriarchal conceptions of sex difference that feminists should be trying to challenge: the idea of a fixed, 'natural' substratum, 'sex', upon which gender variations may be (more or less perfectly or awkwardly) superimposed.

At the same time, I was careful to emphasise that the answer does not lie in the renunciation of all talk of 'nature' or 'sex difference', restricting ourselves completely to the language of the social. The most general lesson of the discussion above is perhaps a warning against rigidity and one-sidedness. Certainly, one of the more obvious examples of the kind of view to be avoided may be the traditional patriarchal idea – arguably preserved in the approach of some feminists – that the difference between men and women is, at the most fundamental level, a natural difference (where 'natural' is assumed to be a pre-social and pre-political category): some things are nature and some things are nurture; nature sets the ultimate constraints on what nurture can

---

[30] See Haslanger (2005) for a defence of this approach.

[31] Haslanger (2012) suggests as a criterion: being subordinated on the basis of presumed female sex. But see Jenkins (forthcoming) for a critique of Haslanger's account, focusing on its inability to accommodate the cases of certain trans women.

achieve – and there is an end to it. But a contrasting approach, also one-sided, which sees gender identity as something infinitely malleable, is just as fraught with problems and has just as much sinister political potential. It's striking that many testimonies of trans and intersex people emphasise an early conviction of a 'true' gender identity, not adequately expressed by the sex and gender assigned: 'I always knew I was really a girl.' It's important to see that this is neither a vindication of gender essentialism (the view, often biologistic in its elaboration, that there is some fixed 'essence' which makes people women or men), nor merely confused or deluded. Such statements are both an expression of a subjective truth – a truth about a person's experience and sense of self – and also a rational reaction against a certain kind of social and intellectual context: a context characterised by the attitude that gender can be cultivated and engineered in whatever way society deems appropriate. John Money, the psychologist famous for advising in the case of identical twin boys, one of whom had lost his penis in a botched circumcision, took the view that gender identity was completely unfixed before the age of three: if a child was raised as a boy or as a girl from before that age, they could develop into a healthy boy or girl, man or woman. Money's theory is generally regarded as having been falsified in tragic fashion by the outcome of the 'experiment' involving the twins: the child raised as a girl never adjusted to this gender identity, and both siblings ultimately committed suicide. The temptation for many has been to take this episode as a grim reminder that nature is destiny: girls will be girls and boys will be boys. But the experiences of many others – of some intersex and trans people, who see their destiny as lying in a departure from the sex assigned to them at birth – tell a different story.

Sex, or gender, is never *just* natural, physical, or biological, and never *just* social or political, but always – simultaneously and inextricably – both. Both natural or biologistic and also social concepts and categories can be used to capture aspects of what it means to be female and male, women and men. And giving a dogmatic and inflexible primacy to either kind of conception is equally liable to contribute to oppressive and often devastating social practices.

I have conspicuously skirted around the issue of transsexual and trans-gender identities – and the situations of trans women in particular. This is an issue which looms ever larger in debates within contemporary feminism, although it has for some time been a point of contention for some radical feminists. Certain of these feminists – most notoriously, perhaps, lesbian feminists Sheila Jeffreys and Janice Raymond – have attacked both male-to-female and female-to-male transsexuals as imposters and deserters respectively.[32] The sometimes viciously transphobic tendency within radical feminism (a label which in some circles has in fact become virtually synonymous with transphobia)[33] has festered into a fraught and ugly antagonism among self-described feminists.[34] I confess that I have avoided dealing in depth with the subject partly because it can be such a minefield, at times a mind-achingly complex hotspot of fear and hatred, confusion and division. A more positive way to put it – and also true – would be to say that transfeminism is a rich body of work and practice worth studying in its own right. It would be especially unwise to try to wade right into the set of issues around trans people and transfeminism at the *end* of a chapter. But it also would be negligent not to acknowledge this cluster of arguments and concerns at all, and not to say something about how the thoughts laid out in this chapter might bear on them. An understandable suspicion might be that the kind of construal of the category of 'women' that I've been most sympathetic to, i.e. the one which understands it as a kind of class or caste term, tends towards a feminism that is inhospitable to trans women. The thought is especially understandable given the fact that some transphobic or trans exclusionary radical feminists have held precisely this view, and have used it to support their contention that a person born male can no more become a woman by sheer fiat than a white person can acquire an identity as e.g. 'black' or 'African American' just by colouring his or her skin.[35] Those who hold this position argue that trans women (whom they typically refuse to call 'women' and seek to exclude from women-only spaces) enjoy 'male privilege' due to having lived as men before living as women – a privileged history which cannot be shed or shared.

If these were inescapable implications of a 'positional' account of what it means to be a woman, then that would be troubling indeed. But this does

---

[32] Raymond's 1979 book *The Transsexual Empire: the making of the she-male* went as far as to claim: 'All transsexuals rape women's bodies by reducing the real female form to an artifact, appropriating this body for themselves'. Jeffreys (2003), meanwhile, accuses female-to-male transsexualism as capitulation to misogyny.

[33] Another label commonly used is TERF ('trans exclusionary radical feminist').

[34] For an interesting discussion of this, see Goldberg (2014).

[35] This is the position of members of the eco-feminist group 'Deep Green Resistance', as discussed in Goldberg (2014). See also Raymond (1994, p. xvi).

not seem to me to be the case. What we do have to reject, I think, is the idea that being a woman is no more than a state of mind, a way that we 'feel inside'. There is much more to it than that, of course: women are those who occupy a particular position in society relative to men (regardless of how anyone feels about it), and who face particular kinds of discrimination and oppression. We also have to reject at all costs any account which denies the significance of differences among the oppressed class that we associate with the term 'women'. Just as a woman is oppressed in a different way depending on whether she is white or black or brown, middle, upper or working class,[36] it is also true that she is oppressed in a different way depending on whether she is cis-gender[37] or whether she was originally categorised by society as male. Each of these identities might carry with it certain kinds of privilege: in the case of white and upper- or middle-class women, this is obvious enough; but it may also be true that black and working-class women are exempt from certain forms of oppression which apply in particular or predominantly to more privileged women – for instance, affluent white women have historically been more likely to be confined to the home, while black and working-class women have been not only allowed but compelled to work – *and this kind of exemption might itself be described, in a very thin sense, as a form of privilege (even, at a stretch,* male *privilege, in the sense of being a treatment that is disproportionately applied to men rather than women).* Clearly, none of this means that (e.g.) black and working-class women are not 'women'. By the same logic, we can allow that the situation of trans women is not equivalent to that of cis women, and even that this situation sometimes carries an exemption from certain aspects of oppression which apply to cis women, without concluding that they must therefore be denied their identity as women.

It seems clear enough that trans women are oppressed in many of the same ways that cis women are – this is so insofar as society treats them 'as women'.[38] To the extent that this treatment stops short of full recognition

---

[36] This has come to be known as the phenomenon of 'intersectionality' (see Crenshaw 1991; Hill Collins 1998, 2000).

[37] The term 'cis-' indicates that the person to whom it is applied has a gender identity which corresponds to the sex they were assigned at birth (simply put: if you are not trans, you are cis).

[38] This is presumably so in a case where a trans woman is taken by others to be a cis woman, but may also be so in the case where she is not: it is quite possible to treat someone as X (in various ways), whilst simultaneously (in other ways) refusing to

and acceptance of their gender identities, trans people of whatever gender may also be oppressed *as trans* – and as we've seen, this often takes place within movements which have women's liberation as their stated objective (and which trans women might otherwise turn to for support). It is also clear that the situation of trans women is then *not* akin to that of privileged subsets within the class of women – e.g. white women – where the privilege attached to membership of those subsets far outweighs any disadvantages. On the contrary, trans women suffer extraordinary levels of formal and informal discrimination and violence.[39] In the last instance, the question of whether and when to call someone a woman is not a metaphysical or conceptual question – a question about what that person ('really') *is* – but a fundamentally *practical, political and ethical* question:[40] it is a question about the sorts of social practices which are inflicted on them and which shape their experiences; and it is also a practical question in the sense of being answerable to the feminist goal of bringing the oppression that centres around the categories of sex and gender to an end. On both counts, it seems to me, respecting people's self-ascriptions of gender is a no-brainer. There is room in feminism for women who have lived as men or boys. Moreover, feminism as a movement stands to benefit from trans insights into the system of patriarchy. If the epistemic vantage point of trans women is discussed, it is often to make the argument that the latter can never really know what it is like to have been born female and to have been socialised from your earliest moments in line with what is expected of a woman or girl. What is less often acknowledged is that the situation of a trans woman, or a person transitioning to womanhood, can also carry epistemic advantages which are not available to cis women. What to women who have always been (treated as) women or girls may be

recognise them as X – take, for example, the practice of trying some children as adults in US courts.

[39] As Goldberg (2014) observes: 'although radical feminism is far from achieving all its goals, women have won far more formal equality than trans people have. In most states, it's legal to fire someone for being transgender, and transgender people can't serve in the military. A recent survey by the National Center for Transgender Equality and the National Gay and Lesbian Task Force found overwhelming levels of anti-trans violence and persecution. Forty-one per cent of respondents said that they had attempted suicide.'

[40] See Bettcher (2009). Bettcher, a trans woman and feminist philosopher, argues for the principle that trans people have 'first-person authority' over their own gender identities, and argues that this is an *ethical* principle above all.

so 'normal' as to be invisible can, for someone entering the social identity of womanhood as a conscious adult, be unmissably vivid. Trans feminist blogger Lisa Millbank describes her experience of transition as one of watching various male privileges dropping away but leaving their residue behind:

> As I've moved from 'male' to 'freak', I've found that my *social* male privileges have been largely suspended in that, by people not treating me as male, I'm not offered most social privileges. As I've moved from 'freak' to 'female', most of these haven't returned. In general, I've experienced these privileges as ones which are *removed from me* by society based on its perception of me. Broadly, I characterise the removal of these privileges as misogyny, i.e. the normal condition of being a woman under patriarchy . . . [O]n the subject of *internalised* privileges . . . my sense of when to speak up in a group is sometimes still closely matched to the patterns taught to men, which given that I spend increasing amounts of time in women-only organising spaces means that I need to work hard to consciously speak less. As I've moved from 'freak' to 'female', I've begun to experience some of the policing mechanisms experienced by women since birth and which act to suppress self-worth and confidence in women under patriarchy. Nowadays I can expect to be censured if I speak in a way that's perceived to be 'too confident' for a woman, in the same way as most people *assigned female at birth* (AFAB) are censured. Because it hasn't been happening to me for as long as it has to AFAB women, it hasn't had as much effect yet. Like with loss of *social* privilege, I characterise this as misogyny.[41]

For Millbank, feminists should not rest content with the critique of the binary division between male and female, man and woman, and all that this entails. We have to address a gender 'ternary': a three-part structure comprising men, women and 'freaks' (i.e. those who, like many transsexuals and intersex people, are not accepted as belonging to any of the approved sex or gender categories). As she puts it: 'That is why I want radical feminism and transsexual feminism to work together to destroy patriarchy.'[42]

* * *

In this chapter, I've been concerned with the way in which the subject matter of feminism is decided and defined, questioned and contested. In the next, I turn to its history.

---

[41] Millbank (2011).   [42] Ibid.

5   Whose story?

'Herstory' is a term associated with the ideas of (a) telling women's history, (b) *women* telling their own history and (c) feminist critique of the way the discipline of history is practised, with a particular critical focus on language-use (e.g. making a big deal out the fact that it's *his*-story not *her*-story).[1]

I decided to include a brief comment on the idea of herstory here because it is a point on which feminism is particularly likely to attract ridicule – in fact, the term is probably used more often by those taking the piss out of feminists than by feminists themselves. It is ridiculed on the following main grounds:

1. 'History' is just a word! Why not focus on the things that actually matter to women, rather than engaging in this tedious policing of language?
2. Feminists are simply mistaken about the etymology anyway! 'History' doesn't come from 'his' + 'story'. So the 'herstory' brigade are not only tedious but laughable.

As far as the second point goes, it is certainly true that 'history' doesn't come from 'his' plus 'story'. The actual etymology, for what it's worth, is as follows. The two terms, 'history' and 'story', were used interchangeably in Middle English, and are cognate, i.e. they come from the same source: the Latin term *historia* (taken over from Greek). The Greek term comes from *histor* ('judge' or 'wise man'), which gives rise to the verb *historein* ('to enquire'), so that *historia* refers to the results of that process: an 'enquiry' or 'account'. Very much nothing to do with the male possessive pronoun. But are we really supposed to believe that these feminists simply don't know that? That they haven't

---

[1] For a fascinating example of this, see part III of Andrea Dworkin's first book, *Woman Hating*, entitled 'The herstory', and also the Afterword to the same text: 'The great punctuation typography struggle'.

bothered to look it up?[2] Instead of assuming so, we would do better to ask *what feminists might be trying to do* by introducing and using the term 'herstory', and thus how they might also respond to the first charge above. Here is what they might say:

Of course we don't want to suggest a mere change in the use of words, keeping our practices the same. What feminist would be satisfied with that? The term 'herstory' stands for a different way of *practising* history, after all. And of course we should focus on things that are politically significant, things that matter. But, crucially, we claim that language *is* politically significant, and *does* matter. This is so in two main ways.

First, it has an *epistemic* significance – i.e. it can bring things to our attention, increase our knowledge. Politics leaves traces in our language, so that it is possible to *read the world back off* the language we use, much as we can infer something about the diet of an individual owl, of owls in general, and even about the surrounding ecosystem, by dissecting its pellets.

Secondly, language *constitutes* a certain kind of political practice. As I suggested in the first main chapter of this book, there can be no sharp separation between theory and practice, between sayings and doings. The way in which history is told, and the way in which language is used, *cannot be politically neutral matters.*[3] And if that is right, it means that language is not just an enemy for us to fight, but also one of the political weapons at our disposal: we can *do* things with words, and one of the things we can do with words is *resist* the things that others do – including what they do with words.

And sometimes, if we want – as a way of provoking, or of drawing attention to something – we can even make words up.

There are any number of ways to tell the history, or herstory, of feminism. My aim here is not to argue for any particular version of the story. What I will

---

[2] A more recent but equally notorious feminist made-up word might be applicable here: 'mansplaining'.

[3] Nor, for that matter, is the telling of 'herstory' – and the understanding of what it means to tell herstory – a politically neutral matter among feminists. As Carby (1997, p. 120) points out: 'The herstory of black women is interwoven with that of white women but this does not mean they are the same story. Nor do we need white feminists to write our herstory for us; we can and are doing that for ourselves. However, when they write their herstory and call it the story of women but ignore our lives and deny their relation to us, that is the moment in which they are acting within the relations of racism and writing history.'

do instead is set out a very familiar version, and then show what is wrong with it – not by holding it up against The Full And True Story of feminism (I offer no such thing), but by selecting a few relevant facts and examples, case studies or snapshots (many of which are remarkably underacknowledged). These are very far from constituting an alternative comprehensive history of feminism, but I think they are sufficient to show that whatever an adequate history of feminism would look like, it would *not* look much like the story that we are often told.

* * *

A summary of the sort of account that is most often given or assumed, as to the historical origins and development of feminism, would go roughly as follows:

> Women were oppressed and mistreated for most of human history, until people began to realise, in the nineteenth and early twentieth centuries, that this was wrong. It was only a few people to begin with – like John Stuart Mill, who was one of the first to advocate giving women the vote. But gradually more and more people were convinced. There was also a militant movement, the 'Suffragettes'; but it's unclear whether their aggressive tactics were effective or not – there is some case for thinking that they were counter-productive. When women finally got the vote in Britain, in 1918,[4] it was probably more out of recognition of their hard work during the First World War than because of their chaining themselves to railings.
>
> That was the first wave of feminism – all about votes for women. After this goal was achieved, for many years, nothing happened. The second wave came in the late 1960s and 1970s. Feminists began arguing that it was not enough to have formal legal equality, as enshrined in voting rights, for example. They wanted more, to make this equality fuller and more meaningful: things like equal pay for equal work, access to reproductive healthcare and birth control, different and 'freer' kinds of sex, a more equal division of domestic chores. And that was fair enough – although some of them went a bit far, burning bras and living in lesbian communes and so on.[5]

---

[4] Women did not get the vote *on equal terms with men* until 1928 in the UK.

[5] Whilst there were many lesbian separatist movements and communities, the bra-burning thing is over-blown. That idea comes from a protest staged by feminists at the 1968 Miss America Pageant, at which women hurled various items which they associated with women's oppression – including bras, high-heeled shoes and dish rags – into a 'Freedom Trash Can'.

So in sum, the nineteenth century was about voting, and the twentieth century was about sex and the body. Just as the first wave achieved its objective and then died down, the second wave made many gains (such as the UK Equal Pay Act of 1970). There are still some residual injustices, but we – we in the West, at least – have come a long way.

The strictly factual claims made here are not false. The dates are right: there was indeed an upsurge of high-profile feminist activism in the late sixties and in the seventies. And sex and the body certainly were central themes of the so-called second wave. Nevertheless, we might still dispute the picture that is conjured up by the familiar account just given. That account is not simply identical with the individual factual claims of which it is composed. By what it does *not* say, as well as by what it says, it implies a whole lot more than this. It paints feminism as a fairly recent discovery – at times, we could be forgiven for thinking that it was a nineteenth-century invention of J. S. Mill himself.[6] In reality, however, feminist ideas go back much, much further than this (I'll discuss some examples of earlier feminist thought later on in this chapter). We might also criticise the way in which the received view underplays the work undertaken *between* the so-called 'waves' – even if we confine ourselves to considering only relatively recent efforts to resist male domination in Europe and the US, the emphasis on 'first-' and 'second-wave' feminism ignores the ongoing resistance to male domination between the 1920s and 1960s, as well as much of the work that has taken place outside 'mainstream' politics (particularly by black and working-class women).[7] As many feminists have pointed out, progress is not steady or unidirectional, but subject to breaks and reversals, periods of backlash or co-option.[8] The idea that such progress as there has been was simply a matter of people gradually realising that the status quo was unjust, and then doing something about it, is also highly misleading (as I'll argue throughout this chapter): the development of feminism cannot be adequately understood in terms of the

[6] Alison Stone goes one better, and opens her introductory book on feminism with the astonishing sentence: 'Feminist philosophy arose in the early 1970s and has developed most strongly in Western Europe, North America, and Australasia' (2007, p. 1).

[7] See Cott (1987).

[8] Millett (1969) refers to the period between 1930 and 1960 as a 'counter-revolution', whilst Faludi (1993) examines the 'backlash' that followed the successes of the 'second wave'.

imposition of *ideas* on a passive reality; social reality plays an active role, affects what ideas arise, when they arise, and when and whether they catch on. It is important to notice, finally, that the received view as laid out above not only suggests that the West is more advanced *now* in terms of the position of women, but also implies – at least by omission – that feminist progress has historically been a matter of the West leading 'the rest'. What room is there, in this picture, for the twelfth-century Islamic scholars (both male and female), who espoused ideals of equality between the sexes not advocated by Western thinkers until the eighteenth and nineteenth centuries?[9] What room is there for the fact that in the first Muslim societies, women possessed the independent property rights which Caroline Norton was fighting for in the nineteenth century in Britain?[10] The point here is not to idealise any society or epoch, but just to point out that the usual story is bullshit (in the strict, Frankfurtian sense of the term)[11] – and suspiciously convenient bullshit, at that.

The rest of this chapter – the rest of this book, in fact – is meant as an antidote to the received wisdom. The standard account laid out above, it should already be clear, is a mess. It is much easier to make a mess than to clear one up, and I won't try to address everything that is wrong with the received view at once. In this chapter, I'll concentrate on offering some correctives to two interconnected errors embodied in that view: the illusion of a young feminism; and the bias towards views of history which privilege theory over practice. In the process, however, I'll also be able to emphasise the importance of contributions from women writers and activists – and to shrink John Stuart Mill back down to his correct, bean-like size.

So how old is feminism *really*? In order to get anywhere with this question, we first have to distinguish between the *word* and the phenomenon that it refers to. The word 'feminism' itself *is* quite new. The term does not seem to have been used to refer to the advocacy of the advancement or emancipation of

---

[9] For example: Ibn Asakir, who argued that women should be able to receive degrees and become scholars; or Ibn Rushd (Averroes), who regarded men and women as equal in all respects, including military capabilities.

[10] The Acts of 1870 and 1882 (written by Richard Pankhurst, husband of Emmeline and father of the Pankhurst sisters) finally gave women, respectively, the right to independent earnings and property in the UK.

[11] The relevant criterion here is that those who say these things have *no interest in their truth-value, one way or the other* (see Frankfurt 2005).

women until the late nineteenth century – although it was occasionally used before that (from 1851), to refer to the *quality or state of being feminine*. It was only after the First International Women's Conference in 1892 that it took on its current significance (following the use of the French *féministe*). During the 1860s–80s in America, the different term 'womanism' was used, and some contemporary feminists have proposed reverting to this term in order to evoke a feminism more inclusive of black and working-class women,[12] more responsive to what some have termed the 'problem of intersectionality'.[13]

But although the term 'feminism' is fairly new, feminist concerns, sentiments and actions are not. On the barest definition – where 'feminism' is anything that represents or enacts the view that there is something wrong or unjust about the way in which women are treated in society, and that this should change – feminism is probably as old as women's subordination. In any case, instances of something recognisable to us as feminist thought and action certainly go back a lot further than the eighteenth or nineteenth century.

For want of a better starting point, let us go back to the fifteenth. According to Miriam Schneir, the first work of explicit praise and defence of women to be written *by a woman* – although by 'woman', it may be that we should read 'Western woman' – was Christine de Pisan's *The City of Ladies*, published in 1405.[14] Unfortunately, this seems to have been pretty awful. The book features the characters of Lady Reason, Lady Justice and Lady Rectitude, who appear to Christine in order to instruct her on the construction of a city for 'virtuous' women (the non-virtuous, it is made clear, are to be strictly banished to outside the city's walls). But it does exhibit an enduring theme of later feminism, namely the defence of the appropriateness of education for women; and it suggests some (rather basic) 'error theories' – ideological explanations, at a push – for the prevailing misogynistic wisdom, mostly by referring to what we might now call 'male pride': 'Thus, not all men (and especially the wisest) share the opinion that it is bad for women to be educated. But it is very true that many foolish men have claimed this *because it displeased them that women knew more than they did*.'[15]

---

[12] E.g. Alice Walker (1990, p. 370).   [13] See Crenshaw (1991).

[14] Schneir (1996, p. xii).

[15] Pisan (1405; emphasis added). In addition, she tells us: '[t]hose motivated by the infirmity of their bodies are cripples with misshapen bodies and crooked limbs.

The following century yields something more exhilarating, in the shape of a spate of anonymous pamphleteers in Elizabethan England. In the second half of the sixteenth century, shortly after the beginning of Elizabeth's reign, a number of pamphlets appeared under the name 'Jane Anger' (which may or may not have been the real name of the author, but in any case has to be up there with Sojourner Truth, Shulamith Firestone, Nina Power and Felicia Herrschaft in any 'best feminist name' contest). In 1559, Anger was already railing against the popular attitude that 'to shun a shower of rain and know the way to our husband's bed is wisdom sufficient for us women',[16] hitting on a thought better known from the work of John Stuart Mill three centuries later (i.e. the idea that the horizons of women's knowledge and understanding were artificially constrained rather than naturally limited), as well as making the critique, characteristic of more contemporary feminism, of the reduction of women to sex objects. This passage, from 'Her Protection for Women', even anticipates an important insight of feminists of the second wave, namely the idea that women are trapped in a series of 'double-binds' which have to do with their sexual significance to men:

> They have bene so daintely fed with our good natures, that like jades (their stomackes are grown so quesie) they surfeit of our kindnes. If we wil not suffer them to smell on our smockes, they will snatch at our peticotes: but if our honest natures cannot away with that uncivil kinde of jesting then we are coy: yet if we beare with their rudenes, and be somwhat modestly familiar with them, they will straight make matter of nothing, blazing abroad that they have surfeited with love, and then their wits must be showen in telling the maner how.[17]

Compare this with the words of an anonymous feminist activist quoted in a publication called *The Torch* in 1987:

> if we enjoy sex we're nymphos and if we don't we're frigid and if we love women it's because we can't get a 'real' man and if we ask our doctor too many questions we're neurotic and/or pushy and if we expect childcare we're

> Their minds are malicious and sharp, and they have no other means of vengeance for the misery of their impotence than to blame those [women] who bring gladness to others . . .'. In short, then: men are misogynistic because they are insecure, either because they're stupid or because they're ugly (or both).

[16] Cited in Schneir (1996, p. xiii).   [17] Anger (1589).

selfish and if we stand up for our rights we're aggressive and 'unfeminine' and if we don't we're typical weak females and if we want to get married we're out to trap a man and if we don't we're unnatural and because we still can't get an adequate safe contraceptive but men can walk on the moon and if we can't cope or don't want a pregnancy we're made to feel guilty about abortion and . . . for lots of other reasons we are part of the women's liberation movement.

The idea of the 'double-bind'[18] is that of being in a situation where you get punished (or 'negatively reinforced') *whatever you do*: however you react to the situation. Both Anger and the much more recent commentator quoted above might be interpreted as picking up on exactly this phenomenon, which is a crucial feature of the way in which what I have been calling 'patriarchal ideology' works: if we look, we can begin to detect an endless series of 'damned-if-you-do, damned-if-you-don't' laws which apply to women in particular; that is to say, a succession of double-binds which are imposed on women *qua* women – perhaps the pithiest summary of this is given by contemporary feminist Gail Dines, who describes women as being faced with two basic alternatives: be 'fuckable', or be 'invisible'.[19]

Also striking is the sheer *anger* of Anger's prose. Her injunction is simple – 'Hate those who shall speak anything in the dispraise or to the dishonour of our sex'[20] – and she has a devastatingly short way with would-be critics: 'it is to be feared that your setled wits wil advisedly condemn that, which my cholloricke vaine hath rashly set downe, and so perchance, ANGER shal reape anger for not agreeing with diseased persons . . .' The message is clear: you won't like what I have to say, because it threatens the status quo and the comfortable complacency ('setled wits') with which you regard it; my anger ('cholloricke vain') will make you angry, you will succumb to it like an infectious disease ('ANGER shal reape anger'), precisely because you have aligned yourself with the object of my anger and have so far been enjoying the benefit of *freedom* from anger; but your freedom is no freedom, and you will catch no real disease from me; your 'freedom', your alignment with the

---

[18] Cf. Bateson (1972).

[19] Dines (2010). This is of course not to deny that men can be placed in double-binds – although feminists might be more reluctant to accept that there are any such binds which affect men *as men*.

[20] Cited in Schneir (1996, p. xiii).

existing state of things, *is* your disease – and one of its symptoms is that it makes you highly intolerant of any attempt to diagnose it. What Anger is doing here is describing, and raging against, the ideology of patriarchy.

A feature of the standard history of feminism is the sense that the anger of and on behalf of women was something that built up slowly, that earlier feminists were polite, later ones more militant and uncompromising: peaceful, constitutionalist suffragists making way for the ball-breaking suffragettes; Wollstonecraft making way for Mill making way for provocative figures of the 'second wave'. It's not hard to see how this encouragement to believe that this is how things have happened (and that the process has yielded slow but steady and substantial progress) might also encourage us to accept that this is how things *should* happen – and therefore that we are too impatient, if we get angry within our own lifetimes. But it is not at all clearly the case that this is how the history of feminism has worked, as the example of Jane Anger, a sixteenth-century writer who rivals later radical feminists in terms of polemical verve, illustrates very well.

In fact, many would also want to make a case for the polemic power of figures such as Wollstonecraft and Mill, who do certainly have their moments (as witnessed by the dignity and defiance of Wollstonecraft's statement, 'I might have expressed concern on a lower key; but I am afraid it would have been the whine of affectation, and not the faithful expression of my feelings, of the clear result which experience and reflection have led me to draw').[21] We will deal with Mill soon enough. But it is worth pointing out here that if there is any era that stands out for the timidity, acquiescence, deference and conciliatoriness of tone with which any vaguely feminist sentiments are expressed, it may well be the great era of 'I'm not a feminist, but...':[22] the era in which we now live.

---

[21] This comes from Wollstonecraft's 1792 *Vindication of the Rights of Woman* – see Wollstonecraft (2004, p. 13).

[22] See Dries (2013) for a collation of examples of high-profile women unwilling to identify themselves as 'feminists'. The desire to avoid confrontation can also be seen in the approach of many who *do* openly identify with (and argue for) feminism. In her introduction to feminism, Saul (2003) addresses herself to those who are not already feminists, and expresses the hope that they will 'find something of interest', even whilst they may not agree. Imaginatively replacing the word 'feminist' with 'anti-racist' can be an instructive exercise here.

Now we will deal with Mill: the best-known feminist of the nineteenth century, or at least of nineteenth-century Britain – showered with endless praise for overcoming the twin disabilities of being a man and being a Victorian (whilst simultaneously having his limitations excused on the same grounds). Mill was, as is repeated ad nauseam, the first to bring the issue of women's suffrage to a vote in Parliament (which defeated it decisively), something for which he had to endure a good deal of ridicule. He is the author of *The Subjection of Women* (written in 1861, though not published until 1869), which called for what Mill saw as complete equality between the sexes. He was also, as is slightly less well known, arrested as a teenager for distributing information about birth control. So it is not that he is without feminist credentials. But nor does he remotely deserve his central place within the standard history of feminism. The simple reason for saying so is that his only written contribution to this cause, *The Subjection of Women*, doesn't really say anything that hadn't already been said, and said better, by earlier feminists (sometimes *much* earlier), some of them women. For that matter, it doesn't really say anything that his own wife hadn't said over a decade earlier, and in a much more elegant and concise form, in her essay 'The enfranchisement of women' (1851).[23]

Take, for example, Mill's extended argument to the effect that we haven't yet seen what women can achieve, since they have been artificially constrained by an unequal society. This is an important point but also quite an obvious one – and not just to 'us nowadays'. Marie de Gournay, a protégée of Montaigne's and now not particularly widely known, argues in one of her two main works[24] on the position of women, *Grief des dames* (1626), that women's failure to achieve on a level with men is due to social restrictions rather than innate inferiority – two hundred years before Mill's much better known expression of the same essential point.

More broadly, Mill's two main themes of education and political rights for women were not new ones. The Dutch prodigy and linguist Anna Maria van Schurman had published, in 1638 (in Latin), a defence of the suitability of women for a life of scholarship (this appeared in English as *The Learned Maid* in 1659);[25] and towards the end of the same century, the English philosopher

---

[23] H. T. Mill (1998).   [24] The other is her 1622 work, *Egalité des hommes et des femmes*.
[25] Van Schurman was at that time being allowed into lectures at the University of Utrecht only on the condition that she listen from behind a curtain.

Mary Astell published *A Serious Proposal to the Ladies*, advocating the establishment of a women's educational institution, which would also serve as a space for single women. Calls for greater inclusion of women in education in Europe date back at least to the 'humanism' of the sixteenth century – although at that point the suggestion was for women to be provided with a specially tailored *women's* education, not that they should be able to participate on equal terms. The theme of education for women continued to be dominant in seventeenth-century feminism, but it was now, relative to the sixteenth century, more recognisable *as feminism*: increasingly, the demand was for *parity* with men, and the demand was more often made by women themselves. The century also saw some prominent examples of women who *enacted* this drive for education by becoming accomplished intellectuals and learned commentators on social issues, including their own cause – de Gournay and Schurman among them.

This emphasis on women's education continues into the eighteenth century, where it gets supplemented by an additional emphasis on the extension of political rights – e.g. Abigail Adams's plea to her husband John (the second president of the United States) to 'remember the ladies' (a plea which was met with his laughter). In 1790, Catharine Macaulay, a well-respected British historian admired by Abigail Adams, published her *Letters on Education*, arguing for the extension of education and political rights to women. This was reviewed in glowing terms by Mary Wollstonecraft who, two years later, published *A Vindication of the Rights of Woman*.

Mill's ideas may be relatively progressive for his time, then, but they are hardly new. The most interesting parts of *The Subjection of Women*, to my mind, are the couple of places where he indirectly comments on patriarchal ideology. On the first page of the book, he complains: '[t]he very words necessary to express the task I have undertaken, show how arduous it is. [This difficulty] exists in all cases in which there is a mass of feeling to be contended against.'[26] He continues to talk about the 'burthen' on those who attack universal opinion: the difficulty in getting a hearing; the double standards employed in the assessment of evidence and argument. This is not only the trivial point that dissenters from conventional views find themselves – at least initially – in the minority. Mill is suggesting that the odds are stacked against them in a further sense: the *very fact* that they are opposing conventional wisdom

---

[26] See excerpt in Schneir (1996, p. 163).

is itself taken as a weighty piece of evidence against them – enough to shift the burden of proof onto them, and to raise the standards of evidence and argumentation demanded to a level higher than in the case of proponents of the conventional line, and often higher than can feasibly be reached. Now, there will be contexts in which this is legitimate, where we *should* give weight to the fact that a certain view is held by the majority, as a kind of testimony – many will take this to be a *generally* legitimate policy. But Mill argues that in the particular case of sex inequality, there are reasons *not* to be impressed by mass testimony, since this rests on something which has nothing to do with truth or evidence; rather, the conventional view is based on the brute facts of the desirability of women to men and of the dependence of women on men. In other words, Mill is offering a 'debunking'[27] ideological explanation of sex inequality and of the opinions sustaining it: (Victorian) people may think that the unequal status quo is supported by various arguments; but once they see why they *actually* hold the attitudes they do, the practices and views associated with this inequality will (might? should?) lose their grip on them.

A particularly interesting feature of Mill's comments on the difficulty of his own task, and on the reasons underlying it, is that the profundity of this difficulty is identified as a function of the fact that patriarchal ideology – although of course he doesn't call it by that name – pervades the very language that is his main weapon in combatting that ideology and the system it upholds. His comment about 'the very words necessary to undertake this task . . .' suggests that dissenters are disadvantaged *by the language itself*. Conventional wisdom is so deeply ingrained in language as to make the dissenter's task laborious and difficult. (Combine this difficulty with a natural talent for long-windedness and repetition, and you get *The Subjection of Women*.) Conventional wisdom, as well as the practices underlying it and sustained by it, is then protected and reinforced by the language it has shaped. This begins to paint a picture of conventional wisdom as a self-protecting system, almost akin to an organism. Mill reinforces and adds to this picture when he says that rational argument tends to be ineffectual or even counterproductive in cases where a dogma

---

[27] A debunking explanation is an explanation which removes the credibility of the thing explained. A classic example would be the famous reply by Mandy Rice-Davies, a former model and 'showgirl' who was one of the central figures of the so-called Profumo Affair that scandalised British politics in the 1960s. When it was put to Rice-Davies that Lord Astor had denied having an affair with her, she replied, 'He would, wouldn't he?'

is 'strongly rooted in the feelings...While the feeling remains, it is always throwing up fresh intrenchments of argument to repair any breach made in the old.'[28] It is not *arguments* that are in charge: the case of sex inequality is one where there is a strong and widespread feeling in favour of the status quo; and a legion of forces – including language and argumentation – serving to protect that feeling and its object.

However, the insight is not developed any further than in the couple of sentences cited above; and Mill certainly does not connect the problem he identifies with the Marxist notion of ideology. The working lifespans of Mill and Marx overlapped, but the two did not exactly have a lot in common. Mill seems to have been oblivious to Marx's existence, whereas on the one occasion when Marx comments on J. S. Mill (as opposed to his father, James), the result is not flattering: 'On the level plain,' Marx reflects, 'simple mounds look like hills; and the imbecile flatness of the present bourgeoisie is to be measured by the altitude of its great intellects.'[29]

But the relationship between the ideas of Mill and Marx repays reflection. In Marx's case, the notion of ideology is clearly bound up with his other theoretical commitments – in particular, with his theory of history. Very roughly, Marx rejected the prevailing 'idealism', which cast *ideas* as the highest reality or as the motor of history, in favour of a view which acknowledged the importance of the underlying material conditions of a society in shaping both subsequent material circumstances and the attendant sphere of ideas. Mill, on the other hand, enthusiastically embraces a kind of idealism – namely, the 'Whig' view of history, whereby ideas (notoriously, the ideas of 'great white men') drive society slowly but steadily along the path towards reason and enlightenment. His appreciation of the immense difficulties he faces, in confronting the status quo of sex inequality, is combined throughout *The Subjection of Women* with a more fundamental optimism – referring, for example, to the 'great modern spiritual and social transition' towards freedom and equality.[30]

Mill's nascent awareness of what a Marxist would call ideological false consciousness sits uncomfortably against this Whiggish background. The notion of ideology is a notion of ideas being subservient to something other than ideas – namely, the interests of a certain social group and the means at their

---

[28] Mill (2006, p. 133).   [29] See *Capital*, vol. I, end of chapter 16.
[30] Mill (2006, p. 134; see also p. 151).

disposal to protect those interests: in Mill's case, the interest that men have in securing access to and control over the objects of their desire, and the superior physical strength that is the origin of their success in doing so. Yet on the Whig view, it is ideas that progressively transform and rationalise material circumstances. Of course, there are glitches in this process – cases where matter gets the upper hand over mind. No idealist could afford to deny something so obvious. But these 'glitches' cannot be acknowledged to be *too* many, too big or systematic, without this pushing us away from an idealist picture of history towards one which places more emphasis on the material and its impact upon the sphere of ideas. It is therefore not surprising that Mill seems to treat the sort of profound difficulty he confronts at the start of *The Subjection of Women* as an exceptional case – although the whole sphere of ideas and attitudes surrounding the relations between the sexes would still have to count as a pretty big 'exception'. This probably goes some way towards explaining why he managed to be so progressive on the issue of women whilst at the same time being such a keen colonialist and racist.

There are a couple of points where Mill does seem to lean towards a view of ideology as something general rather than exceptional. Responding to a form of objection still common today, which meets feminist criticisms and proposals with the charge that these violate the 'natural' order of things, he asks, 'But was there *ever any* domination which did not appear natural to those who possessed it?'[31] And he notes earlier on that the 'law of force' is now only practised 'under cover of some pretext which gives ... the semblance of having some general social interest on [one's] side.'[32] These observations are instantly forgotten, however, when elsewhere he praises the French 'civilising mission' in Algeria and advocates the extension of the British colonisation of India, even though this may provoke 'obloquy' from Europeans – a result, he thought, of their inability to comprehend the unique selflessness of Britain's foreign policy.[33]

All in all, Mill's positive contribution amounts to a semi-accidental and severely limited account of the phenomenon of ideology, plus a selection of the reheated ideas of his female forerunners. Puzzling, then, that he enjoys such fame as a feminist pioneer – until, that is, we remember the phenomenon of patriarchal and other kinds of ideological distortion, at which point it

---

[31] Mill (2006, p. 144; emphasis added).   [32] Ibid., p. 138.
[33] Cited in Chomsky (2003, pp. 44–5).

becomes quite easy to imagine a promising explanation in only three words: *great white man* (and possibly a fourth: *liberal*).

* * *

This chapter has so far been rather haphazard and disjointed, but it has been intentionally so. Since I could not possibly provide anything like a full or adequate 'history of feminism' – and a reductive '*brief* history of feminism' would perhaps be even worse – I wanted it to be clear that what I offer here makes no pretence to be anything of the sort. Instead, I wanted to make vivid the point that the way in which we tell the story of feminism is itself an important feminist issue. I wanted to set out, even if only in crude caricature, a view of the historical development of feminism which I suspect will be familiar from mainstream culture and, to some extent, from academic representations. I then tried to give a sense of what is wrong with that view, not by giving an in-depth, point-by-point response to it but mainly by holding up two case studies alongside it: the case of Jane Anger (little-known sixteenth-century polemicist); and the case of John Stuart Mill (inescapable nineteenth-century bore). What I've tried to draw out of my brief discussions of each of the figures I've mentioned is: first, that not only feminism in general but specific feminist ideas, arguments and even styles of expression go back *much earlier* than is often assumed; and, secondly, that this observation, *as well as the notion of ideology which I've made central to the approach of this book*, casts serious doubt on the naïve 'ideas-first' approach implicit in the received version of the history of feminism.

Whereas we might initially think of any approach based on the notion of 'ideology' as carrying with it a focus on ideas rather than on concrete reality, the lives and needs and actions of flesh-and-blood human beings, we have seen a sense in which the opposite is the case. The more seriously we take the phenomenon of ideology, the more pressure this puts on us to lean away from forms of historical 'idealism' and towards approaches which place more emphasis on the importance of material conditions (including social relations). And the same imperative may be drawn from the observation about the sheer *oldness* of particular feminist ideas. It is not as if, for most of history, nobody stopped to think that the position of women might not be right, or that it might not be beneficial to them or to human society in general, or that maybe women were only as frail and incapable as they apparently were (the middle-to-upper-class ones, anyway) because they had lived their whole lives in a radically restrictive environment. People noticed and said these things, but mostly it had little impact either on the shape of the broader sphere of ideas or on social practices. And if this is so, if many of the ideas associated with Mill and even with feminists of the second wave have been cropping up for centuries, then why do they catch on only when and where they do (if, indeed, they catch on at all)?

I make no real attempt to answer a question as big as that – in fact, it must surely divide into innumerable more particular questions, about particular feminist ideas and their reception. The point here is just that this sort of question can't be answered in terms of features of the *ideas* – the same idea falls flat in one context and takes off in another. The more we notice this sort of phenomenon, the more we will need to look outside the sphere of ideas – to contingent historical factors, material conditions and social practices – in order to explain it. The more we do this, the further we move away from a naïve idealism whereby ideas – and above all, *good* ideas – are in the driving seat of history.

And the more we move away from such a view, the more important it becomes to recognise that a phenomenon like feminism is about more than just ideas. This chapter has concentrated on the words of feminists. The next concentrates on their actions.

6   Deeds not words

The argument of the broken window pane is the most valuable argument in modern politics.

– Emmeline Pankhurst

Depending on whether we look at feminism through the lens of 'theory' or through the lens of 'practice', we will see different things. Disagreements and issues which are visible through one lens may not be visible through the other. The same is true of political theory and practice more generally. We know that Marxists, non-Marxist socialists, anarchists and liberals all have different analyses of the world and its workings, but that they can also unite (at least to some extent) in struggles such as the fight against higher student fees and the marketisation of education. In the context of that struggle, there might be substantial overlap between the things that all these parties say about the policies they are opposing: e.g. that these will tend to increase the inequality between rich and poor, and that they will seriously damage the quality and diversity of the education that is available. Conversely, there will be cases where people seem to agree at the level of theory, but come into conflict with one another in their efforts to put their commitments into practice. These may be disagreements about the means and ends which are permissible or impermissible, or likely to be effective, ineffective, or counterproductive. They may concern the forming of alliances – who should and should not count as an ally? They may have to do with the connections we draw (or don't draw) between the issue in question (e.g. student fees) and other issues (e.g. privatisation or capitalism).

The sorts of issues that I've suggested might be visible only in practical contexts are issues of strategy and transition, but they can also be issues of morality (what are the limits to the means we think are *morally* acceptable to attain some end? What are the limits to the people or groups we are prepared to co-operate with?), and of our underlying view as to how the political world works ('Power concedes nothing without a demand', to take the famous words of abolitionist and former slave Frederick Douglass as one example).[1] Clearly, there is nothing about these issues which means that they *can't* appear at the level of theory: what is Marxism if it is not an analysis of how the world works and of how history develops? What is pacifism if it does not imply a view about the sorts of means that are acceptable in the pursuit of social change? So I am not trying to draw a line between 'theoretical' issues and 'practical' ones: all of these issues are both theoretical *and* practical.[2] The point is just that it sometimes takes a practical situation of a certain kind to force an issue onto the agenda, or to bring certain deep-seated disagreements to light, and that this is one of the major reasons to look at feminism as practice and not just as theory. The need is particularly strong in the context of trends in contemporary political philosophy which orientate it more towards what we might call 'static', rather than 'dynamic' theories: a 'dynamic' theory would be one which focused its analysis and recommendations on the manner of *transition* between one social state of affairs and another (e.g. the Marxist theory of history, the commitment to 'gradualism' espoused by Fabian socialists, the pacifist rejection of those means considered violent, or the 'constitutionalism' of early suffragists who shunned the militancy and law-breaking tactics employed later by the Suffragettes); an example of a 'static' theory, on the other hand, would be the theory set out by John Rawls in his hugely influential *A Theory of Justice*, which sketches an 'ideal theory' of what a just society would look like, but says nothing about actual historical or political processes (including the processes necessary or appropriate to realise Rawls's vision).[3] Whereas a dynamic theory – or, more properly, a dynamic *element* in a theory[4] – focuses on the way in which change does or should happen, static theory describes or recommends states of affairs considered as fixed or frozen: it says, 'This is how things are', or 'This is how things should be.'

Nowadays, political philosophers (including feminist political philosophers) are more likely to express and categorise themselves according to the sort of society they think exists or, more likely, according to the sort of society they think *should* exist (whether under the guise of 'ideal' or 'non-ideal'

[1] Douglass (1857).   [2] See my brief comment on theory and practice in Chapter 2.
[3] See Rawls (2005).
[4] In practice, all theories will contain both static and dynamic elements.

theory): they may take sides, for instance, on the question of whether pornography should be restricted,[5] or whether women should be paid a wage for housework and childcare.[6] They are much less likely to categorise themselves and each other according to whether they are reformists or revolutionaries, constitutionalists or militants. Partly, this may be because it is assumed that nobody is a revolutionary anymore – certainly, it is often assumed that nobody still advocates *communist* revolution. Partly it may be that questions of means and ends are considered too 'practical' to be 'philosophical'. I can see no reason why describing an ideally just society is more 'philosophical' than analysing and prescribing mechanisms of social change. If we insist on defining such issues out of philosophy, then so much the worse for 'philosophy': the issues remain crucial. Moreover, the suggestion that some issue is uninteresting or irrelevant is often a thin cover for a forced and stale consensus on that very issue. We therefore have a strong reason to try to bring these questions into the open; and to the extent that contemporary political theory tends to be of the 'static' variety, doing this will require that we switch lenses, from 'theory' to 'practice' – or, to borrow one of the mottoes of the Suffragette movement, 'Deeds not words'.

* * *

A notion that is absolutely central to Marx's vision of how history and social change happen, and which I think is usefully applied in the case of the feminist movement, is the notion of 'praxis'. In order to make proper sense of this notion, it's crucial to recognise that, although the Marxist model of history insists on a greater attention to material conditions than is paid by 'idealist' approaches to history, Marx himself also vehemently rejected the idea of a clean divide between the 'material' and 'ideal' spheres of reality: he never called himself a 'materialist';[7] and he railed against 'the old materialism' of Feuerbach as well as against the 'idealism' of the 'Young Hegelians'. Whilst

---

[5] The debate over pornography might also count as a dynamic issue, i.e. it might be a question of how feminists should best react to pornography in the project of fighting a patriarchal society. In fact, I think this is the best way to understand the debate. But my impression is that this is not the way the debate is most usually viewed. I discuss feminist arguments over pornography in Chapter 9.

[6] Again, the demand for wages for housework may be understood as part of *either* static or dynamic theory (for example, Selma James – who will reappear in Chapter 8 – advocates this as part of a broader agenda of revolutionary transformation of society).

[7] 'Historical materialism' is a termed coined by later thinkers to describe Marx's view of history.

there is a clearly a sense in which he wants to prioritise the 'material' over the 'ideal' – as witnessed by statements like, 'It is not the consciousness of man that determines his being, but rather, his social being that determines his consciousness', or (as paraphrased by Engels in his speech at Marx's graveside in 1883) that we have to have food, shelter and other necessities before we can pursue art or philosophy – it is equally clear that he sees social reality as an inextricable fusion of both elements: 'practical, human-sensuous activity'.[8] Just as I suggested earlier that we should reject a gulf between 'descriptive' and 'normative', seeing these instead as simultaneously present aspects of claims and theories – with the context and our purposes determining which of these aspects it is more appropriate to emphasise in a given case – so Marx, I believe, views the material and ideal as ever-present elements or aspects of reality, each of which may be emphasised as appropriate (and in an intellectual context dominated by Hegelian idealism, it may be appropriate to emphasise the material more often than not).

The notion of *praxis* exhibits this fusion of 'material' and 'ideal' very clearly. Praxis, for Marx, is something extremely general: basically, it is his conception of human activity. It is the process by which human beings act on the world in a way that is simultaneously active, conscious or sensuous as well as practical. The 'world' on which they act, too, is understood as embodying this fusion: hence, it is a world which is made up not only of material objects and resources – wood that becomes tables and chairs – but also of human beings and their ideas, experiences and desires. Praxis, then, is the process by which humans work on and transform both the world around them *and also themselves*.

The notion of praxis helps to bring out the importance of practical action in the history of feminism. Feminists have long been engaged not only in theoretical reflection, but in practical action on the world: a world which is not just the dead lump to which Marx accuses the 'old materialists' of reducing material reality, but which includes human beings, their practices, and their ideas.

Feminist praxis, then, might be seen as having three dimensions:

(i) practice on *practice*;
(ii) practice on *thought*;
(iii) practice on *ourselves*.

---

[8] See Marx's 1845 *Theses on Feuerbach* (Thesis V), in e.g. Marx (1967).

For instance, the UK Equal Pay Act of 1970 was not simply *argued* into existence – the idea of 'equal pay for equal work' was not, in any case, a new idea, but was being argued for by such figures as American feminist Susan B. Anthony over a hundred years earlier. The arguments of feminists are one part of the picture, but so are certain *practical* interventions, such as the strike by female machinists at a Ford factory in Dagenham in 1968.[9]

Then there is the impact of practice on thought and ideas. Part of the point of feminist activism is, of course, to change how people think – in particular, how women are thought about. Contrary to a very common expectation, which any activist will have encountered, this needn't be a matter of 'winning people round': in the case at hand, it need not necessarily be a matter of persuading people to look upon women more favourably, or of convincing them of the desirability of equality between the sexes. The communicative function of a practice might also be that of issuing a demand, a threat or statement of defiance. In an address in 1913, the matriarch of the Suffragettes, Emmeline Pankhurst, makes this abundantly clear:

> 'How are they going to persuade people that they ought to have the vote by breaking their windows?' you say. Now, if you say that, it shows you do not understand the meaning of our revolution at all, and I want to show you that when damage is done to property it is not done in order to convert people to woman suffrage at all. It is a practical political means, the only means we consider open to voteless persons to bring about a political situation, which can only be solved by giving women the vote.[10]

As Pankhurst explicitly avows, the action of window-breaking is not intended to persuade. But it is still *communicative*, and it clearly supposed to work by affecting people's *consciousness* in a particular way. Broken windows alone don't force people to do anything – other than, perhaps, replace the windows. If people had had no idea why this group of women had suddenly started breaking windows, or if they had assumed that the damage was the result of freak weather events, then this action could not have had the intended effect. The action conveys a message: what it communicates is a non-negotiable demand for the right to vote, and an intention to continue a policy of strategic destruction and disruption of social life until this goal is achieved. It is a

---

[9] This strike was made the focus of a 2010 film, *Made in Dagenham*.
[10] See Schneir (1996, p. 298).

practice which changes the situation, where a crucial part of the *way* in which it changes the situation is through changing the way people *view* the situation: the way they regard women, their capabilities and wishes, and the way they balance the feasibility and costs of maintaining the status quo relative to letting go of it. This sort of effect is not limited to those activities we would normally identify as 'activism'. A much wider range of events and practices, from the presence of a strong female head of state[11] to the sudden entrance of large numbers of women into traditionally male workplaces in the nineteenth and early twentieth centuries – can dramatically affect the ways in which women are perceived and thought about. The practices in question, then, may be deliberate feminist interventions, or accidental catalysts. They may be instances of collective action, or individual acts of rebellion, such as those performed by the nineteenth-century novelist George Sand, or the American sisters and campaigners Victoria and Tennessee 'Tenny C' Claflin, who advocated and practised sexual freedom and performatively challenged norms of feminine conduct and dress.

These examples lead naturally to the third dimension of feminist praxis: *self*-transformation. Clearly, those involved in feminist struggle have changed themselves, and have done so both as a *means* of changing society – as, for instance, with the bodyguard unit of the Suffragettes, who learned the martial art of jujitsu[12] – and as a (deliberate or incidental) consequence of their efforts

[11] For instance, the ascent of Elizabeth I to the throne arguably had the effect of sparking the activity of pamphleteers such as Jane Anger (discussed in the previous chapter), and clearly inspired American poet Anne Bradstreet, who wrote the lines: 'Let such as say our Sex is void of Reason, / Know tis a Slander now, but once was Treason.' I stress that I do *not* mean to encourage any similar claim about the late Margaret 'milk snatcher' Thatcher, whose existence has done considerable harm to women, along with the rest of the British population (and the populations of many other countries besides). In her 2003 introduction to feminism, Jennifer Saul mentions the fact that there has been a female prime minister in the UK, 'and an exceptionally strong one at that', as if somehow the mere fact of Thatcher's possession of ovaries and a handbag was sufficient to produce a benefit to womankind the moment she stepped into Number Ten, regardless of what she then *did* (Saul wisely makes no suggestion that Thatcher's policies were beneficial to women). Even the claim that Thatcher was a 'strong' leader is questionable. Thatcher benefited from an extremely weak and fragmented opposition, and never enjoyed a high degree of popular support, and in that sense, was not strong at all.

[12] The bodyguard unit of the WSPU ('Women's Social and Political Union' – the official name of the Suffragettes) was formed in 1913 in response the 'Cat and Mouse Act',

toward social change. Perhaps the clearest example of self-transformative activity in feminism is the second-wave technique of 'consciousness-raising' (briefly discussed in Chapter 3), in which women would meet to try to come to understand their situations through group discussion.[13] But the importance of self-transformation in the context of the 'first wave' of feminism is made clear, too, by testimonies such as this one (from English suffragist, Ida Alexa Ross Wylie):

> To my astonishment, I found that women ... could at a pinch outrun the average London bobby. Their aim with a little practice became good enough to land ripe vegetables in ministerial eyes, their wits sharp enough to keep Scotland Yard running around in circles and looking very silly ... The day that, with a straight left to the jaw, I sent a fair-sized CID officer into the orchestra pit of the theatre where we were holding one of our belligerent meetings, *was the day of my own coming of age* ... [14]

To understand feminism as a practical movement, then, is to understand it as a process in which people – women in particular – act so as to transform not only the practices and the systems of thought that surround them, but also themselves.

* * *

The history of feminist praxis is a history of alliance as well as conflict. Feminists have worked not only with one another but with other movements, such as those opposing racism, war and capitalism. But these alliances have also produced tensions, and some of the most dramatic rifts in the feminist movement have come out of disagreements over whether and when the feminist movement should follow, stand by, or break away from its allies.

---

which authorised the temporary release and re-arrest of hunger-striking prisoners. They were trained in jujitsu by Edith Margaret Garrud, one of the first female martial arts experts in the Western world, in secret locations around London. Quoted in the *New York Times* on 12 August 1913, Sylvia Pankhurst underlined the importance of this training: 'We have not yet made ourselves a match for the police, and we have got to do it. The police know jiu-jitsu. I advise you to learn jiu-jitsu. Women should practice it as well as men. Don't come to meetings without sticks in future, men and women alike. It is worthwhile really striking. It is no use pretending. We have got to fight.'

[13] See Morgan (1970).

[14] Cited in Schneir (1996, p. xxv, emphasis added; as Schneir indicates, this citation also appears in Friedan's *The Feminine Mystique* – see Friedan 2013).

The connection between feminism and anti-racism is longstanding: many nineteenth-century American feminists – figures such as Frederick Douglass, Sojourner Truth and Abby Kelley Foster – were also deeply involved in the movement for the abolition of slavery. Douglass, a freed slave and prominent anti-slavery campaigner, stated that he was to proud call himself a 'woman's rights man'. The parallels between the situations of women and of black Americans made this alliance seem a very natural one: both were groups of people who were treated as chattel, denied education, social respect, and the right to vote. And for someone like Sojourner Truth who, as a black woman and former slave, stood at the intersection of these two vast systems of oppression, neither struggle made sense without the other.[15]

In the twentieth century, too, feminist movements maintained close links to the struggle against racism, and to the political left more generally. Many feminist groups, in fact, were *born out of* left-wing movements which initially failed to make space for women's concerns – movements such as 'Students for a Democratic Society' (SDS), formed at the University of Michigan in 1960, which organised around the issues of withdrawal of troops from Vietnam, student control over education, and fighting poverty and racism (but showed no interest in or even acknowledgement of the oppression of women until the late sixties, when women began to change this). This case illustrates both the ties and the tensions between the different causes. 'Second-wave' feminism in the US was marked by a fierce division – albeit a necessarily complicated, fuzzy and exception-prone one – between 'radical feminists' and 'politicos': the former insistent on a distinctive or even separatist women's liberation movement; the 'politicos' identifying more closely with the traditional political left, which included and was usually dominated by (if not exhausted by) concerns *not* specifically to do with women, such as class, poverty and war.

One example of this is the 1969 split of the New York Radical Women,[16] into two rival groups: the Redstockings, headed by Ellen Willis and Shulamith Firestone (the latter of whom soon left to form the New York Radical

---

[15] See the speech attributed to Truth, 'Keeping the thing going while things are stirring', excerpted in Schneir (1996, pp. 128–31).

[16] This organisation, the creation of radical feminist Shulamith Firestone, was structured as a network of small 'brigades'. Faludi writes: 'Each brigade would name itself after a historical feminist, and write a biographical booklet about its namesake. '"We are committed to a flexible, non-dogmatic approach", Firestone wrote. "WE DO WHAT WORKS"' (Faludi 2013, p. 57).

Feminists); and WITCH (an acronym which could be filled in however the members saw fit – popular choices included 'Women Inspired to Commit Herstory', 'Women Interested in Toppling Consumer Holidays' and (my personal favourite) 'Women's International Terrorist Conspiracy from Hell').[17] Of the two groups, WITCH was the more 'politico' – although Robin Morgan, one of its most prominent members, later repudiated any 'New Left' affiliations. Redstockings, an autonomist radical feminist group, focused its attention on issues such as abortion, and propagated its messages through street theatre. The group disbanded in 1970, but was later reformed – by Carol 'The personal is political' Hanisch,[18] among others – and exists to this day.[19]

An important point here is that *you might not be able to tell*, just from looking at the statements avowed by a given feminist or group of feminists, whether the position is 'radical feminist' or 'politico' (for example). On paper, the positions may seem to agree: for instance, those calling themselves 'radical feminists' emphasise the reality of the oppression of women and the need to oppose it, and those calling themselves 'socialist feminists' will say the same; 'socialist feminists' will emphasise the need to be attentive to problems facing working class women, and 'radical feminists' are unlikely to object to that. Some differences *will*, of course, appear on paper; but often these will come down to differences of emphasis, and in the debates between those who place emphasis in different places, it may appear that the two sides are talking past each other – that there is no *real* disagreement here at all. Looking at the formations of alliances and rifts in the context of practical feminist struggles can allow us to see who stands where, where the fault-lines are, and also that the disagreements in question are very real indeed.

It is helpful, I think, to distinguish three major areas of conflict.

6.1 Priorities

Positions which may look similar on paper can diverge very sharply according to the order of priority they impose on their various commitments, or

---

[17] WITCH members were known for their 'hexings' of public officials or institutions, on one occasion taking it upon themselves to 'hex' the United Fruit Company.

[18] Hanisch published an article in 1969, entitled 'The personal is political', which became an important slogan for the 'second wave', and for radical feminists in particular.

[19] See the website: www.redstockings.org. The writer Kathie Sarachild is the group's only remaining original member.

according to which of these they treat as fundamental. In the USA, for example, when the 14th and 15th Amendments were proposed, giving the vote to black men but not to women of any race, a rift emerged between what had thus far been allied movements. Many who had campaigned on both fronts took the view that this was – as Douglass put it – 'the negro's hour'. Others such as Susan B. Anthony and Elizabeth Cady Stanton, on the other hand, opposed the amendments and called on suffragists to hold out for universal suffrage, all or nothing – in some cases, this position was bound up with an underlying racism that was quite common among the members of the American women's movement at that time, its alliance with the abolitionist cause notwithstanding (Stanton, for example, protested: 'We educated, virtuous white women are more worthy of the vote'). Still others, like the feminist and abolitionist Lucy Stone, found themselves profoundly torn. Neither opposing the amendments nor supporting them in the form in which they appeared, Stone reflected: 'I will be thankful in my soul if *any* body can get out of the terrible pit.'[20]

6.2 Means and ends

Positions which appear to agree at the level of theory sometimes only do so because the theory is of what I've called the 'static' variety: e.g. it describes a society in which gender justice prevails, but says nothing about how to get there. In practical contexts, however, disagreements over the appropriate means become inescapable, and can prise apart those whose ends appear indistinguishable. To take a very familiar example, those who agreed on the moral and practical necessity of extending the franchise to women were deeply divided between those who favoured more genteel tactics such as letter-writing, and those who favoured the militant approach adopted by the Pankhursts and their fellow Suffragettes. This divide also extended to the matter of internal organisation: the WSPU was deliberately and self-consciously structured along military lines, stressing hierarchy, loyalty, and obedience to those in positions of authority in the organisation (i.e. above all, to Emmeline and Christabel Pankhurst) – a feature which, along with the organisation's enthusiasm for the First World War, eventually drove Christabel's younger sister, Sylvia, to break away. The leaders of the WSPU had judged that an organisation with this kind of internal structure was the only appropriate

---

[20] Quoted in Schneir (1996, p. 129).

means to the end of attaining female suffrage – a position which many others, including Sylvia Pankhurst, strongly rejected. As we'll see later on,[21] this issue of means and ends, especially in relation to the internal structuring of movements for social change, has been a key point of contention between socialist and anarchist currents within feminism.

6.3 Separability and interconnection

The issue of what to separate and what to run together is a fundamental one for all political criticism.[22] Some approaches, such as the approach of 'critical theorists', emphasise the need for radical critics to recognise the interconnectedness of the social world, to treat society as a 'totality'.[23] At the same time, the practice of *distinguishing* or *separating* is obviously indispensable, and even captures the etymology of the word 'criticism' (from the Greek *krinein*, meaning 'to separate or take apart'). In the context of practical struggle, it is often necessary to take a stand on the extent to which our various commitments – and the things those commitments oppose – are interconnected, and the extent to which it is possible to hold them apart: e.g. for socialist feminists, capitalism is so deeply implicated in the current system of patriarchy that it isn't really possible to criticise one without criticising the other; for some radical feminists who are also socialists, such a separation is not only possible but necessary. Just as it is instructive to look at the feminist movement with an eye to alliance and division, I'm suggesting, one of the major things people divide (and unite) over turns out to be precisely the matter of where to draw connections and where to draw divides. This is a staple dispute or dilemma for activists: on one side, there will be those who argue that there is no point criticising one thing (e.g. student fees) without locating it in a certain context (marketisation, privatisation, capitalism, etc.); on the other side, there will be those who warn against 'issue pollution', often arguing that the broadening of the target of criticism and opposition will result in a narrowing of the movement's support base.[24]

---

[21] See Chapter 10 below.

[22] Come to that, the practices of separating and connecting seem about as central to the way we deal with the world as you can get.

[23] See Horkheimer (1999).

[24] This was certainly a common dispute during the occupation that took place at my university in 2010 against the 'reforms' to the higher education system.

The three themes – priorities, means and ends, separability and interconnection – are themselves closely interconnected. They do not take turns to crop up in activist settings, but tend to crop up all-at-once and all-in-one. When the conflict broke out over the proposed 14th and 15th Amendments, for example, this was partly a question of which struggle to prioritise: the struggle for black (male) voting rights, or the struggle for votes for women. But tensions between abolitionism and feminism clearly also had to do with questions of separability: is it really possible to separate the one system of oppression, and the fight against it, from the other? In 1852, Sojourner Truth, who steadfastly refused to do so (or rather, regarded it as impossible), rose to speak at a meeting, whereupon a number of people cried out that she should be prevented, lest 'every newspaper in the land' should have the cause of votes for women 'mixed with abolition'.[25] The objection here was not just that Truth was connecting two things which could conceptually be distinguished, but rather that associating them was not going to be an effective *means* to the end of achieving suffrage for (white) women (which, evidently, was their first priority). Truth's speech was recorded,[26] and contains what has since become a classic expression of resistance against the attempt to separate racial, class and sex oppression, and against the tendency on the part of white feminists to forget that some black people are *women* too:

> That man over there says that women need to be helped into carriages, and lifted over ditches, and to have the best place everywhere. Nobody ever helps me into carriages, or over mud-puddles, or gives me any best place! And ain't I a woman? Look at me! Look at my arm! I have ploughed and planted, and gathered into barns, and no man could head me! And ain't I a woman? I could work as much and eat as much as a man – when I could get it – and bear the lash as well! And ain't I a woman? I have borne thirteen children, and seen most of them sold off to slavery, and when I cried out with my mother's grief, none but Jesus heard me! And ain't I a woman?[27]

* * *

[25] Schneir (1996, p. 93).

[26] As some have pointed out, the most common rendering of Truth's speech (which is the one given here) is unlikely to be historically accurate, insofar as it renders Truth as speaking in a Southern dialect (in fact, she never lived in the South, and her first language was Dutch). The woman who recorded this version, Frances Gage, is thought to have done so twelve years after the event. See Painter (1996) for a history of Truth's life, and see also Haraway's (2004) discussion of 'inappropriate/d others'.

[27] See Schneir (1996, pp. 94–5).

It is very common to hear the following complaint applied to activists of various kinds: 'They share the same goal – what a shame they can't just co-operate with each other so as to achieve it. Why are they fighting amongst themselves, undermining their common cause? They should be allies.' Perhaps still more common is the old joke about the political left and how prone they are to in-fighting and fragmentation: usually this takes the form of a reference to the *Monty Python* sketch about the People's Front of Judea and their arch-enemies, the Judean People's Front.

Those who make these comments have probably either never known what it's like to fight something bigger than oneself, or else have forgotten. On a moment or two's reflection, it is not at all surprising if the left and feminists alike have a tendency to fight one another and to fragment. They are fighting an opponent which, at the moment at least, has the upper hand – and is in that sense stronger than they are. When fighting an enemy who has the upper hand, it is (almost inevitably) a lot more difficult to 'just get along' than when one has the upper hand oneself. Suppose you and I are in a relatively stable position of power – e.g. we are the ludicrously wealthy CEOs, the Koch brothers – and we agree on some end we want to realise. We, qua ludicrously wealthy, well-connected CEOs, have vastly many more options – things that are securely in our power to do – than most people have. We have the resources and personnel on hand to bring about our ends through all sorts of channels – inject funds into this or that PAC, lobby this or that politician, produce a propaganda film – and if one means doesn't work, we can always try another. If Charles and David Koch disagree on the best means to an end, they may fall out over it, but it is much easier for them not to than it would be for some other partners. Each can *afford* to yield or compromise. The situation of the relatively powerless is completely different. The range of things we might actually be able to achieve is much narrower. There are fewer means at our disposal to pursue our ends. If what we want to achieve can be achieved by us at all, the details of how we pull it off might be absolutely critical: there might be only one plan that would have a chance in hell of working, and everything hangs on our getting it right. If I think you've got it wrong, I can't very well afford to be tolerant. We also know that if we do get it wrong, our opponents have the resources at their disposal to crack down on us in ways which will not only be painful but will also further limit the options available to us – we may not be able to just try something else. This should be enough to account for the greater brittleness of the left, or the tensions between feminists of different stripes.[28] It's not that believing in the equality of men and women, or in socialism, in itself makes a person unable to get along with others, or unable to tolerate disagreeing (and perhaps also agreeing) with them. We are in a situation of pressure, and pressure produces cracks.

The next chapter examines the continuities and tensions between three rival feminist factions which do not get along.

---

[28] Though I guess it still leaves out something important, something we might call the 'problem of false friends'. My image of cracking under pressure presupposes that the group in question really are on the same side, all fighting for the same end. But clearly, at least when it comes to relatively larger movements, this is an idealisation. One of the mechanisms by which dominant groups maintain their dominance is by producing false friends for their enemies. A very literal and straightforward example of this is the police's use of *agents provocateurs*, and of undercover officers who infiltrate 'green' and student movements. In the case of feminism, we might think of the 'feminism' of Sarah Palin, or of 'consumer feminism' (both examples are discussed by Power (2009)). At least some of what appears to outsiders as fragmentation, in that case, may in fact be the justified and necessary refusal of feminists to embrace feminism's false friends. I discuss such cases of the 'co-option' of feminism in Chapter 11.

7   Faces and facades

In the first chapter of this book, I defined the core of feminism, the common thread running through various different feminisms, in terms of (i) a descriptive recognition of the fact of patriarchy, and (ii) the opposition to this state of affairs. These bare bones are fleshed out in very different ways by different schools of feminist political philosophy. The way in which patriarchy is characterised will vary, as will the manner of opposition to it.

Feminism is often divided into three main traditions,[1] with the expectation that contemporary feminist philosophers will fall unambiguously into one or other of them:

(i) liberal feminism;
(ii) radical feminism;
(iii) Marxist feminism.

There are two points to make about this division straightaway. First, it by no means exhausts the range of feminist perspectives. It does not include anarchist feminists, such as Emma Goldman, who wrote on the status of women in the early twentieth century.[2] It leaves no obvious place for the black feminists who have been critical of all mainstream feminist traditions, or perhaps for self-described 'eco-' and 'techno-feminists'.[3] (It leaves no obvious place for Sarah Palin, either, but we might be less worried about that.)

The second point to note is that the three categories distinguished above are not particularly transparent, either in themselves (what *is* e.g. 'liberal' feminism?) or in their relation to one another (is liberal feminism compatible

---

[1] For a much more in-depth study arranged around these categories, plus a further category of 'socialist feminism' (which the author defends), see Jaggar (1983).
[2] See Goldman's 1910 *Anarchism and Other Essays* (Goldman 1969).
[3] See e.g. (on ecofeminism) Mies & Shiva (2014); (on technofeminism) Wajcman (2004).

with radical feminism?). So not only do these three labels not cover everything; it's not even all that clear what they *do* cover. And the lack of clarity is not just a product of a lack of information. We cannot simply go and look the terms up in a dictionary. There is a slipperiness inherent in the categories themselves. There can be no simple and satisfying fact of the matter as to what defines these varieties of feminism: definitions are products of agreement, and this is an area where people simply do not agree.

So if we assume that these three categories are all there is to feminism, then our horizons will be unduly narrow. And if we assume that these are three discrete, non-overlapping, clearly defined types, then we will be disappointed, and will also tend to misunderstand the force of various usages of the terms. That said – and since these labels show no signs of going away – it is worth outlining some of the characteristic views or assumptions and priorities (loosely) associated with them.

7.1 Liberal feminism

Contemporary liberal feminists, quite often, do not talk in terms of 'patriarchy' much at all, preferring terms like 'gender injustice'. They tend to emphasise a certain characteristic set of values and concepts: instead of 'oppression' and 'domination', they are likely to use the vocabulary of 'justice'/ 'injustice', 'rights', 'equality' and 'autonomy'. This vocabulary, it's worth noting, just *is* the vocabulary of contemporary (liberal) political philosophy. As far as I can see, it is not the case that liberal feminists' approach to feminist issues is any *more* liberal than their approach to anything else (or 'liberal' in any interestingly different way). Rather, liberal feminists are, very simply, liberals who are feminists: as liberals, they are concerned with justice and equality; and as liberal *feminists*, they are concerned with *gender* justice and *gender* equality.

This all sounds boring and commonsensical enough, but it already raises a worry. The worry is that, within the liberal feminist approach, feminism is something that is simply tacked onto the pre-existing framework of traditional liberal political philosophy – to produce a 'liberal political philosophy *of women*' – whereas that framework should be shaped, from the word go, in a way that takes due account of women's experiences and social situations. It should be acknowledged, at this point, that many liberal political philosophers do demand that we revise our understanding of traditional liberal values (such as 'freedom' or 'autonomy') in response to the specific concerns of women.[4] Even so, we might still have doubts about the radical potential of any methodology which begins from – and then tweaks – values which have been handed down to us overwhelmingly by men who crafted them only or primarily with men in mind.[5]

A further thing to note straightaway is that liberal feminists are not necessarily more likely than other kinds of feminist to couch their discussions in terms of the value of *freedom*. It is very easy to assume that the defining characteristic of liberal feminism is a concern for women's freedom – and the attempt to overcome the obstacles to and enemies of that freedom: whilst radical feminists might be concerned with domination or oppression, liberals, it is assumed, put freedom first. The problem with this interpretation is that it plays into the common idea that liberals somehow have a monopoly on this value – as if, simply through the adoption of the word 'liberal', they had succeeded in placing a copyright on liberty. But to go along with this idea is to beg the question against liberalism's main rivals. Marxists will almost invariably avow a central commitment to freedom as well – and some Marxist feminists might say that the *freedom* of women is what their position is most fundamentally about. Even more obviously, anarchists place the value of freedom at the heart of their political philosophy – although, of course, both they and Marxists are likely to understand that value in a way importantly different from liberals' understanding of it (and perhaps from each other's).[6] Interestingly, in fact, the central values of Marxism and liberalism are more or less the opposite way around from the way in which they are usually portrayed: liberals, despite the name, talk constantly of 'equality'; whilst

---

[4] The work of Iris Marion Young is an important case-in-point here (see, especially, her *Justice and the Politics of Difference* (1990)). Cf. also: Susan Moller Okin's 1989 book *Justice, Gender, and the Family* (which seeks not just to extend Rawlsianism to the case of women, but to revise it in the process); or Marina Oshana's 2006 book *Personal Autonomy in Society* (which argues for a 'social-relational' theory of autonomy).

[5] This point, if it is a sound one, might well work against other approaches to feminism too. But in the case of Marxist feminism, at least, this is already well recognised: the most common criticism of Marxist feminism (from within feminist ranks) is that it awkwardly and inadequately attempts to incorporate feminist concerns within a framework which has not been constructed with these concerns sufficiently in mind. My suggestion is not that this is a worry solely for liberals. Rather, my point is that we should not forget that it is one which applies to them *too*.

[6] I discuss this further in Chapter 10.

Marxists could be quite plausibly interpreted as being primarily interested in human *freedom* (understood, in part, as freedom from 'alienation'), and *not* – contrary to popular belief – with 'equality', which Marx scorned as a pointless, abstract notion, and unambiguously disowned as an end-in-itself.[7]

In addition to focusing on a set of characteristic values, and employing characteristic terminology, liberal feminism is associated with particular *interpretations* of those values and terms – although, of course, for any generalisation we might wish to make, there will be numerous deviations and exceptions.[8] Generalising regardless, we might highlight the following features:

(a) *Individualism:* the values of 'autonomy', 'freedom' and 'rights' are traditionally understood in terms of the situation and point of view of the individual (e.g. in terms of the rights or autonomy of individual women), as opposed to the dynamics of a society or some other social group.[9] This approach seems so commonsensical to many that they do not even think of it as an 'approach' at all, since they are scarcely able to conceive of any other way of doing things. Yet liberal individualism might be thought to contrast quite starkly with, for example, the radical feminist focus on 'sisterhood', or the Marxist focus on class struggle.

(b) *Distribution:* the values of 'equality', 'justice' and 'fairness' tend to be understood in terms of the way in which the state parcels out *distribuenda* (i.e. whatever is to be distributed) to individual citizens. Contemporary liberal theorists often conceptualise their concern for 'equality' (for example) as a matter of the distribution of wealth or other goods, on the one hand, and of costs or burdens, on the other.[10] The issues of concern to feminists,

[7] See above all Marx's 1875 *Critique of the Gotha Programme.*

[8] All of the tendencies I'll mention have also attracted a good deal of criticism, some of which has come from theorists who see themselves as belonging to a liberal tradition, and much of which has been grounded in feminist considerations (see e.g. Baier 1995). I still stand by my generalisations, as accurately identifying a dominant style against which there has been a degree of inevitable rebellion.

[9] Jaggar (1983) connects the individualist approach of liberal feminism also with a characteristic emphasis on the rationality, autonomy and self-centredness of human beings.

[10] Rawls makes the classic statement of this approach in *A Theory of Justice*: 'principles of social justice ... define the appropriate distribution of the benefits and burdens of social cooperation' (Rawls 2005, p. 4).

too, have often been approached from within this framework – a framework which in certain contexts starts to seem highly questionable (e.g. when liberal theorists start to talk about the 'just' distribution of *love* or *respect*). Perhaps the most perverse example of this is the argument that what is problematic about rape is that it distributes fear unequally across the population, so that the right remedy is for fear to be 'redistributed'.[11]

(c) *Abstraction:* each value among this whole cluster I've associated with the liberal approach tends to be understood in fairly abstract terms. Rather than beginning from a systematic analysis of, e.g., economic or social history, the liberal theorist may begin from a reflection on the *concept* of 'equality' or 'justice', drawing on this reflection to produce normative principles. The figure most strongly associated with this abstract approach is, of course, Rawls, famous for the device of the 'Original Position' (a thought experiment in which we imagine the deliberations of a group of agents who are artificially deprived – by a 'veil of ignorance' – of knowledge of crucial information on such matters as their social class, talents, disabilities and 'conceptions of the good').[12] Whilst Rawls's work has provoked a good deal of criticism as well as adulation, his approach has been extraordinarily influential, and many feminist critics of his theory retain and reinforce its basic elements, including its abstract nature: Susan Moller Okin, for example, criticises Rawls for not drawing out the full feminist implications of his device of the veil of ignorance – and indeed, for writing patriarchal assumptions into its construction – but embraces a duly modified version of this device.[13]

The three tendencies mentioned above have been well canvassed (and criticised, defended and denied). I'd like now to mention two more, which are rarely acknowledged – partly, I think, because most mainstream theorists take them to be so obviously unobjectionable or positively good. Not everyone finds it so obvious, however – not outside the liberal tradition, anyway. And these features strike me as being at least as significant as the ones mentioned so far. They are:

[11] Burgess-Jackson (1999, pp. 44–9). Presumably he doesn't have in mind here the introduction of state-sponsored surprise sexual assaults on men, although that would seem to fulfil his criterion for an adequate solution.
[12] Rawls (2005).   [13] Okin (1989).

(d) *Positivity:* liberal feminists tend to be in the business of offering positive descriptions of, or proposals for, 'gender justice'. This might take the form of either 'ideal' or 'non-ideal' theory: either way, they are issuing suggestions as to what should be done. Their main emphasis – it seems to me, at least – is on this positive project, and not on critiquing and exposing existing forms of patriarchy – which is not to claim that they don't do this *at all*, just that this is not the main focus of attention. This point will be extremely important when we come to contrast liberal feminism with the radical feminist and Marxist feminist positions.[14]

(e) *Capitalism:* the final and, perhaps, most crucial thing to emphasise about liberal feminism is that this is an approach which is (implicitly or explicitly) committed to a capitalist economic framework of one kind or another.[15] In fact, it would make more sense, in some ways, to use the label 'capitalist feminism' rather than 'liberal feminism': if we allow that Marxists, too, are interested in freedom, then the former label better captures the disagreement between the two approaches than the latter does. Admittedly, liberal feminists do not usually identify themselves as 'pro-capitalism', nor do they recognise a need to *defend* capitalism as a political and economic system. As with liberal political philosophy more broadly, liberal feminism generally just *assumes* the desirability or necessity of private ownership of the means of production (enforced by state violence) and of some kind of market mechanism (albeit often more or less tightly constrained and regulated), coupled with redistributive

---

[14] I would also suggest that most liberal theory is of the 'static' variety, in the sense identified in the previous chapter. As I acknowledged, however, that distinction is not a hard-and-fast one. In the case of a given 'policy proposal' put forward by a liberal feminist theorist in the context of a 'non-ideal' theory, for example, some might take the view that this is 'dynamic', since the theorist is putting forward a view about how we can get from here (i.e. from a situation of gender injustice) to a more just social system; on the other hand, some might class the proposal as belonging to 'static' theory, on the grounds that it only names a measure that 'should' be taken, without saying enough (or anything at all, perhaps) about *how* we might actually either get those in power to implement that measure or get rid of those in power.

[15] This point is obscured partly by the fact that some liberal feminists – in particular, those from the US – describe their positions as 'socialist'. This sense of 'socialist', as far as I can see, is not one which precludes capitalism, but is rather a by-word for a managed capitalist economy of the kind traditionally championed by 'social democrats'.

taxation: thus far, the system which we already have. Economic matters are not usually discussed at all, except to provide more exact specifications within this agreed framework: for example, to address the question of which sorts of 'disadvantages' do and do not need to be compensated for by the redistributive mechanism.[16]

Liberal feminism, then, may be identified by such tell-tale signs as a focus on 'equality' (often interpreted as a project of offering suggestions for 'just' distributive schemes), an individualistic or abstract methodology, and by a stance that is *pro-capitalist*, at least by implication or omission. For if we encounter someone who is engaged in the project of describing a better society, and does not mention that the society envisaged would have a completely different economic system from the one we now have, then it is fair to assume that their intention is that it wouldn't. In general, one of the privileges enjoyed by the status quo is that it requires only omission for affirmation. You might know someone for a very long time, without their ever mentioning that they broadly approve of capitalism – it kind of goes without saying; but you will probably *not* know an anti-capitalist for long before it comes up in conversation. Here is a context, then, where silence equals assent.

7.2 Radical feminism

If liberal feminists characteristically talk about autonomy, equality, rights and justice, 'radical' feminists are more likely to talk in terms of 'oppression', 'domination', 'exploitation', 'violence' and 'subordination' – often with the aid of extremely graphic descriptions and examples. As a very rough rule of thumb, whilst liberal feminists are interested in questions of justice and equality, radical feminists focus on *concrete relations of power*: what real men do to real women. Of course, this is not to say that radical feminists are uninterested in justice and equality for women – it is just that they think that the best way to respond to these concerns is through looking at the real phenomena of domination and subordination. It is often possible to identify the sort of feminist philosophy that is usually classed as 'radical' by its more incendiary or polemical language – e.g. talk of 'de-humanisation', of patriarchy as violence or 'war' against women – and by a characteristic focus

---

[16] See e.g. Dworkin (2000).

on issues such as sexual violence and rape, pornography and prostitution, as central to women's oppression under patriarchy. It is a sign both of radical feminism's influence and of its stigmatisation that this is the kind of feminism from which many women are eager to distance themselves, when asked about their views: e.g. 'I'm not a feminist [i.e. militant, hairy man-hater], but I do believe in equality', or 'I'm a feminist, I believe in equal rights, but I'm not extreme – I don't hate men.'

The other thing that is immediately noticeable is radical feminism's apparently *negative* emphasis, as compared with what I described as the 'positivity' of liberal feminism: rather than talking about the rights women should have, or the autonomy, opportunities and share of resources they should enjoy, radical feminists are interested above all in illuminating, analysing and explaining the horrific reality of patriarchy.

The above gives a superficial sense of what is meant by the category of 'radical feminism' – the styles and habits associated with that label – but it doesn't yet say anything much about what 'radical feminism' *means*. In particular, what is *radical* about radical feminism?

As far as its etymology goes, the word 'radical' just indicates something *having to do with roots*. This gives us a double sense in which radical feminism might be 'radical': first, by *going to the root of the problem of patriarchy*; and second, by identifying patriarchy as the problem *at the root of other social ills*. The first of these ideas, perhaps, is shared by all feminists: everyone, I guess, thinks that they (and perhaps only they) are getting to the heart of the matter – although different positions will of course have different views as to what the 'heart of the matter' is when it comes to patriarchy. The second idea, however, is certainly not universal. You don't have to think that patriarchy is *the* fundamental problem at the root of all others in order to think that it is both real and bad. The feminism of some liberals will not be 'radical' in this sense, and the feminism of a Marxist might not be either – a common radical feminist criticism of Marxist feminists is that they try to reduce everything to class, which is what *they* see as being at the root of everything.

It is not clear, however, that *all* radical feminists are 'radical' in this second, more controversial sense. And depending on what exactly is meant by 'at the root', here, it's not even clear that all of those who take patriarchy to be 'at the root' of other social ills are radical feminists. Engels, for example, describes the division of labour between the sexes as the first division of labour, which precedes and makes possible all others – so although in an obvious sense he (with Marx) treats class as the fundamental category of human societies, he also depicts *sex* as fundamental to *class*. Yet it would be unusual to describe Engels as a 'radical feminist'.

At this point, it becomes very difficult to be sure of what radical feminism involves. It looks plausible to say that all radical feminists take themselves to be going to the root of patriarchy, but this doesn't help to distinguish them from other feminists: i.e. it's necessary, but not sufficient, for being a radical feminist; and it's not so clear that locating patriarchy at the root of things is *either* necessary *or* sufficient. Admittedly, it is almost certainly a mistake to look for strict necessary and sufficient conditions in an area like this – imperfect clusters and tendencies are all we can hope to find. But the problem is that it's not even clear what tendencies or clusters of properties we should associate with this kind of feminism – except, *maybe*, the tendency to see patriarchy as underlying other problems. I think we can do better than that. But it will mean looking critically at the status of labels such as 'radical', its corollaries and contrasts.

Many feminists conceive of theirs as a 'revolutionary' kind of feminism, and are highly critical of what they describe as the 'reformism' of liberal feminists.[17] The latter, they complain, merely advocate equal rights for men and women within the same social structures that we now have: e.g. advocating equal opportunities for men and women to become CEOs, lawyers, or frontline soldiers. Radical feminists, by contrast, see themselves as *revolutionaries*, in the sense that they want to transform the structures themselves.[18] In an illuminating article about the life of radical feminist Shulamith Firestone (who died in 2012), Susan Faludi describes the sharp divergence between radical feminism and the liberal mainstream, as institutionalised in the National Organisation for Women (NOW), which sought, Faludi reports, '"to bring women into full participation in the mainstream of American society," largely by means of equal pay and equal representation. The radical feminists, by contrast, wanted *to reconceive public life and private life entirely*.'[19]

This seems to be connected with the point noted above: that radical feminists take themselves, but not their opponents, to be going to the roots of patriarchy. Radical feminists want to effect more 'structural' change not because they have accompanying (non-feminist) commitments to other

---

[17] See e.g. hooks (2000b); Ehrlich (1977).   [18] See e.g. hooks (2000b).
[19] Faludi (2013, p. 54; emphasis added).

values, although they might well have such commitments – for instance, a feminist who is also a pacifist will want to criticise the institution of the military, rather than arguing for women to be allowed to fight alongside men on the front line. One gets a clear sense that radical feminists are critical of those they label 'reformists', primarily for not being sufficiently revolutionary *in their feminism*: the latter are accused of failing to get to the root of patriarchy, of failing to realise that patriarchy cannot be got rid of whilst various social structures – such as those embodying class or racial or colonial domination – remain in place.

However, just as liberal feminists are likely to insist that they *are* tackling patriarchy at its roots, it is also quite possible for them to deny the charge that they envisage keeping social structures the same. For one thing, they might say, to achieve equal access for women *already is* to change existing structures. And liberals may be well aware that there will also be various changes which are *prerequisites* for achieving equal rights. In order to achieve a society where women can compete with men in all professions on an equal footing and be accorded equal respect in their public and private lives, all sorts of things would have to change: for example, we might have to start valuing care – and housework – properly, making proper provision for paternity leave, changing the way children are educated about gender roles, or changing the expectations of employers so that they are not implicitly shaped to fit the heterosexual man with a wife who stays at home to care for the children. What more does the radical feminist want?

The liberal feminist, then, may argue that she *does* acknowledge the need for structural change, and that the radical feminist is not telling her anything she doesn't already know.

The possibility of such a reply, however, does not mean that the radical feminist is mistaken – either in her criticism, or in her sense that there is a real disagreement between her and the reformist. It is clearly not meaningless to accuse somebody of holding the structures of the political status quo too fixed, merely proposing alterations to the gender or racial balance of the people who move through those structures – and in some cases the accusation will surely be correct: the radical feminist may be perfectly justified in wanting more. What the possibility of the sort of reply sketched above actually shows is just that categories such as 'radical', 'revolutionary' and 'reformist' cannot have their meanings fixed in a way that is neutral between different political standpoints. Who and what counts as radical depends on your politics, i.e. on what sort of place you think the world is, and what sorts of change you think are necessary or appropriate in order to address a problem like patriarchy – and any proposal or analysis that falls short of that, you may call insufficiently radical (the sources of the same proposal or analysis, unsurprisingly enough, are likely to disagree). There are real disagreements here, all right. But they are disagreements which can only be understood and addressed as disagreements over specific views and assumptions about what the world is like, and what is required in order to change it: which is simply to say, they are *political* disagreements.[20]

7.3 Marxist feminism

Another approach which would criticise liberals for focusing too narrowly on equality within a fixed system, but which makes this criticism from a different point of view, is Marxist feminism. Unlike radical feminism, how-ever, Marxist feminism – and perhaps also the related category of 'socialist feminism'[21] – is often seen as embodying a tension or contradiction, or at the very least, a potentially awkward fusion of two components which have little to do with one another. Yet Marxist feminists do exist, and have done so for quite a while, seeing profound affinities where others see potentially irre-solvable tensions. Women, too, are workers, whose labour – whether directed

[20] Carol Ehrlich gets it right, I think, when she says: 'I know that "reformist" is an epithet that may be used in ways that are neither honest nor very useful – principally to demonstrate one's ideological purity, or to say that concrete political work of any type is not worth doing because it is potentially co-optable. In response, some feminists have argued persuasively that the right kinds of reforms can build a radical movement. Just the same, there are reformist strategies that waste the energies of women, that raise expectations of great change, and that are misleading and alienating because they cannot deliver the goods' (Ehrlich 1977, pp. 3–4).

[21] I am concentrating on the category of 'Marxism' rather than 'socialism' here, purely because this is a chapter about the three schools of feminism that are most often dis-cussed, and my impression is that socialist feminism is more usually ignored, or sim-ply equated with Marxist feminism. I will pay more attention to non-Marxist socialist feminism (in the guise of anarchist feminism) in Chapter 10. For the moment, I will simply note that I am understanding Marxism as a subset of socialism, and using 'socialism' to denote a broader category of anti-capitalist, collectivist politics (contra the usage of some US theorists, as acknowledged earlier), which does not necessarily imply a commitment to everything I associate with Marxism below – not all kinds of socialist, for example, advocate the *revolutionary* overthrow of capitalism.

towards the production and care of male workers and future workers or (as increasingly the case from the mid nineteenth century onward) as industrial wage labour of a kind formerly performed by men – is indispensable to the survival of the capitalist economic system. As the socialist and feminist August Bebel (1840–1913) observed in his *Women and Socialism*, 'The Socialist Party is the only one that has made the full equality of women, their liberation from every form of dependence and oppression, an integral part of its program; not for reasons of propaganda, but from necessity. *For there can be no liberation of mankind without social independence and equality of the sexes.*'[22] Bebel's statement makes clear his view that the connections between socialism and feminism are not (or not just) a matter of the necessity of proletarian revolution for the emancipation of women, but vice versa – a sentiment echoed by the Marxist feminist Clara Zetkin (1857–1933), in her 1896 article, 'Only in Conjunction With the Proletarian Woman Will Socialism Be Victorious'. The Suffragette Sylvia Pankhurst agreed, and – unlike the rest of her family – was a lifelong socialist and anti-colonialist alongside her feminist convictions.

Just as liberal feminists are feminists who are liberals, so Marxist feminists can be initially described simply as feminists who are Marxists (note that this doesn't appear to work in the other remaining case: radical feminists are not just 'feminists who are radicals'). It is therefore necessary to say something – if only something very crude and general – about what a Marxist is. A plausible answer to this would be to say that a Marxist is someone who displays the following three characteristics:

(i) a commitment to some kind of 'materialism'[23] about history and social change;
(ii) an emphasis on social class[24] and class struggle;

---

[22] Excerpted in Schneir (1996, p. 211; italics in original).

[23] Recall that the more plausible versions of this will not involve a crude reduction of all social existence to 'blind' material forces, leaving no room for human agency and conscious experience. By 'materialism', here, I only mean to designate a view which takes seriously the role of material as well as 'ideal' factors in explaining social change, and which sees this as necessitating a corrective against the emphasis of the liberal idealist views which remain dominant – i.e. as necessitating an *emphasis* on the material as against the ideal.

[24] It's also important to add that Marxism and socialism are associated with particular *ways of understanding* the notion of class, ways which do not neatly correspond to liberal or everyday conceptions (which, in the UK at least, are often understood in

(iii) an expectation and/or advocacy of the revolutionary[25] replacement of capitalist relations of production with communist ones.

The question is then how Marxism, understood in terms of the three commitments just delineated, relates to feminism. There might be some examples of people who have identified themselves both as Marxists (or socialists) and as feminists without saying anything very systematic about the connection or relationship between them. But it is also possible to connect the two, in a variety of ways:

(a) *parallels* – many Marxist feminists have suggested that sex is to feminism what class is to Marxism, and hence that there are instructive parallels between the two approaches.[26]

(b) *overlap* – Marxist and feminist theory have a shared emphasis on oppression and domination, practical social change, as well as the concepts of ideology and of ideology-critique.

(c) *intersection* – as Marxist and socialist feminists have been quick to point out, class and sex oppression intersect in the social situation of working-class

terms of an ambiguous and complex mixture of economic and 'cultural' capital). Marxists are primarily concerned with class as understood in terms of a person's relationship to the means of production: if you own nothing but your labour power, and have to sell your labour power in order to live, you are technically proletarian (even though you may be a highly educated, well-paid lecturer or manager); if you possess the means to profit from the labour of others, instead, you are bourgeois. I can't get into the complexities and objections to which this gives rise here. The exact understanding of 'class' is not something that remains constant across different Marxisms and socialisms, and I'm concerned here with roughly defined common themes or threads. But it must be borne in mind that 'class', as emphasised by many socialists and Marxists, is not necessarily the same 'class' that is acknowledged (albeit increasingly seldom) by theorists and commentators of the liberal mainstream.

[25] It must also be borne in mind that 'revolutionary' is not a straightforward term. We often assume that we know what we mean by 'revolution', and that it involves sudden, wholesale political change, effected through violent means. But it's important to note that not all revolutionaries share these assumptions – and, indeed, it is not clear that Marx himself shared them: at certain points, he entertains the possibility of gradual as well as sudden revolutions, and of revolutions without bloodshed (see Eagleton 2011).

[26] Catharine MacKinnon entertains this thought at the beginning of her book, *Towards a Feminist Theory of the State* (1989), but ultimately rejects the idea. It is partly for this reason that she does not define herself as a Marxist feminist in any straightforward sense.

women, a situation which cannot be understood by simply lumping together a male-centred analysis of class with an analysis of sex relations which implicitly equates 'women' with 'middle- to upper-class women'.

(d) *entanglement* – capitalism and patriarchy are seen as mutually reinforcing structures, which are so entangled with one another in practice as to be inseparable.

Their perception of these connections has led some feminists to attach particular importance to the situation of working-class women, and to seek to apply socialist analyses, strategies and solutions to the problems faced by women of all classes through a focus on women's *labour* (as opposed to the traditional liberal focus on their civic and property rights).[27] One example of this is the socialist (but non-Marxist) feminist Charlotte Perkins Gilman, who advocated the collectivisation of traditionally female labour such as cookery. Though perhaps not a typical example of a socialist feminist, she is worth quoting for the sheer eloquence and fury with which she manages to discuss so tedious a topic as food preparation:

> one would naturally suppose that the segregation of an entire sex to the fulfilment of this function would insure the most remarkable results. It has, but they are not so favorable as might be expected...As it stands among us today,...it is the lowest of amateur handicrafts and a prolific source of disease; and, as an art, it has developed under the peculiar stimulus of its position as a sex-function into a voluptuous profusion as false as it is evil. Our innocent proverb, 'The way to a man's heart is through his stomach,' is a painfully plain comment on the way in which we have come to deprave our bodies and degrade our souls at the table.[28]

One promising way to understand Marxist and socialist feminisms, then, is as seeking to highlight and correct the mistakes and oversights of other approaches: Marxist feminists, on this picture, are simply feminists who are also Marxists, and who think that other, perhaps more dominant forms of feminism – e.g. liberal feminism – *at best* lack certain insights which a Marxist perspective can provide. For instance, mainstream feminism has been criticised by Marxists (among others) for being too narrowly focused on the concerns of (white) middle-class women, too preoccupied with formal rights and freedoms like suffrage, at the cost of neglecting the issue of the material

[27] See e.g. Vogel (1995).   [28] In Schneir (1996, pp. 239–40).

deprivation suffered disproportionately by women, and too little conscious of the barriers that class erects between women, who for that reason cannot be regarded as a homogenous group.

As mentioned earlier, however, a common charge against Marxist feminism is that it treats patriarchal oppression as an issue of derivative or secondary concern. And this is undeniably true of some Marxist and other left-wing organisations, which have frequently been deeply sexist in their commitments and internal practices.[29] But it is not as if liberalism does not also have a history of perpetuation of and apologetics for misogyny and patriarchy. Nor is it at all surprising, from a point of view attuned to the notion of ideology, that patriarchal ideology will be found in the thought of Marxists too – this just reinforces the need for greater self-reflection and criticism. The strongest form of the charge, however, is not just that Marxists aren't immune to patriarchal forms of thought and practice – no-one is – but that there is something about Marxism which entails a dismissive or belittling attitude towards feminist concerns. Marxist feminists, unsurprisingly, deny this charge, and often say that for them, Marxism and feminism are not competing commitments, such that one could be ranked above the other. Rather, they are two sides of the same coin – mutually indispensable. They insist: you can't get rid of capitalism without getting rid of patriarchy; and you can't get rid of patriarchy without getting rid of capitalism.

The problem is that these claims are fundamentally ambiguous – rather like the claim: 'A necessary part of clearing up is finding the vacuum cleaner.' This could mean *either* that you need to find the vacuum cleaner in order to clear up properly, *or* that if you clear up properly, you cannot fail to find the vacuum cleaner at some point (because it must be under there somewhere). Of course, both of these might be true. But the point is that they are

---

[29] Faludi relates the story of what happened at an early 'new left' conference, when Shulamith Firestone and Jo Freeman 'drafted a resolution calling for equitable marriage and property laws, "complete control by women of their own bodies," and a fifty-one-per-cent representation of women on the conference floor. The chairman skipped over it. "They laughed at us," Freeman recalled. "The chair said, 'Move on little girl. We have more important issues to talk about here than women's problems.' And then he literally reached out and patted Shulie on the head"' (Faludi 2013, p. 55). Firestone later wrote, in a letter to a radical New York newspaper: 'Fuck off, left. You can examine your navel by yourself from now on. We're starting our own movement' (see Faludi 2013, p. 57).

obviously different claims. The key question, I think, is what sense of 'can't' is at play in the statement, 'You can't get rid of capitalism without getting rid of patriarchy'. This could mean either of two things: (a) that if you get rid of capitalism, patriarchy cannot fail to wither away too, as if by magic; or (b) that getting rid of patriarchy is a *precondition or necessary part of the process of getting rid of capitalism* – the position of major figures such as Bebel and Zetkin, as we saw above.[30]

Marxist feminism seems clearly opposed to liberal feminism, if the latter implies a commitment to capitalism and the former a commitment to its overthrow. But as we've seen, the relationship between radical feminism and Marxist (or socialist) feminism is not so clear. The connection between liberal feminism and capitalism does not appear to exist between capitalism and radical feminism. In fact, some radical feminists also see themselves as Marxists, in at least some sense of the term. For many Marxists, there is no disagreement between them and radical feminists: there is a disagreement only in the sense that radical feminists *think* there is a disagreement, whereas Marxist feminists do not – a war, as the Leonard Cohen lyric puts it, between those who say there is a war and those who say there isn't. Many radical feminists see it differently: there *is* a disagreement with Marxists, because the latter want to reduce gender to class, or at least to treat it as of secondary importance. It is not clear to me whether there is any necessary connection between being a Marxist and being guilty of that. But what *does* seem clear is that we should extremely suspicious of the line, 'Yes, yes, but you just have to wait!', wherever that line comes from. This trope of being asked to 'just wait' has an ugly history in politics. And as the economist John Maynard Keynes reminds us, in the long run we are all dead.

* * *

A number of analytic philosophers, working in the theory of knowledge, have been very keen on a set of thought experiments where – in order to work out what knowledge is – you imagine yourself in a landscape populated by 'barn facades' (fake two-dimensional screens that look like barns), false cows, cows standing in front of sheep, and the like. There is a certain irony in the fact that philosophers are so partial to these sorts of games, and at the same time so oblivious to the fact that the intellectual landscapes they already inhabit

---

[30] Cf. the 'motivation objection' to the Marxist idea that revolution is inevitable, discussed and rejected by Eagleton (2011).

are as deceptive as any they could conjure in imagination. The sketch I've laid out in this chapter, of the landscape within which insiders and newcomers to feminist philosophy are expected to move, is itself a sketch of a landscape where nothing is as it seems. Liberal feminism has no special claim on the value of liberty or freedom, and is most usually not even couched in terms of it. It might be better described as a particular kind of 'reformist' feminism,[31] where one of the structures that it holds in place is the economic system of capitalism. But whilst an affirmative attitude to capitalism distinguishes liberal feminism from Marxist feminism (a distinction which there was never much difficulty in drawing anyway), it may not succeed in distinguishing liberal from what is called *radical* feminism, which does not always incorporate an anti-capitalist stance.

Radical feminism, too, emerges as a deceptive object. Its radical credentials consist, in large part, in the adherence to a kind of 'revolutionary' feminist politics, as opposed to the 'reformism' most closely associated with liberals: it is not just capitalism the latter want to keep intact, radical feminists would allege, but much of the fundamental structure of patriarchy. But thinking of this under the category of 'radical feminism' can tend to give an erroneous impression: that this is a category whose meaning and membership can be determined in a way acceptable to all sides. In actual fact, terms like 'radical' and 'revolutionary' only make sense as terms of allegiance or castigation, usages of which come already loaded with contested political judgements of value and fact:[32] to describe one's own feminism as 'radical' or 'revolutionary' is to declare that it goes *deep and far enough* in its analysis and critique; and to call someone a 'reformist' is often to accuse them of failing to do this. At least as often, the term 'radical feminism' is used with a pejorative force, to indicate the kind of 'extreme' or 'outdated' view from which the speaker wishes to disassociate herself.[33] Interestingly, many of the thinkers usually classed as 'radical feminists' reject that label, preferring to describe what they

---

[31] Jaggar (1983) shares this verdict.

[32] There is nothing wrong with this kind of loading, in itself. What is important is that we know what we are carrying, and declare it openly to others and to ourselves.

[33] The (unfortunately little-known) feminist philosopher, Denise Thompson, observes the dual action of the terms 'radical' and 'old-fashioned' in order to dismiss the kind of feminism she favours: 'I'm fascinated to note that feminism seems to have gone from being too radical (for "the women out there") to old-fashioned with nothing in between' (Thompson 2003/2004).

do simply as 'feminism' (a point which Catharine MacKinnon underscores by adopting the alternative term 'feminism unmodified').[34]

In fact, all three categories discussed here are probably more likely to be employed as terms of denunciation or abuse than anything else: a 'liberal' is an individualist who can't think past formal rights; a 'radical feminist' is an extremist, prone to hyperbole and paranoia, an 'anti-sex' attitude and the denial of the value of women's experiences; a 'Marxist feminist' is someone who belittles the specificities of patriarchy as a system of oppression, either by side-lining it altogether or by seeking to reduce it to the issue of class. If there is one thing in all this that is clear, it is the extent and deep-rootedness of the *unclarity* inherent in these categories. They emerge as slippery, contested and essentially value-laden.

What is the best response to this? Not the analytic philosopher's kneejerk solution of definition-building, that's for sure. To try to fix clear definitions for any of these categories would be to impose a coherence and simplicity on what is inherently vague and disordered. And to try to impose definitions which are *universally acceptable* would be to overlook the political loaded-ness of the terms. Just as we can't get anywhere with this by reading the dictionary, nor are we likely to get far by rewriting it. The trick is, I think, to refuse to be constrained by the three categories outlined in this chapter, but to do this without ignoring them. Even barn facades are real objects to be navigated around – they are just not the objects they seem to be. So in what follows, I'm not going to have a full chapter on each 'kind' of feminism – apart from anything else, this is a tired format which could quickly get boring. I'm also reluctant to do what some advocate, and forget about different 'approaches' in favour of 'issues'. This tends to mean attempting to look at topics of feminist significance – such as abortion, work, or the family – in a way that is artificially apolitical (apoliticality is always artificial). The suggestion that we should look at 'issues' rather than at the affinities and tensions between broad approaches, such as socialism, Marxism and liberalism, often turns out to be code for

---

[34] Thompson shares this position. Railing on her webpage against the title of her own book, *Radical Feminism Today* (2001) – a title forced upon her by her publishers – Thompson argues: 'There's only feminism; and what's usually called "radical feminism" (that is, what's usually called "radical feminism" by those who agree with it, not what is usually called "radical feminism" by its enemies who distort and trivialise it) comes closest to being only feminism unmixed with anything else.'

the intention to work solely within the *liberal* approach that is currently dominant.

Instead, I'll aim to shed some light on the way in which the political commitments of different approaches to feminism conflict and intersect in the attempt to grapple with particular questions. In the next chapter, I'll look at some of the issues which feminists have made their own – issues belonging to what has traditionally been regarded as the 'personal' or 'private' sphere, but which, feminists have insisted, are no less political for that.

8 Everyday rebellions: revolution in the private sphere

He said: There was, in Medina, a shameless woman called Sallama al-Khadra (the Green). It happened that she was caught with an effeminate man while she was fucking him with a dildo; so she was hauled up before the governor, who punished her with a beating and had her paraded on a camel. A man who knew her looked at her and said: 'What is this, oh Sallama?' So she said: 'By God, shut up! There is nothing in the world more oppressive than men. You have been fucking us since the beginning of all time, and when we've fucked you one single time you are killing us!'

– From Jahez, *Rasa'il* (Epistles)[1]

In the last chapter, I outlined the three most widely recognised approaches within feminist philosophy: liberal, Marxist and radical feminism. I warned against the reification of these categories, and stated my intention to focus on those places where real disagreements between feminists emerge most clearly and concretely. Among those places, there is no place like the home. Radical, liberal and Marxist feminisms are associated with quite different attitudes to what has traditionally been called the 'private sphere', clashing over issues such as the unpaid labour of women in the home, the rearing of children, and the institutions of marriage and the family. Radical feminists have accused Marxist feminists not so much of getting these issues wrong, but of treating them as unimportant – tending to privilege the role and perspective of the (male) waged industrial worker above all else. Some Marxist feminists have sought to remedy this by emphasising the role of unpaid 'reproductive' labour (mostly performed by women in the home) in sustaining

---

The title for this chapter is borrowed from Gloria Steinem's 1983 book, *Outrageous Acts and Everyday Rebellions.*

[1] Translation LF. From al-Jahez (1964, vol. 2, p. 135).

capitalism and producing wealth.[2] We briefly encountered, in the last chapter, the preferred solution of socialist feminist and economist Charlotte Perkins Gilman: the collectivisation of household labour.

Meanwhile, those usually considered 'radical feminists' have produced a wide array of controversial suggestions, some of which will be mentioned in the course of this chapter. Liberal feminists, for their part, while stopping short of calling for the abolition of the family (a demand notoriously characteristic of some radical feminists), have been keen to advocate its reform – breaking with the traditional liberal view of the 'private sphere' as a realm of 'individual choice' into which politics should not intrude.

This chapter deals with all things private and personal – issues to do with the home, the family, the body, love, sex and reproduction. These are matters which have been so centrally important for many feminists that it would seem strange for a book on feminism to omit discussion of them. Of course, they haven't been entirely absent in the chapters so far. Chapter 4, for example, was in large part concerned with the body and sexual identity. Private issues are never really private. They are always impinged upon and shaped by a range of medical and social and academic practices. This is part of what is meant by the feminist claim that the personal is political. But another part of what is meant is that the personal is important – *politically* important – in its own right.

Beyond this, there are few certainties and endless disagreement. Feminists may all have something to say about the importance of the private or personal, but they do not all say the same thing (why would they?). Besides disagreeing on the particular significance of various practices and phenomena such as marriage, heterosexuality, abortion or motherhood, they disagree, too, on what it *means* to say that 'the personal' is politically significant. I'll take these two areas or levels of controversy in turn. First, I'll say something about feminist thought and action with respect to the institutions of marriage and the family. Then I'll look more closely at the idea that 'the personal is political', what it meant for second-wave feminists and what it might mean for us now.

* * *

If there is any place to talk personally in this book, I suppose this is it. And so I will break for a moment with the book's usual mode and say something

---

[2] E.g. Benston (1969); Dalla Costa & James (2012); Federici (1975); Hennessy (2003); Malos (1975); Vogel (1995).

from my own perspective. I have to admit that I find myself particularly out of my depth when trying to discuss the subject of marriage and 'the family' (something about that definite article makes it sound as though there is one and only one thing – probably the neat package of mother, father and children – that is being referred to). I grew up thinking of marriage as something completely foreign, something other people did. The main thing it symbolised for me was a kind of respectability, something from which I felt semi-proudly, semi-painfully excluded. My parents were never married, and after they separated I was raised by a single father. I don't think it had ever even occurred to either of them to get married. My mother (who had not married my brother's father either) was explicitly influenced in her outlook, to some extent, by second-wave feminism. As for my father, I think he just didn't see any need for marriage – and besides, he would have found the prospect of the actual ceremony almost impossibly embarrassing.

This all seemed perfectly natural to me, of course – it was other people who were odd. But I do remember that, in the context of village life, this set-up was the object of a certain amount of disapproval, curiosity and gossip. Many people, I later learned, were horrified that a *mother* could have left her child, as they saw it (she actually only went to the next village). Partly, this is just because there is not much to do in the countryside, and so people are desperate for some kind of intrigue or outrage. But it was not only in the village that my family arrangements were an issue. From a distance, certain relatives were ashamed of what they saw as the stigma of my brother's and my own illegitimacy, to the point where contact was minimal or non-existent for many years. It might be tempting to assume that these sorts of attitudes are confined to the very parochial and the very elderly, and that 'nowadays', not marrying – and having children outside marriage – is completely normal and accepted. Whilst there is some truth to this, I think it is often exaggerated. Ironically, the exaggeration may be the product of a media-fuelled anxiety over the idea that people are not getting married anymore – an anxiety which utterly belies the idea that non-marriage is fully accepted. All this is more vividly apparent to those who stand at some distance from the institution of marriage. I still notice that people tend to assume that my parents were married once, if not anymore, so that if the fact that they live separately comes up in conversation, a common question is 'When did your parents divorce then?' For some reason, I always feel an urge to correct the misapprehension, without being quite sure why it matters, and feeling slightly ashamed of being so pedantic. The usual response at this point is 'Well OK, separated' – as if to confirm that there is no real difference. But I suspect that the difference, too, is more important from the outside than from the inside.

Still more noticeable is the reaction of many people to the idea of a five-year-old being 'abandoned' by her mother, a thought which I have seen bring tears to the eyes of grown feminists (many of whom are surprised and somewhat troubled by their own response). This is not substantially different from when I was a small child, puzzled and embarrassed by certain people's evident pity, and vainly trying to persuade them that there was nothing particularly tragic about being raised by your dad instead of your mum. My dad and I even accepted an invitation to be part of the audience for the TV show of a pre-UKIP Robert Kilroy (a mistake that would not have been made had my dad had any idea who Kilroy was and what his show was like). I remember my sense of rage at Kilroy's opening line: 'Fathers are ten-a-penny, but a *mother...*'. My dad put his hand up to speak, but the studio assistants must have seen the look on his face and whispered some wise words into Kilroy's earpiece, because he studiously avoided us for the duration.

Although marriage is declining in Britain and the United States, it remains the norm. Most people still get married. The right-wing British broadsheet *The Telegraph* reported with horror in 2011 that married couples were now officially a 'minority', as the rate of married people (among those old enough to marry) had dipped to 47 per cent.[3] Shocking as this figure may have been to *Telegraph* readers, it of course does not mean that only a minority marry *at some point in their lives*. It mostly means that people are getting married later (in large part because of an increased student population). According to a 2014 report by the Pew Research Center: 'When today's young [American] adults reach their mid-40s to mid-50s, a *record high share* (roughly 25%) is likely to have never been married.'[4] Imagine that: the percentage of people married by middle age *might* drop as low as 75 per cent. This kind of presentation tells us much more about the persistence of traditional expectations of family structure than it does about the alleged decline of marriage.

If we turn to the rates of single parenthood, the results are similarly un-shocking. Another right-wing British publication reported in 2012 that 'more than one in four families – 26 per cent – are now led by a single parent'.[5]

[3] Bingham (2013).   [4] Luscombe (2014; emphasis added).
[5] Data from the Office for National Statistics (ONS), reported in the *Daily Mail* (Doughty 2012).

So, three-quarters of families are not. As for families headed by single fathers, these were much rarer, accounting for 13.5 per cent of all single-parent households in the UK in 2012 (meaning that only around 3.5 per cent of families were headed by single fathers).[6]

Two points are already clear. First, marriage is still the most common and approved family structure – even in countries such as the US and UK, which have higher rates of single-parent families than many other countries (and in which certain sections of society seem to be very worried about it). Second, family patterns are still very heavily gendered: when parents split, the mother almost always becomes the main caregiver; when she does not, this is often treated as something either tragic or heroic (heroic on the part of the father, that is). Mothers are clearly seen as more naturally suited to raise children, whilst it is also noticeable that absent fathers are generally blamed for perceived social problems such as crime and the lack of 'discipline' among young people.

So although feminist critiques of marriage and the family have been going on for centuries, they have by no means ceased to be relevant. I can't hope to give anything like a comprehensive coverage of them. All I aim to do here is to introduce some of the main themes of these critiques, and to say enough to show what is suspect about the kind of story that is standardly told or assumed about the history of the private sphere. As on previous occasions where I've made a point of this kind, the misconceptions I want to speak against are those which stem from and exhibit an attitude that is both ethnocentric and generally subservient to a desire to glorify the (or 'our') present as the culmination of a process of steady progress. In the case of the private sphere, the story – which is only a more specific, zoomed-in version of the 'standard history of feminism' that I argued against in Chapter 5 – might run roughly as follows:

Historically, the institutions of marriage and the family have meant oppression and exploitation for the women that they have included, along with an additional stigmatisation and other penalties for those excluded – a function of the unjust and unequal laws that surrounded and partially constituted those institutions. At least on the legal side, things are now very different – even gay marriage is being legalised in some countries. We also now have new birth control technologies such as the pill, and

---

[6] '400,000 families were headed by lone fathers in 2012, representing 13.5%. With an average family size of 2.32, that figure represents 927,000 people in the UK' (Chalabi 2013).

progressive liberal laws have made both contraception and abortion safely available to more women.

Where we still have some way to go is in the sphere of culture and attitudes – for example, to end the 'second shift' by getting men to do their fair share of the housework, childcare and so on. Some more legislation may also be needed (especially as regards parental leave), so that women can finally be on a level playing field with men when it comes to competing for careers.

One immediate problem with the whole project of trying to construct a simple, continuous narrative like this is that there is no constant item or institution here, which we can chart and compare across different social and historical contexts. Marriage, for instance, is not one thing but many, varying according to the historical moment and the social and geographical location. So when 'marriage' is criticised, there is more than one importantly different thing which may be meant: we might be talking about a state institution, or we might be talking about a civil or religious one (prior to 1837, for example, births, marriages and deaths in England and Wales did not have to be registered by the state, and were typically recorded in parish records). Besides this, we can distinguish between different marriage forms – e.g. monogamous versus polygamous marriage. Many feminist critiques of marriage are, at least implicitly, critiques of *state* (monogamous) marriage – although the fact that marriage as those critics know or knew it is a state institution may not always be essential to the critique. The point is worth bearing in mind, however, as it draws attention to the historical specificity and recentness of an institution which has taken on a familiar aura of naturalness and permanence.

Beyond this fundamental complicating factor, the pleasant narrative arc drawn by the kind of story given above fails to accommodate certain basic points of historical fact, some of which have already been raised: as I noted in Chapter 5, for example, women in early Muslim societies had independent property rights – such as the right to inherit property (albeit not on equal terms with men). Medieval Islamic societies also permitted easy divorce and remarriage, contraception and (usually) abortion.[7] By contrast, in recent years in the United States, a series of Republican interventions, dubbed the 'War on Women', has eroded women's reproductive rights and control – especially in the case of poor and black women.[8]

---

[7] Musallam (1983).   [8] Finlay (2006).

This points to a third problem with this narrative: its Whiggish conviction that the story of marriage and the family has been one of smooth but steady progress, culminating in a relative positivity about the present which does not always sit well with reality. Partly, this owes to the tendency – characteristic of some strands of liberal thought – to recognise only two sources of problems and solutions: laws and attitudes. In this case as in many others, the verdict is that things are more or less OK on the legal side, but that there is a bit more work to do in terms of changing people's attitudes. What this leaves out, of course, are the material and economic aspects of women's subordination to men in the home and the private sphere. Nor is what radical feminists have regarded as sexual domination easily subsumable under either the 'legal' or 'attitudinal' category. I'll discuss both of these aspects further shortly. But even if we restrict ourselves to looking at the legal aspect of women's situations vis-à-vis the personal or private, it is not an entirely straightforward matter to uphold a rosy view of progress extending to the present and projected into the future – a point which the example of the Republican 'War on Women' serves to underline.

Once again, I will not attempt to replace this with a history of my own. My aims are extremely limited: to make some basic conceptual distinctions in order to draw out some of the main aspects and varieties of the critiques which feminists have formulated; and to offer a few examples by way of (partial) illustration of the range of those feminist critiques, and of associated practices of resistance and rebellion.

* * *

The tradition of feminist critique of marriage is long and diverse, and (like every other aspect of feminism) has both theoretical and practical manifestations. Marriage has been criticised from liberal as well as from socialist (including Marxist) and radical feminist positions. Mary Astell advised educated eighteenth-century women to avoid marrying. Mill regarded marriage (under the laws of his time) as 'slavery'.[9] Caroline Sheridan Norton – although

---

[9] 'The law of servitude in marriage is a monstrous contradiction to all the principles of the modern world, and to all the experience through which those principles have been slowly and painfully worked out. It is the sole case, now that negro slavery has been abolished, in which a human being in the plenitude of every faculty is delivered up to the tender mercies of another human being, in the hope forsooth that this other will use the power solely for the good of the person subjected to it. Marriage is the only actual bondage known to our law. There remain no legal slaves, except the mistress of every house' (Mill 2006, p. 220).

she did not class herself as a 'feminist' – committed much of her life to campaigning for the reform of laws that unjustly penalised women, and her efforts eventually influenced the UK Matrimonial Causes Act of 1857 (which extended the availability of divorce). Feminists have rebelled against marriage not just through their writings and arguments, but through their practice – through the ways in which they have actually lived their lives. When the black sheep of the Suffragettes, Sylvia Pankhurst, began living with the Italian anarchist Silvio Corio, and had a child with him, she refused to marry Corio or to take his name (prompting her mother Emmeline to cut ties with Sylvia and her family). In Chapter 6, I also mentioned the examples of George Sand and of the Claflin sisters, women who rebelled against conventional expectations of marriage and sexuality and practised 'free love'.

These critiques have differed greatly in their angle and emphasis – for instance, in their view as to which particular aspect of traditional or prevalent family structures is problematic, from a feminist perspective. Is it marriage itself that is the problem, or certain other things that have traditionally accompanied it (e.g. inequitable property laws, or gendered schemes of the division of household labour)? Perhaps it doesn't make all that much sense to talk about 'marriage itself' in this way: marriage is just *constituted* by certain laws, conventions or relations, so that it cannot meaningfully be distinguished from them. So perhaps the question is better put as one of reform versus revolution – or in this case, abolition. Is the task to reform marriage so that it is no longer a patriarchal institution, or to abolish it, because it is an *inherently* patriarchal institution? In turn, can the abolition of marriage be thought of as an isolated aim – so that we might target marriage directly, aiming to abolish it even while holding the rest of social reality basically fixed – or is it to be thought of only as part of a wider project of social transformation?

To return to the two senses of 'radical' distinguished in Chapter 7 above, critics of marriage have often been radical critics in the sense of pinpointing marriage as the *root* of the other problems affecting women, and as the primary obstacle to their liberation. Locating the origin of both class and sex oppression in the emergence of monogamous marriage, Engels wrote that the latter institution

comes on the scene as the subjugation of one sex by the other; it announces a struggle between the sexes unknown throughout the whole previous prehistoric period . . . The first class opposition that appears in history coincides with the development of the antagonism between man and woman in monogamous marriage, and the first class oppression coincides with that of the female sex by the male.[10]

Prominent members of the nineteenth-century women's movement in Britain and America, too, saw marriage as fundamental, underlying the other inequalities they were struggling against. In the late nineteenth century, Elizabeth Cady Stanton clashed with the broader women's movement by trying to expand its platform to include the issue of marriage and divorce alongside that of suffrage. She wrote to Susan B. Anthony: 'How this marriage question grows on one. *It lies at the foundation of all progress.*'[11]

Whilst seeing marriage as being at the root of other problems, however, Stanton's attitude was, in another sense, reformist rather than radical – she did not advocate the abolition of marriage, but rather its reform as a contract between two completely equal parties. Here she parts ways with other feminist critics of marriage, such as second-wave radical feminist Sheila Cronan, who argued that freedom for women 'cannot be won without the abolition of marriage'.[12] For many such critics, marriage itself is *at root* the domination of men over women; at least, this is so under conditions of patriarchy – something which many radical feminists also say about heterosexual sex, and which some have extended to the nuclear family (whether or not it involves marriage) and to existing practices of reproduction and childrearing.[13] So we have a preliminary distinction between those feminists who see the patriarchal family as a problem which can be pruned into submission, and those who see it as something that needs to be uprooted and discarded if women's liberation is to be successful.

But what, more precisely, have some feminists found so disturbing about the institutions of marriage and the family?[14] Some of the components of the

---

[10] See Engels (1844), II.4 'The monogamous family'. Also excerpted in Schneir (1996, p. 193).

[11] Quoted in Rossi (1973, p. 392; emphasis added).   [12] Cronan (1973, p. 219).

[13] See e.g. Firestone (1971).

[14] It's worth acknowledging that the feminist emphasis on problematising the family has come in for criticism by some black feminists, who point out that the family does not necessarily mean the same thing for black women as it does for whites: for black people, including black women, the family is not *only* a sphere of oppression, but is equally significant a source of strength and resistance against racism (see Carby 1997, p. 112).

answer to that question have been mentioned already. First, and perhaps most obviously, there is a set of concerns about the economic and legal significance of marriage for women. This was an important focus for nineteenth-century critics such as Caroline Norton, who had been denied access to her own earnings, and to her three children, by her abusive and violent husband after the couple's separation. Prior to the Married Women's Property Acts of 1870 and 1882,[15] married women in Britain were not entitled to hold or receive property, income or inheritance in their own right: everything a married woman received would automatically go to her husband, under whose identity her own was legally subsumed upon marriage. Norton's case also highlights the lack of legal recognition of what we would now call domestic violence.[16] Until the middle of the nineteenth century, it was considered permissible in the UK and most parts of the US for a husband to use physical 'discipline' against his wife, and it was not until the 1878 Matrimonial Causes Act that it was possible for British women to seek legal separation from an abusive husband.[17]

Most of these more obvious legal inequalities and problems surrounding marriage have by now been eliminated. One of the most visible remaining areas of struggle is the exclusion of same-sex couples. While many gay and lesbian activists have campaigned to be allowed to marry on equal terms with heterosexual couples, arguing both that this is a requirement of equality[18] and also that it could have a positive, diversifying and liberating effect on the character and social significance of marriage,[19] others have criticised this approach as overly 'assimilationist': too uncritical of the institution of marriage, and too willing to model same-sex relationships on a heterosexual marital ideal.[20] Lesbian feminist Claudia Card, for example, argues that

---

[15] The 1882 Act applied in England (and Wales) and Ireland (after Irish independence in 1922, only in Northern Ireland), but did not extend to Scotland.

[16] The term 'domestic violence' was first recorded in 1973.

[17] By contrast, it was not until 1991 that marital rape was criminalised in the UK.

[18] Mohr (2005); Rajczi (2008); Williams (2011).

[19] Mohr (2005); Halwani (2003, esp. chapter 3).

[20] See e.g. Ettelbrick (2004); Card (2007). Butler (2004, p. 5) summarises the dilemma to which these thoughts can give rise: 'The recent efforts to promote lesbian and gay marriage also promote a norm that threatens to render illegitimate and abject those sexual arrangements that do not comply with the marriage norm in either its existing or its revisable form. At the same time, the homophobic objections to lesbian and gay marriage expand out through the culture to affect all queer

'current advocacy of lesbian and gay rights to legal marriage and parenthood insufficiently criticizes both marriage and motherhood as they are currently practiced and structured by Northern legal institutions', that 'we would do better not to let the State define our intimate unions', and that 'parenting would be improved if the power presently concentrated in the hands of one or two guardians were diluted and distributed through an appropriately concerned community'.[21] Card and others add that same-sex marriage would extend the undesirable effects of heterosexual marriage to homosexual relationships – for example, by producing economic incentives to stay in bad partnerships, and making it more difficult for people to escape domestic violence and abuse.[22]

It's worth emphasising that taking a critical line on marriage as an objective of the struggle for gay liberation need not mean denying that the exclusion of gay people from marriage is a facet of homophobia (as it surely is). Nor does it have to mean taking the position that the state should *not* allow same-sex marriage (why shouldn't it?). Rather, the point may be that we are asking the wrong question by asking what forms of relationship the (in reality, homophobic and sexist) state should and should not endorse. And certainly, these critics are challenging the idea that the institution of marriage as we know it – i.e. a heteronormative, repressive and patriarchal institution – is something to which gay people ought to be expected to aspire. The thought here is parallel to a line of radical feminist criticism of liberal feminism, discussed in an earlier chapter:[23] we should not understand liberation merely as a matter of achieving equality of access to existing institutions which are treated as fixed; rather, any truly liberatory struggle will be aimed at transforming (or abolishing) those institutions and the kind of society of which they are a part.

Whilst the contemporary legal situation differs in obvious ways from that of the nineteenth century, later feminists have frequently pointed out that marriage remains an institution in which women tend to be economically dependent on men, partly because, under current social conditions, women's

lives. One critical question thus becomes, how does one oppose the homophobia without embracing the marriage norm as the exclusive or most highly valued social arrangement for queer sexual lives?'

[21] Card (1996, p. 1). [22] Card (1996, 2007); Ettelbrick (2004).
[23] See Chapter 7 above.

role as primary carers for children leaves them at a disadvantage in terms of pursuing a career.[24] This helps to account for evidence that women are at far greater risk of poverty than men are in the event of a divorce.[25] It's worth noting that this problem is one that applies to heterosexual couplings in general (especially those in which there are dependent children), rather than being tied exclusively to the relationship of marriage.

The same goes for the related issue of the division of household labour – which stands as a contributing factor relative to the phenomenon of women's economic dependence on male partners. According to a common but misleading view of labour within the household, we can distinguish two importantly different historical stages: a traditional period, where women performed the majority of the housework and cared for the children at home while men earned money through external employment; and a modern period in which women – beginning from the time of the industrial revolution, and powered by surges during and following each of the two World Wars – have entered the workforce in far greater numbers, thus rendering the traditional, stereotypical division of labour between the sexes a thing of the past (although gendered inequalities in earnings and in access to certain careers may persist).

In an influential contribution to twentieth-century feminist theory, Arlie Russell Hochschild has shown that this picture is mistaken. Based on intensive interviews with fifty couples and observation of their family lives, Hochschild found that an equal division of labour in the home was actually very unusual, even among those couples whose professed attitudes to gender and marriage Hochschild classed as 'egalitarian'. Instead, women who were in paid employment worked a 'second shift': upon returning from their formal jobs, they performed the lion's share of household tasks as well (which was also associated with various tensions, marital problems, and negative effects on the women's well-being).[26]

The disproportionate burden of household labour borne by women has been an important focal point for many feminists, but different kinds of feminist have understood its significance in very different ways. For liberals,

---

[24] See e.g. Bergmann (1986); Folbre (1994).

[25] According to a study cited by many contemporary feminist commentators, men's 'standard of living' rises significantly (by 42 per cent) after a divorce, whereas women's is reduced by 78 per cent. See Weitzman (1985).

[26] Hochschild (1989). Hochschild's findings are confirmed by more recent studies (see Sifferlin 2014).

the division of household labour is a matter of justice or equality, including equality of opportunity: it is *unjust* that women should carry more of the burden than men; and it damages women's ability to compete with men on an equal footing in their careers outside the home. For others, this is not the main point at all. Rather, the phenomenon of women's unpaid labour is important because it shows us something about the way in which capitalism functions. The acknowledgement of this labour has an important place in the critique of capitalism. From a feminist point of view, capitalism may then be criticised in terms of what it does to women – namely, exploiting their unpaid labour. Marxist feminists, in particular, have argued that the capitalist economy rests on this 'reproductive' labour (so called because it reproduces and maintains the conditions under which 'productive' labour is possible, e.g. by clothing and feeding the male worker and his dependent children).[27] Selma James and Mariarosa Dalla Costa explain:

> [The ability to work] is a strange commodity for it is not a thing. [It] resides only in a human being whose life is consumed in the process of producing. First it must be nine months in the womb, must be fed, clothed, and trained; then when it works its bed must be made, its floor swept, its lunchbox prepared, its sexuality not gratified but quietened, its dinner ready when it gets home, even if this is eight in the morning from the night shift. This is how labour power is produced and reproduced when it is daily consumed in the factory or the office. To describe its basic production and reproduction is to describe women's work. The community therefore is not an area of freedom and leisure auxiliary to the factory, where by chance there happen to be women who are degraded as the personal servants of men. The community is the other half of capitalist organization, the other area of hidden capitalist exploitation, the other, hidden, source of surplus labour. It becomes increasingly regimented like a factory, what we call a social factory, where the costs and nature of transport, housing, medical care, education, police, are all points of struggle. And this social factory has as its pivot the woman in the home producing labour power as a commodity, and her struggle not to.[28]

This analysis has led a number of Marxist feminist theorists to demand that household labour be paid like other forms of labour. It's important to stress

---

[27] Benston (1969); Dalla Costa & James (2012); Federici (1975); Hennessy (2003); Malos (1975); Vogel (1995).
[28] James & Dalla Costa (2012, pp. 51–2).

that, when the demand is made from a Marxist point of view, this is *not* a demand for the realisation of some ideal of distributive justice. Rather, it is demanded as part of the project of empowering women in the revolutionary struggle against both patriarchy and capitalism.[29] When in 1972, Selma James[30] launched the International Wages for Housework Campaign, the point of this was not only to call for economic renumeration for domestic work, but also to disrupt and to draw attention to the dependence of the capitalist system on the hidden exploitation of women's unpaid labour – in other words, to point out the deep political significance of the personal.

So far, I've been focusing on the legal and economic aspects of feminist critiques of the family. But these are inextricably bound up with a third aspect: the role of sex and the use of the woman's body. The passage from James and Dalla Costa quoted above, for example, observes that part of the reproductive labour of women is to 'quieten' (if not gratify) the sexual desires of the male worker. And indeed, from liberal and radical feminist as well as Marxist perspectives, a link has been made between marriage and prostitution – for example, Sheila Jeffreys, a second-wave lesbian separatist feminist, is known for her bold statement that '[m]arriage is a form of prostitution'.[31] Whilst this is likely to be seen as one of the typically outrageous excesses of radical feminism, it's worth noting that this kind of statement is far from being without precedent. In fact, the comparison between marriage and prostitution is virtually a cliché, and goes back at least to the eighteenth century. Mary Wollstonecraft, along with her contemporaries Sarah Fielding and Mary Hays, argued that marriage was no more than a state of 'legal prostitution'.[32] Engels argued that marriage 'turns often enough into the crassest prostitution – sometimes of both partners, but far more commonly of the woman, who only

---

[29] Silvia Federici explains: 'In our view, when women fight for the wage for domestic work, they are also fighting against this work, as domestic work can continue as such so long as and when it is not paid. It is like slavery. The demand for a domestic wage denaturalized female slavery. Thus, the wage is not the ultimate goal, but an instrument, a strategy, to achieve a change in the power relations between women and capital' (Federici & Gago 2015).

[30] Other advocates of wages for housework include Mariarosa Dalla Costa (see Dalla Costa & James 2012) and Silvia Federici (see Federici 1975).

[31] Jeffreys (2008). Jeffreys is now perhaps better known (along with fellow radical feminist Janice Raymond) for her transphobia – see the discussion in Chapter 4 above.

[32] See Spector (2006, p. 51).

differs from the ordinary courtesan in that she does not let out her body on piece-work as a wage-worker, but sells it once and for all into slavery'.[33] And from a very different perspective, Elizabeth Cady Stanton, too, regarded marriage as unpaid prostitution and domestic labour, adding – in a line reminiscent of twentieth-century feminists such as Catharine MacKinnon – that '[w]omen's degradation is man's idea of his sexual rights'.[34] There is a clear connection between this idea and the aspect of the feminist critique of family life which focuses on economic aspects. The flipside of women's economic dependence on men, which is also the situation of their receiving certain economic benefits – albeit in a process which feminists have depicted as one of exploitation – is that they are obliged to provide the 'reproductive' labour that is not even recognised as labour. And this labour, as the quotation from Dalla Costa and James makes clear, includes sexual services.

Under this aspect of the critique, focusing on sex and the body, we also find a long history of feminist argument and action centring on the role of reproduction – now no longer in the Marxist-feminist sense but in the usual sense of the production of offspring – and the control of women's sexuality: feminists have attacked sentimentalised notions of motherhood, and what they have seen as the treatment of women's bodies within the traditional family as machines for the production of babies; and in general, they have been at the forefront of 'pro-choice' activism, arguing that access to abortion as well as contraception is necessary if women are to have control of their own bodies and lives. Some feminists have identified women's reproductive role as the fundamental factor underlying their subordination and oppression – including, notably, the radical feminist Shulamith Firestone, who memorably described childbirth as like 'shitting a pumpkin', and childhood as 'a supervised nightmare'.[35] Firestone argued that women's liberation will only be achieved once human beings have developed technologies which can free women from the 'tyranny' of biology and reproduction:

> The reproduction of the species by one sex for the benefit of both would be replaced by (at least the option of) artificial reproduction: children would be born to both sexes equally, or independently of either, however one chooses to look at it; the dependence of the child on the mother (and vice versa) would

[33] Engels (1844). Also reproduced in Schneir (1996, p. 197).
[34] Quoted in Rossi (1973, p. 392).   [35] Cited in Faludi (2013).

give way to a greatly shortened dependence on a small group of others in general, and any remaining inferiority to adults in physical strength would be compensated for culturally. The division of labour would be ended by the elimination of labour altogether (cybernation). The tyranny of the biological family would be broken.[36]

Whatever we think of the more sci-fi aspects of this vision, it's worth noting, the idea that there is something artificially isolating and impoverished about the way in which many people (mainly women) are expected to raise children is one with undeniable force. Modern Western capitalist societies are typically arranged in such a way that the responsibility of having a child falls almost exclusively on one or two persons – the adults of the nuclear family – on whom it can often weigh very heavily indeed. The burden is not only that of having to do all or most of the work associated with childcare. It also has to do with the deprivation of other kinds of experience and contact: most people cannot take their child with them to work, many social engagements are such that children are excluded (sometimes officially and even by law), and childcare must typically be vetted, organised and paid for by the individual – a situation incompatible with spontaneity if not with the caregiver's financial means. For all the truth in the point that childcare is not *only* a burden but can also be one of life's greatest sources of joy and fulfilment, there is no particular reason to think that this joy or fulfilment is increased by social arrangements that make everything other than childcare practically inaccessible. However much you may love your best friend, having no real alternative but to spend every day and night with that one person is unlikely to do wonders for any relationship – especially if doing so is also difficult to combine with doing anything else or seeing anyone else. But what the modern nuclear family effectively does is to put many women in exactly that position, placing an often unbearable strain on them, their relationships with their children and (if they have them) with their husbands.[37]

This last point about the *isolation* of wives and mothers connects with what may for the want of a better expression be termed the 'existential' aspect of women's oppression in the private sphere. The most well-known treatment of this aspect is almost certainly Betty Friedan's seminal 1963 work, *The Feminine Mystique*. In this work, Friedan exposes what she calls 'the problem

---

[36] Firestone (1971, p. 12).   [37] Cf. Friedan (2013).

that has no name': a widespread malaise, a barely place-able boredom and unhappiness that afflicted suburban, middle-class, usually college-educated American housewives of the 1950s and early 1960s – despite their relative material comfort, and despite the fact that their lives appeared to satisfy the ideal to which women were taught to aspire.[38] It should be noted that Friedan has been criticised for focusing so heavily on affluent middle-class, relatively educated women, and for allegedly treating their situation as though it were representative of the situation of women in general. The grounds for this come out most clearly in Friedan's proposed solution to the 'problem with no name': that women need to reject the life of a housewife and enter into the world of employment outside the home. For working-class women, of course, this is a pretty useless suggestion. Like working-class men, many working-class women have long had little or no choice but to be in paid employment (and it has conspicuously failed to bring them liberation). But to acknowledge this is not to deny that Friedan is identifying something real and important. The point is that her approach will be inadequate, and her proposed remedy insufficient (or at least, insufficient for all but a small subset of privileged women), unless brought into contact with a more critical analysis of the institution of wage labour under capitalism. We might also note that the kind of ennui and sense of meaninglessness that Friedan identifies certainly has its working-class variants. What Friedan has discovered, perhaps, is nothing more or less than the middle-class American housewife's particular brand of alienation.

In addition to problematizing the near-compulsory status of (a certain kind of) motherhood, lesbian feminists have pointed to a phenomenon of 'compulsory heterosexuality' – a term first employed by Adrienne Rich to underscore her claim that heterosexuality is a 'political institution', rather than either a 'preference' or an 'innate orientation'.[39] In her 1980 paper, 'Compulsory heterosexuality and lesbian experience', Rich attacked other feminists for failing to acknowledge this political character of heterosexuality, understood as something *enforced* on women,[40] and condemned 'the virtual or total

---

[38] Ibid.   [39] Rich (1980, p. 633).

[40] As discussed briefly in Chapter 4, the work of Foucault acts as an important exemplar for the project of attacking 'ahistorical' understandings of social identity (see Foucault 1980, 1985, 1986), and he has had a profound influence on gay, lesbian and 'queer' theorising (see e.g. Spargo 1999; Stychin 2005).

neglect of lesbian existence in a wide range of writings, including feminist scholarship':[41]

> I am suggesting that heterosexuality, like motherhood, needs to be recognized and studied as a political institution – even, or especially, by those individuals who feel they are, in their personal experience, the precursors of a new social relation between the sexes.[42]

This sort of critique seems to run parallel to the feminist objections to the sex/gender distinction discussed in Chapter 4: the point is to avoid naturalising the categories of sexual orientation (i.e. treating them as if they were simply *given* in nature, ahistorical and pre-social), and to see them instead as the *political* institutions that they really are – here, Rich and others are able to point to the long history of coercive and violent means of enforcement of heterosexuality, which have co-operated with more subtle pressures to *produce* the heterosexual as the norm (and continue to do so).[43] But whilst humans are compelled to be *either* men or women, the pressure to be heterosexual is universal: the lesbian, like the intersex individual, is deviant or invisible. Thus both critiques might once again be understood as attempts to reveal the deeply political character of the 'personal'.

Feminist reactions in practice to these critiques – i.e. those focusing on the relationship between sex or sexuality and the patriarchal family – have varied widely. One example already considered is the struggle for the inclusion of gay people in the institution of marriage (although it's hard to imagine radical critics like Rich being very satisfied with this). Another which has also come up already is the rejection of marriage,[44] a stance modelled by several prominent figures in the history of feminism: rather than campaigning for gay marriage, on this approach, we should reject the institution of marriage as inherently heteronormative as well as patriarchal. Some radical feminists have gone further, and enacted practices such as separatism and 'political lesbianism', choosing to live apart (as far as possible) from men, or to renounce

---

[41] Rich (1980, p. 632).   [42] Ibid., p. 637.

[43] Furthermore, Rich makes the same suggestion in the case of the categorisation of sexuality that certain critics of the sex/gender model make in the case of sex difference: the replacement of a binary division with a spectrum – in this case, what Rich describes as a 'lesbian continuum'.

[44] Rich frequently refers to the example of the women she calls 'marriage resisters' (Rich 1980).

sexual activity with them (activity which some described as 'collaboration'). A particularly strong statement of this position comes from a group which included the radical feminist Sheila Jeffreys (who featured as a representative of trans exclusionary feminism in Chapter 4):

> Heterosexual women are collaborators with the enemy. All the good work that our heterosexual feminist sisters do for women is undermined by the counter-revolutionary activity they engage in with men. Being a heterosexual feminist is like being in the resistance in Nazi-occupied Europe where in the daytime you blow up a bridge, in the evening you rush to repair it... Every woman who lives with or fucks a man helps to maintain the oppression of her sisters and hinders our struggle.[45]

This kind of position has become fairly familiar as a kind of caricature which has often been used in an attempt to discredit feminism or to warn 'moderate' feminists against getting 'too extreme', and it's worth emphasing that it is only one strand within radical feminism (let alone feminism more broadly). Whilst it's not a position I would try to defend,[46] it is important, I think, to make the effort to understand its internal logic and motivation. Speaking in 1980 about her involvement with the radical women's movement, Ti-Grace Atkinson makes this logic very clear:

> It's a cliché of course now, in most places when you first get together with women, you always thought you were the only woman in the world who always met nothing but jerks... People would say, 'Oh you have a way of always finding the guy who's the jerk in the crowd', right, and you're alone so you never tell anybody about it, because obviously you have terrible taste. And then you meet all these other women who *also* met all the jerks in the world, and you put all those jerks together and you realise that men are a

---

[45] Leeds Revolutionary Feminist Group (1981, p. 7).

[46] One of the less well-aired criticisms of 'compulsory separatism' has been made by black feminists who have suggested that this sort of policy is indicative of racial privilege and of the associated tendency to treat the situation and experiences of white women as universal: 'Although we are feminists and lesbians, we feel solidarity with progressive Black men and do not advocate the fractionalisation that white women who are separatists demand. Our situation as Black people necessitates that we have solidarity around the fact of race, which white women of course do not need to have with white men, unless it is their negative solidarity as racial oppressors. We struggle together with Black men against racism, while we also struggle with Black men about sexism' (Combahee River Collective 1983, p. 267).

problem. So, taking that position, I didn't see how you could say that men are the enemy, and walk around with them. It was really quite simple...

[A]s far as not speaking to a man and not walking down the street with men, the reason that attracted so much attention at the time was not that what I was doing was so peculiar, but what everybody else was doing was so peculiar. That is, they were saying 'Men are the enemy!', and they were associating with them constantly. So it became 'Isn't that strange? She doesn't speak or associate with men, wow!'. But there was really nothing at all strange about that position because that was the rhetorical position taken by radical feminists at the time, it was just that there was a gap between the rhetoric and, um, the actuality.[47]

For radical feminists like Atkinson, then, there was nothing 'extreme' about the policy of separatism. On the contrary, in the climate at the time, for some women it was just common sense (albeit a common sense that was not always easy to implement – as even the authors of the polemical pamphlet quoted earlier were prepared to acknowledge). Atkinson clearly saw the policy of not associating with men as dictated by a value of *consistency* ('I didn't see how you could say that men are the enemy, and walk around with them'). Of course, many would take issue with the premise that men are the enemy, and perhaps rightly so.[48] But again, it's important to be clear about what is and is not meant by that sort of statement. Atkinson herself is careful to emphasise the strategic and contextual status of the attitude she held, as a separatist, towards men:

I feel very strongly that one should live one's beliefs. And *at that time, tactically, I believed that men were the enemy. I did not believe that biologically they were necessarily and incurably the enemy.* I didn't believe, in other words, in some racial superiority theory. But I did believe that women *were not going to be able to overthrow their own oppression without banding together as a group and putting their anger together,* and that their anger would propel them forward into a unity, against men.[49]

---

[47] Ti-Grace Atkinson, speaking in the documentary film *Some American Feminists* (Brossard *et al.* 1980).

[48] Another point on which we might have doubts is the very idea that it is possible to live in a way that is consistent with one's principles – to 'live one's beliefs', as Atkinson puts it. I'll touch on this worry again later in this chapter.

[49] See Brossard *et al.* (1980; emphasis added).

A further thing that has motivated proponents of controversial policies such as separatism is, precisely, the fact that they are controversial: *they piss people off*. It might seem bloody-minded to relish this feature, but there is a simple and serious political point here. It seems obvious enough that those in positions of power and privilege will be reluctant to concede that power and privilege. They will therefore not take kindly to acts of resistance which threaten their superior position. Acts which are relatively ineffectual, on the other hand, might actually be a blessing for the dominant group: they distract and absorb the energy of the subordinated into something 'harmless'; they can sometimes be invoked to support the claim that the dominant group is in fact oppressed or under attack; and if the dominant group is savvy enough to be seen to welcome and encourage – at least up to a point – the subordinated group's activities and campaigns, then a convenient impression of progress, dialogue and even alliance can be maintained, masking a fundamental opposition of interests. This does not mean that *anything* which annoys men is a promising strategy for women's liberation. But it does suggest that if we are not doing anything to disturb or anger or irritate, then we are not doing anything that is really subversive of the structures that we are aiming to subvert. And in that case, it makes a certain amount of sense for feminists, and others involved in movements of resistance against oppression, to hold the question 'Will this piss them off?' firmly in mind, when approaching questions of political practice.

* * *

In this chapter so far, I've discussed some of the main ways in which feminists have opposed – in theory and in practice – the patriarchal structures that they detect within the traditionally 'private' or 'personal' realm of family life. Their critiques range over the legal, economic, sexual and existential aspects of this realm and of what it does to women. The range of practical political responses feminists have offered is, if anything, wider still, encompassing everything from (militant or genteel) campaigning for legal alterations to the law, to 'marriage resistance' or 'free love', to the establishment of communes run according to feminist principles,[50] to separatism and political lesbianism.

---

[50] One example of this response was the establishment, from 1971, of the Wild communes ('Wild' being the invented surname given to all children born within the communes). Several of these communes (permitting men but aiming to instantiate egalitarian principles within the home) were founded across the UK, and persisted until the mid to late eighties (see Williams 2009).

Not all of the analyses and strategies canvassed sit well with one another. There are feminists who argue and campaign for gay marriage and those who reject the institution outright, those who want equality within heterosexual partnerships and those who want nothing to do with men. In other words, there are disagreements to be had when we come to the question of what the politics of the personal *are* and how we should try to change them. But feminists can all agree on one thing: that the personal is, indeed, political.

Maybe that is true. After all, the statement 'the personal is political' has become one of the top clichés of feminism, to the point where it might be hard to find a self-described feminist who would deny it. I don't want to deny it either. But as I indicated at the beginning of this chapter, I don't believe that all feminists have meant the same thing by this slogan. And the disagreement matters.

The feminist statement that 'the personal is political' first appeared in published form as the title of a 1969 article by Carol Hanisch (although Hanisch makes clear that the title was not her own but was most likely chosen by Shulamith Firestone and Anne Koedt, the editors of the volume *Notes From the Second Year*, in which Hanisch's piece appeared in 1970). It is therefore possible that neither Firestone nor Koedt nor any other particular individual invented the slogan, but that this was simply a motto that was already doing the rounds at the time – it's hard to say for sure.

The more important point, though, is to make clear what the slogan has stood for since it became a motto of the second wave, as this meaning is in danger of becoming lost in certain contemporary appropriations. According to a currently influential way of thinking, political philosophy is equivalent to 'the ethics of the state': the task for political philosophers is to work out what the state should do, just as the task of ordinary ethicists is to work out what individuals should do. Since 'the state' is very often treated as equivalent to 'the liberal state', many questions in political philosophy take the following form: 'What are the limits of state interference? What realms may the state legitimately enter, and from which realms must it be kept out?' For instance, many contemporary liberals would defend schemes to redistribute wealth (by state-backed coercion), but would insist that the state has no business telling us what we can and cannot think, wear or say. These things, it is judged, come under the heading of 'personal freedoms', whereas others are public or 'political' matters, and may be objects of legitimate coercive intervention.

For feminists working within this framework, it will seem natural to attribute a particular sort of significance to the idea that the personal is political. Traditionally, liberal theory has regarded the family (among other things) as belonging to the private sphere, with the consequence that it was not understood as having much (if any) political significance: the only thing to be said about the family, from the point of view of politics, was perhaps that the state should more or less leave it alone. Feminists have consistently pointed out that this effectively defines women out of 'politics': historically, and still to a significant extent, women have been disproportionately confined to the 'private' sphere of the home and family, and excluded from major public institutions such as parliament or court or university. In light of this, liberal feminists have wanted to insist that the personal sphere does have significance for political philosophers – which is often taken to be equivalent to the claim that the family is a legitimate object of state concern and action. As some have correctly pointed out, it is not as though the state hasn't already been involved in the family, usually to the disadvantage of women[51] – through the determination of divorce laws and laws of inheritance, and through being the body that rubber-stamps marriage and continues to recognise it through a system of obligations and privileges. So, as one commentator puts it: 'The issue, for feminists, is not whether the state can intervene in the family and reproduction but how, and to what ends.'[52] This doesn't have to mean that the state may attempt to enforce the equitable division of domestic chores (as liberals are quick to stress). But it might mean, for example, that the state may legitimately encourage some family types rather than others, through educational curricula or other sanctioned means; or that it should take a role in providing care for children and the elderly (a task usually performed, unpaid, by women) and in rewarding the work of caregiving.[53] To say that the personal is political, on this reading, is to say that the project of the ethics of state *can* be a project of legislating for the family, after all.

It's important to emphasise that the above really has very little to do with the way in which feminists of the second wave – and many since – have understood the slogan under consideration. There is, admittedly, *some* continuity. On all sides, part of the point has been to say that dominant ways of defining 'the political' constitute an artificial *narrowing*, the function of

---

[51] See e.g. Fineman (1995).   [52] Satz (2013).   [53] See e.g. Kittay (1999).

which has been to exclude women, rendering their oppression invisible and impeding their liberation (something which we might also want to describe as an instance of patriarchal ideology). But the original context of the slogan is not that of a discussion of the abstract question of what principles of justice a state ought to adopt or embody.[54] Rather, it emerges out of a real political struggle: at a certain historical juncture – roughly, the end of the 1960s and beginning of the 1970s – more and more women begin forming their own groups and organisations to try and change social structures, and especially patriarchy, partly as a response to the sexism they face within existing left and anti-war movements; they then have to contend with the problem that their fellow activists – including some 'political' women and feminists – often do not recognise the issues that they are raising, nor the sorts of means they are using to address them, as *political* at all; they are criticised or dismissed as being preoccupied with 'personal problems' and as attempting to treat these problems through 'therapy', as opposed to concentrating on bona fide political resistance or revolutionary action. The assertion of the personal as political is shaped by this kind of context, and is an act of resistance against it. That is to say, it *comes out of* a context of struggle, *is itself* an act of struggle or resistance, and is an insight which has certain *upshots* for the way in which political struggle is to be conducted.

Hanisch makes this context clear from the opening lines of her (strangely neglected) article:

> I have been participating in groups in New York and Gainesville for more than a year. Both of these groups have been called 'therapy' and 'personal' groups by women who consider themselves 'more political'.[55]

It's worth pointing out that this sort of situation – i.e. women working on distinctively feminist issues, and being met with the accusation that this work is trivial and a distraction from proper political goals – is not peculiar to the period of the second wave. Clara Zetkin's record of a meeting with Lenin in 1920, for example, paints a strikingly similar picture. Immediately upon the

---

[54] The insight embodied in the slogan 'The personal is political' could not easily have arisen purely out of such an abstract discussion, in any case. The moments where we notice that our concepts and language are limited or distorted in some way are the moments where we run up against them, where we realise that they are impeding us from doing and saying the things we want or need to do and say.

[55] Hanisch (1970, p. 76).

meeting's beginning, Lenin begins to lecture Zetkin on what he sees as the insufficiently single-minded dedication of certain women communists to the revolutionary cause:

> I have heard strange things about that from Russian and German comrades... I understand that in Hamburg a gifted Communist woman is bringing out a newspaper for prostitutes, and is trying to organize them for the revolutionary struggle... To understand this is one thing, but it is quite another thing – how shall I put it? To organize the prostitutes as a special revolutionary guild contingent and publish a trade union paper for them. Are there really no industrial working women left in Germany who need organizing, who need a newspaper, who should be enlisted in your struggle?[56]

A little later on, Lenin remarks:

> The record of your sins, Clara, is even worse. I have been told that at the evenings arranged for reading and discussion with working women, sex and marriage problems come first. They are said to be the main objects of interest in your political instruction and educational work. I could not believe my ears when I heard that. The first state of proletarian dictatorship is battling with the counter-revolutionaries of the whole world. The situation in Germany itself calls for the greatest unity of all proletarian revolutionary forces, so that they can repel the counter-revolution which is pushing on. But active Communist women are busy discussing sex problems and the forms of marriage...[57]

I quote Zetkin (quoting Lenin) at length here, partly to re-emphasise a point I've had occasion to make before: that we should be wary of falling into the trap of thinking of ideas, themes and interventions in feminism – in particular, the ones we like – as being much newer than they actually are (a habit which allows us more easily to uphold a highly misleading view of the history of feminism as a tale of gradual, cumulative progress towards greater enlightenment). But the other reason for mentioning it is to make the point that in *neither* of these contexts – the context of second-wave feminism in the US and the context of revolutionary communist struggle in early twentieth-century Europe – does it make sense to think of the issue at stake as being that of whether, how and to what extent 'the state' should intervene in family life (or in other areas traditionally regarded as 'personal'). Lenin's position is

[56] Schneir (1996, pp. 336–7).   [57] Ibid., p. 337.

not that the state – either the Russian or the German one – should stay out of family life. He is making a point about the way in which communist revolution should be struggled for and defended: he sees 'women's issues', such as problems with sex and marriage, as having no proper place within that struggle. Nor were radical feminists of the 1960s and 1970s typically arguing over the proper limits of state involvement in the regulation of the family.[58] For one thing, 'the personal' covers more than just the family. More importantly, feminists have not always been very keen on the state, regarding it primarily as an instrument of patriarchal domination – so why would they be interested in issuing policy recommendations for such an institution? And finally, it would be a mistake to assume that all of these activists were mainly in the business of designing a hypothetical or future society, with or without the state as its centrepiece. Feminists have always wanted to change the world for the better, certainly. But to assume that the attempt to do this could only take the form of a planning exercise is to fail to see beyond the particular view of political philosophy and its purpose that has become dominant in recent years (at least in the Anglophone world).[59]

When you look at Hanisch's original piece, in fact, it ceases to be surprising that many contemporary feminists prefer to adopt the titular slogan and drop the rest, for the content fits very badly into the framework of liberal theory. There is not a single mention of the state in Hanisch's article. Nor does she lay out a vision of a 'just' society. Rather than contributing to an ethics of state, she is engaged in something more like an 'ethics of activism'. And a criticism she wants to press against certain of her fellow activists is that they are defining 'the political' in a way that is unduly restrictive:

> I think we who work full-time in the movement tend to become very narrow. What is happening now is that when non-movement women disagree with us, we assume it's because they are 'apolitical', not because there might be something wrong with our thinking... What I am trying to say is that there are things in the consciousness of 'apolitical' women (I find them very political) that are as valid as any political consciousness we think we have.[60]

---

[58] And to the extent that they *were* interested in this question, those who politicised 'personal' issues like abortion, reproduction and love were most likely to be heard arguing that the state should back off from dictating people's (especially women's) personal choices, rather than involving itself more heavily – one memorable second-wave banner read 'The state has no business in the wombs of the nation.'

[59] I'll discuss this point at greater length in Chapter 10.

[60] Hanisch (1970, pp. 77–8).

Part of the point Hanisch is making here is that by operating with too narrow an understanding of politics, we make not only a mistake, but a *political* mistake. The mistake is political in the obvious sense of being detrimental to the health of the movement ('Women have left the movement in droves').[61] But it is also clear that Hanisch believes that the activists in question are *wrong* in their judgement of certain things as non- or apolitical. If so, their error is 'political' in a further sense: part of the point that is made by saying that the personal is political – although it is not a point which Hanisch herself makes very explicit – is that the way in which we define 'the political' *is itself a political matter* (which means that we can expect dominant ways of characterising it to reflect and perpetuate dominant political structures).

What Hanisch is pointing out is that this is a problem which occurs in left and feminist movements too. This might seem surprising, since the history of feminism suggests very strongly that feminists have been very much aware of the political character of the private and the personal. Many nineteenth-century critiques took aim at marriage and the traditional family. And the idea that men's dominance over women has its roots or, at least, a central manifestation in the realm of sexual relations is hardly new, as I've been at pains to emphasise. In Chapter 5, I discussed the example of the Elizabethan pamphleteer Jane Anger, who railed against the hypocrisy of gendered expectations surrounding sex. And I began the current chapter with a passage from the ninth century which seems to do the same: 'You have been fucking us since the beginning of all time, and when we've fucked you one single time you are killing us!'

What feminist, then, would deny that these sorts of thing – sex, marriage, the family – are political? It is hard to believe that Hanisch's contemporaries would have done so. What this should tell us, I think, is that the slogan 'The personal is political' must be saying something more than that sex, marriage (etc.) are political issues. Everybody knows that. What was and remains more controversial is the question of what counts as political *action*. In particular: what does and does not count as an act of resistance, or a contribution to a political movement against oppression? Hanisch and other radical feminists of the second wave wanted to argue that certain ways of talking and organising – such as the practice of consciousness-raising, and the model of the small group – far from being 'apolitical' or decadent, were legitimate and even indispensable modes of resistance. Pam Allen, a member of the group

---

[61] Ibid., p. 77.

'Sudsofloppen', sketches what she sees as a false dichotomy between personal and political:

> Some said that liberation would come through changing ourselves; thus we should talk about our private lives and our feelings towards ourselves and each other. Others felt that liberation would come by first changing our society; thus we should talk about building a political women's movement. The women who felt that our first and most important task was to change ourselves by growing in self awareness and developing more honest personal relationships, felt that politics were irrelevant if not detrimental to human liberation. They based this on their past experiences in New Left politics (and, of course, from viewing Establishment politics) where they saw people being inhuman to one another in the name of progress and humanity. These women saw this as being in absolute contradiction to the movement's professed goal of learning to be loving and responsive people. For these women politics became equated with inhumanity. But others (and I was one of these) believed that no real changes could be made in our lives unless these changes were societal. We felt that our strength would be in our numbers and that a few women trying to change their personal lives would be too vulnerable. We wanted to build an effective political movement that could both confront the injustices of our society and also protect the right of individual women to change their life styles.[62]

The last sentence of this passage raises a puzzle. I've suggested that we interpret 'The personal is political' as a point about modes of resistance above all. If apparently 'personal' actions and discussions can be forms of political resistance, then it seems to follow that it *matters*, politically, what sorts of personal decisions we make. Not only can talking about experiences of sex and marriage within a small group be a form of political action, but the same might be said of having sex with men (or refusing to) – or any number of individual actions. Certainly, it seemed as though proponents of separatism viewed this above all as an act of resistance – not a response to the innate evil of men, and not necessarily a policy to be adopted in all places and for all time, but a stage in the struggle against the system of male dominance. And they have not been shy to demand that other women follow their example. But the sense encouraged by Allen's phrase, 'protect the right of individual women to change their life styles', is that it is up to individual women to live

---

[62] Allen (1970, p. 13).

their personal lives as they see fit. Likewise, Hanisch explicitly rejects any kind of feminism aimed at dictating the 'politically correct' lifestyle for feminists to adopt:

> When our group first started, going by majority opinion, we would have been out in the streets demonstrating against marriage, against having babies, for free love, against women who wore makeup, against housewives, for equality without recognition of biological differences, and god knows what else. Now we see all these things as what we call 'personal solutionary'.[63]

So what is going on here? The most obvious reasons for rejecting a 'personal solutionary' approach seem to be out of bounds for Hanisch, given the importance she wants to place on the personal. One such reason would be that personal solutions are a distraction from the project of changing society. But as both Hanisch and Allen would argue, to say this is to forget that the personal *is* political: it is a legitimate site of the struggle to change society, and also a sphere of society in need of change. So is the point only that it is strategically unwise to preach to people about whether they should get married (etc.) if you want to keep them on side? I argued that there was more to it than that.

Sure enough, Hanisch suggests a reason why policing lifestyles is a (more than strategic) mistake:

> The groups that I have been in have also not gotten into 'alternative life-styles' or what it means to be a 'liberated' woman. We came early to the conclusion that all alternatives are bad under present conditions. Whether we live with or without a man, communally or in couples or alone, are married or unmarried, live with other women, go for free love, celibacy or lesbianism, or any combination, there are only good and bad things about each bad situation. There is no 'more liberated' way; there are only bad alternatives.[64]

The point here is reminiscent of a statement made by Adorno: that 'wrong life cannot be lived rightly'.[65] Because there is something badly wrong with the world, it is a mistake to think that any individual life can be lived well or 'correctly' while the world more generally stays as it is. It is not just that oppressive social structures will negatively impact the quality of people's

---

[63] Hanisch (1970, p. 77).   [64] Ibid., p. 77.
[65] 'Es gibt kein richtiges Leben im falschen'. Translation from Adorno (1974, p. 39, §18).

lives, whatever personal choices they make in an effort to escape this impact. We are talking here about social movements, where the aim is not to be happy but to bring about social transformation. So if it were true that one particular lifestyle – say, lesbianism – were the key to bringing about that transformation, then someone like Hanisch would surely have reason to promote that lifestyle over others. But, she is saying, it just doesn't work like that. There is no 'correct' or even 'best' lifestyle for a feminist to live ('there are only bad alternatives').

It's not immediately clear how to read these kinds of statements. Is Hanisch saying that every lifestyle is as good as every other? Or, perhaps, that there is a permissible range rather than a single solution? Putting aside the question of what Hanisch herself is saying, what *should* a feminist say on this issue? I don't think I have a satisfactory answer to this question, but it may be helpful to formulate a central dilemma. On the one hand, Hanisch seems to get something importantly right, by rejecting a feminism that consists of a series of imperatives as to how to organise your personal life (especially as none of the options is obviously very satisfactory). A 'personal solutionary' feminism seems overly didactic, divisive and individualistic, shortening women's vision and focusing their attention on evaluating their own and each other's particular ways of existing within a social reality which itself needs to change. By describing her own position as 'the Pro-Woman Line', and criticising the 'anti-woman' interventions of certain other feminists around her, Hanisch is making the point that the imperative of feminism is to foster relations of solidarity among women: 'One more thing: I think we must listen to what so-called apolitical women have to say – not so we can do a better job of organizing them but because together we are a mass movement.'[66]

Moreover, ideas of the 'correct' way to live one's personal life are liable to be reflective of racial and class (and other forms of) privilege. The kinds of clothing that are thought to be most 'objectifying' just happen to be those worn by predominantly working-class women and girls (hence the disparaging of certain styles as 'trashy' while others, thought to express a better and more dignified relationship to one's sexuality, are tellingly described as 'classy'). Yet both the young woman on a Saturday night out in Wetherspoons and the elegantly dressed female academic may often plausibly be seen as responding to the demands of their different social environments in quite a similar way:

[66] Hanisch (1970).

they are fashioning themselves to appear as their environment (an environment numerically or otherwise dominated by men) requires them to appear in order to access certain desired ends, whether sex, sexual attention, or social recognition and positive validation in a more general sense.

On the other hand, it seemed important to insist on the political dimension of the personal. In so doing, second-wave feminists were reacting partly against what they saw as the narrowness of conceptions of politics in some left-wing movements. But the point might now be made with equal urgency against a prevalent brand of feminism which portrays all choices as 'equally valid'. As Michaele Ferguson argues, through its desperation not exclude or upset anyone, or even to make judgements about them, this 'choice feminism' ends up devoid of any political content – and hence incapable of fulfilling the central feminist objective of challenging the status quo.[67]

Many issues that conventionally belong to the private or personal sphere – the family, norms of beauty and sexuality, etc. – have been issues of concern for feminists, and this is presumably because they judge that there is something *wrong or bad* going on in this sphere, something which needs to be recognised as a political problem so that the right kind of action can be taken. If beauty norms are oppressive, then what is the point of insisting that they are so, if this implies no suggestion at all that women (and perhaps men too) should orientate themselves differently with respect to beauty norms (e.g. for individual women to stop wearing make-up, or to stop expecting and rewarding the wearing of make-up by other women)?

Here is another point at which the notions of ideology and ideology-critique turn out to be useful, I think. When feminists say that the personal is political, they are saying that phenomena categorised as 'personal' are also political, particularly in the sense of being sites of women's oppression: women are not oppressed just through being paid less, or by being excluded from certain public institutions; they are oppressed also in the home, and in their own bodies. This is to say something about the kind of beast that patriarchy is (i.e. that it operates through the 'personal' as well the 'public' sphere), and about the significance of such things as sexual and romantic behaviour, habits of dress and personal grooming (i.e. that they are *not* simply 'personal'). That is enough to make us see the world very differently, even though it may not prescribe any *particular* course of action.

[67] Ferguson (2010).

This is a general feature of the way in which the critique of ideology works. Although ideology, as I've defined it, is a kind of *false* consciousness (a 'functionally explained' kind), it's important to notice that ideology-critique need not necessarily proceed by showing, or even claiming, that a given piece of consciousness is false. One obvious reason for this is that it is not always feasible or even possible to prove that a given claim is false (take the claim that God made man high and lowly) – and another reason is that, as we saw in Chapter 3, ideological false consciousness doesn't always take the form of a false belief or an inaccurate perception of a situation (the example I used there was that of 'Stockholm Syndrome'). What ideology-critique does is to take a way of thinking, seeing or feeling that is present and perhaps prevalent, and say the following: OK, one hypothesis is that this way of thinking(/seeing/feeling) occurs because it is true(/accurate/appropriate); but there is also a rival interpretation in the case at hand, namely that it is believed / seen that way / felt to be so *not* because this is in fact correct or appropriate, but because it is very *convenient* for some person or group that this way of seeing things should prevail. Note that, strictly speaking, this structure leaves it an open question whether the bit of consciousness in question is true or realistic or appropriate *in itself*. The claim is that there is something wrong with the process by which it is formed and maintained. It is true, for example, that the earth orbits the sun, but if it is only believed to be the case because this stands symbolically in the society in question for the people's subordination to the great Emperor, then this relation of answerability to the Emperor's interest in having this cosmological picture accepted might form the material for an ideology-critique of the view – even though the view happens to be true.[68] But in the standard case of ideology-critique, the point is to set up a rival, debunking hypothesis: by showing that a way of thinking, seeing or feeling may be responsive to something to which we think it should not be responsive – namely, a certain set of interests – we undermine the grounds for subscribing to that way of thinking, seeing

---

[68] I borrow this example from Rosen (1996, p. 34). We might describe certain cases as cases of ideology-critique, I think, even if the belief in question is *known to be* true (although this would not be the most usual case): the point here would be that the thing would be believed *even if it were false*. This still, arguably, represents a kind of distortion – an error about the *status* of the belief as 'truth-tracking' (cf. the critique of status mistakes that illegitimately ascribe certain true generalisations to 'nature') – even whilst the distortion is not detectable in the belief's *content*.

or feeling (without showing it positively to be false or inappropriate). Our confidence in the thing criticised is thus diminished, and we come to look at it in quite a different way.

Similarly, when it is pointed out to us that some phenomenon which we had previously viewed as merely personal, and thus politically insignificant, is actually an important part of the process through which the dominance of men and the subordination of women is maintained, it is to some extent an open question what should come next. If make-up is part of the picture of patriarchy, *one* possible lesson to infer from this is that feminists should avoid make-up. But what has actually been presented in the critique is not this particular lesson, but rather a story about the *origin, role and function* of the wearing of make-up (not its moral, aesthetic or political worth). If we are persuaded that something has a patriarchal origin and function, that it plays an instrumental, supportive or affirmative role within the system of patriarchy, there is a range of possible responses to this realisation. One response, certainly, is to ditch that thing: stop wearing make-up, or high heels (for example). Another kind of response is not to boycott the practice in question, exactly, but to do it *in a different way*: to experiment with different styles of personal decoration, perhaps subverting dominant expectations as to what women should look like (as in the styles associated with punk and goth subcultures, for example); or even to go on doing what is to all outward appearances the same thing, but adopting a different attitude towards it – there is a big difference, for instance, between (a) wearing make-up because you think your face is unacceptable without it, (b) wearing make-up, but feeling guilty about it because you wonder if it makes you a bad feminist and (c) wearing make-up because that is still what you are inclined to do, preferring your face that way, but recognising this preference as a product of a patriarchal system of beauty norms which has no particular aesthetic validity (in the sense that we would almost certainly not find this so attractive or necessary if it weren't for the kind of patriarchal social form we inhabit), and recognising also that it is *not your fault* (and that, furthermore, there is probably nothing so terribly wrong with your face).

Alongside any one of these options, we might respond to a critique of some-thing like beauty norms by looking for the 'root'. Judging that the problem is not going to be removed by a reform of practices of personal decoration – or not *only* by this – we might turn to the question of what underlies such practices, and their tendency to restrict and confine women and to decrease their power relative to men: only by changing something more fundamental, we may say, can we adequately respond to the problem identified – and this more fundamental change might be taken to involve anything from a change in the law (for example, you might think that only compulsory provision of better paternity leave will bring about changes in gendered norms about childcare), to a gradual process of re-education, to more radical policies such as separatism.

What counts as a good response must depend, at least in part, on a judgement as to what is likely to be a *possible and possibly effective contribution* to the struggle against patriarchy. In some cases, the more obvious responses such as boycotting a given practice will not really be open to us. It may or may not be possible – psychologically, socially and professionally – for a woman to give up make-up and other trappings of femininity (it helps if she is conventionally good-looking, or not employed in an occupation where she is expected to offer a 'presentable' face to clients). It may well *not* be possible for a woman to 'train' herself not to prefer extreme thinness, or for her to be completely at ease with looking roughly the age that she is. And it will not always be possible or desirable for a woman to withdraw from providing care to her children.

If a given response *is* judged to be possible, a question still remains as to what effect or force (if any) this response could have as an intervention. There can be no context-free answer to that kind of question. Showing leg hair might be usefully provocative in certain situations – if, for example, it is virtually unheard of for a woman to do this, there might be a value in showing that the sky does not come crashing down when she does (once leg hair has become a feminist cliché, the situation is perhaps different, and the choice might be evaluated slightly differently).

In short, the slogan 'The personal is political' opens the space for a certain kind of *critique* and multiple forms of *resistance*: there are many possible ways in which a feminist might respond when moved by a critique which touches on the personal, and what counts as a good or useful or 'less bad' response will depend on various features of the context. This open-endedness does not mean that the critique has no force, no practical relevance. It simply means that it does not offer us a single, unambiguous instruction. No critique does that, come to think of it. After saying or showing that something is bad, there is always a further step to any particular conclusion about what we (or anybody) should *do* about it.

If the structure of this kind of feminist critique is similar to the structure of ideology-critique, as I've claimed, then this is perhaps because it basically *is* an ideology-critique. In arguing that women are oppressed in the home and body, the claim is made that certain assumptions about women's proper role, certain preferences on the part of both women and men, as well as commonly held standards of beauty and worth for woman are ideological distortions, operating so as to advantage men by securing their dominance and women's submission; further, the erasure of the 'personal' forms of both oppression and resistance *as political* might also be seen as an instance of patriarchal ideology, having much the same origin and function as the patriarchal perceptions which contribute to women's private oppression in the first place.

Whatever the particular response to feminist critiques of personal life under patriarchy, the *general* force of such critiques is to make us see both the personal and patriarchy differently: the personal can never again be 'merely' personal; and 'patriarchy' is revealed as something bigger, and closer to us, than we might have realised. Rather than being an abstract concept or external structure – one which many women might think does not apply to or affect them (because *they* are e.g. breadwinners, or academic high flyers) – 'patriarchy' suddenly becomes something familiar and very real. The purpose of this may not be to provide advice on state policy. But if we begin to see certain phenomena belonging to personal life as political, then it is possible to see them as consequences of a broader social structure (rather than as consequences of 'nature', or personal choice, or personal failing). We can't triangulate from this to the 'correct' way to live an individual life. But what it does allow us to do is to arrive at a better – more realistic and potentially empowering – view of the difficulties we face as women (i.e. by seeing them as products or aspects of patriarchy), and a better understanding of what it would take to overcome them. The fact that there may be no 'correct' set of personal choices to structure the daily life of a feminist does not mean that the personal cannot be a site of rebellion, resistance and even revolution.

9 The porn wars

At the time of writing, pornography is all over the media. Of course, it is always all over the media, in the sense that our TV programmes, advertisements and newspapers are typically saturated with images of naked and semi-naked women, offered up for our enjoyment, judgement or ridicule. But every so often, alongside these images (sometimes literally alongside them), there are also flurries of identikit journalistic articles about whether porn – in particular, internet porn – is harmless fun or the sign of civilisation's end, degrading to women or a means of liberation. There are self-described 'feminists' on both sides (and never any shortage of undisguised misogyny).[1]

Pornography (and its regulation) is also a controversial topic amongst political philosophers. It divides not only political philosophers, but *feminist* political philosophers; and, increasingly, it divides not only feminist political philosophers, but *liberal feminist* political philosophers.

This debate very quickly gets messy, and one of the main aims of this chapter is to gain a clear overview of the main issues that divide those engaged in it. I'm not so much interested in pushing for one position or other within this standard debate. I'm more concerned to issue some correctives to the course which this debate usually runs and to the assumptions on which it rests. In particular, I want to bring out a couple of points which tend to be lost, insufficiently appreciated, or never raised at all. The first sounds obvious: that porn is an issue belonging to real politics, not an abstract academic

---

[1] One of the notable things about the age of Twitter, Facebook and online 'comment' facilities on news websites is the inevitability with which women who say anything even remotely feminist in a public forum are met with threats of sexual violence – an inevitability which would be tedious if it wasn't so frightening. As I was first drafting this chapter, an ongoing news story was the row over rape threats issued through the medium of Twitter to a number of women including Caroline Criado-Perez, who had successfully campaigned for the face of Jane Austen to appear on the £10 banknote.

problem.[2] And perhaps it *is* obvious, but philosophers in particular are not known for their ability to grasp obvious things, and the signs suggest that many of them have not grasped this one yet. The second, related point is that the issue of porn is not just about censorship. In fact, as we'll see, the issue of porn is not even just about porn.

When it comes to the issue of pornography, feminists argue amongst themselves and with their opponents over three main questions: what is porn? What (if anything) is wrong with it? What (if anything) should be done about it?

I'll take these questions in turn.

9.1 What is porn?

Most of us have a fairly good idea of what we mean by 'porn', but it is equally clear that 'porn' means very different things to different people. To begin with, we might divide the definitional approaches in the philosophical literature on porn into two main camps: 'pejorative' and 'non-pejorative'.

The most famous example of the pejorative strategy comes from Catharine MacKinnon and Andrea Dworkin, who in 1983 defined pornography as 'the graphic sexually explicit subordination of women, whether in pictures or in words'.[3] Here, what is held to be problematic about porn, from a feminist point of view, is built into the definition.[4] By contrast, the non-pejorative strategy – much the more common approach among liberals and liberal feminists – seeks to define pornography in a supposedly more neutral way: most usually as (something along the lines of) 'sexually explicit material with the primary intent to arouse'.[5]

Among those who employ the pejorative strategy, there is a further division to be made, according to whether or not a contrast is drawn between 'pornography' and 'erotica'. Some theorists reserve the term 'erotica' for that portion of sexually explicit or arousing material which is *not* degrading to women. As Gloria Steinem puts it: 'Erotica is as different from pornography

---

[2] MacKinnon continually emphasises this point (MacKinnon 1994, 2012).

[3] This was the definition adopted by the Minneapolis Ordinance of the same year, which was vetoed by the mayor, readopted, and vetoed again the following year.

[4] Russell (1993) uses a pejorative definition which, unlike most, does not require that the material in question be sexually explicit.

[5] See e.g. Williams (1981).

as love is from rape, as dignity is from humiliation, as partnership is from slavery, as pleasure is from pain.'[6] One attraction of this stance is that it sends a clear message that the anti-porn feminist is not the prude or 'anti-sex' fanatic that she is so often accused of being.[7]

On the other hand, some radical feminists have taken a very different approach. For example, in the preface to her book *Pornography: men possessing women* Andrea Dworkin puts the case against the 'pornography'/'erotica' contrast with exceptional clarity and force:

> This book is not about the difference between pornography and erotica. Feminists have made honorable efforts to define the difference, in general asserting that erotica involves mutuality and reciprocity, whereas pornography involves dominance and violence. But in the male sexual lexicon, which is the vocabulary of power, erotica is simply high-class pornography: better produced, better conceived, better executed, better packaged, designed for a better class of consumer. As with the call girl and the streetwalker, one is turned out better but both are produced by the same system of sexual values and both perform the same sexual service. Intellectuals, especially, call what they themselves produce or like 'erotica', which means simply that a very bright person made or likes whatever it is. The pornography industry, larger than the record and film industries combined, sells pornography, 'the graphic depiction of whores'. In the male system, erotica is a subcategory of pornography.[8]

This might seem to generate a dilemma. On the one hand, Dworkin is obviously onto something here: a hypocritical and elitist tendency to buy oneself out of trouble, e.g. by writing class markers into the definitions of problematic practices. But if that is so, do feminists have no choice but to give in and agree to wear the 'anti-sex' label?

Not necessarily – which is fortunate, since many would consider this a heavy cost. Whatever one thinks about Andrea Dworkin's views, she is clearly no prude (as anyone who has read her uninhibited and sexually explicit prose

[6] Steinem (1984, p. 219).

[7] Such accusations come from other feminists as well as from outside the movement: see e.g. Strossen (1996).

[8] Dworkin (1989, p. 11). Or as Ellen Willis (1981, pp. 222–3) puts it: 'In practice, attempts to sort out good erotica from bad porn inevitably come down to "What turns me on is erotic; what turns you on is pornographic."'

can attest). And contrary to a very common misconception,[9] neither she nor MacKinnon regard sex as something *inevitably* violent, degrading or sinister. For them and other radical feminists, a large part of the point of wanting to overthrow patriarchy is to regain for women the control over their own sexuality, not to suppress, stigmatise or deny it – that is what *patriarchy* does (under the guise of a celebration of women's sexuality). Discussing a quotation which envisages a transformation of sexual relations whereby woman becomes like a moving 'stream' rather than like a 'placid lake', Dworkin affirms: 'A stream herself, she would move over the earth, sensual and equal; especially, she will go her own way.'[10]

There need be no inconsistency here. In the first place, Dworkin's resistance to the tendency to fence off what is high-class (or accords with one's own personal tastes), and to call that politically kosher, is technically quite compatible with agreeing that there are some forms of sexuality, and forms of sexually explicit material, which *are* both unobjectionable and valuable: it remains true that we are in danger of being merely snobbish or self-deluding when deciding what does and does not fall into that category. That is one point. It might be interpreted not as a rejection of the 'pornography'/'erotica' distinction *tout court*, but as a call for caution and wariness with respect to its application. But it is also true that there is a more radical and controversial aspect to the attitude of figures like Dworkin and MacKinnon towards sexuality. It is not just that we tend to commit ideologically motivated inaccuracies when judging what is and is not 'pornographic' in a pejorative sense. There is also an important sense, for radical feminists, in which pornography *is* everywhere and nothing is innocent: patriarchy has 'pornographised' our sexuality thoroughly – even though there may of course be sexual acts and representations which are better or worse than others – so that pornography now pervades the sexualised social life of patriarchal societies. On this view, it seems as though a completely non-pejorative category of 'erotica' will be empty. But, crucially, this is not because sex per se is regarded as a bad thing. The view is one about sex, sexual expression and sexual representation *in a certain kind of patriarchal society.*

[9] This has much to do with the oft-cited sentence 'All heterosexual sex is rape', which appears to be a misquotation of Dworkin, and in any case presents her views out of context.

[10] Dworkin (1987, p. 162).

So, which of these definitional strategies is best? The advantage of the pejorative strategy was supposed to be the defence it provides against the charge of being 'anti-sex', a defence facilitated by its greater precision: its ability to single out a *subset* of sexually explicit and intentionally arousing material, holding only this subset to be politically problematic. But it now seems that some radical feminist proponents of the pejorative strategy, at least, cannot so easily lay claim to this advantage: in general, the world cannot be neatly or usefully divided up into 'good' and 'evil'; and titillating material cannot be sorted and either issued with black marks or stamped with seals of feminist approval.[11] As we saw, this doesn't mean that the 'anti-sex' charge sticks. But it does seem to mean that the apparent advantage of the pejorative strategy – an advantage of precision and appeasement – evaporates.

In that case, it might be tempting to judge the non-pejorative definitional strategy as the more appealing. This strategy is often considered to enjoy an advantage of 'neutrality': it defers judgement on the question of what feminists should think of porn, which is often considered to be the main question at issue. By *defining* porn as something which 'subordinates' women, some feel, radical feminists such Dworkin and MacKinnon presuppose the conclusion they are supposed to be arguing for.

This sort of worry about 'question-begging'[12] is one which has great currency among analytic philosophers in particular: to find that one has 'begged the question' is the equivalent to finding that the car's big end has gone (terminally bad news). In this case, however, the accusation is far too quick. Manifestly, radical feminists do not write only in tautologies. They do offer arguments and often empirical support – both anecdotal and statistical – for their positions. That argument and evidence may be criticised, but it is hardly fair to deny its existence.

---

[11] Note that this is not necessarily to rule the genre of 'feminist porn' out of court. The point is that it's not useful to approach the issue of porn by trying to sort what is 'ok', from a feminist point of view, from what is not: everything will be both. But it's possible in principle to subvert any genre, to try to use it for feminist purposes. Whether a given attempt is successful must be judged on a case-by-case basis.

[12] It's worth acknowledging that people outside analytic philosophy departments don't use this phrase with the same technical meaning which analytic philosophers attach to it – in ordinary parlance, 'begs the question' is often used interchangeably with 'raises the question' (or 'makes one wonder...').

In terms of logical structure, it's not clear why it matters at all whether we proceed (a) by defining pornography non-pejoratively, and then arguing that it – or at least, a lot of it – subordinates women, or (b) by starting from a pejorative definition, and then going on to show that it *exists* (and on a large scale). From a political, strategic, or rhetorical point of view, however, it might matter quite a lot. For example, there might be a rhetorical advantage in defining porn in descriptive rather than explicitly pejorative terms: it might be less off-putting for those who as yet see no problem with (at least some) porn. It might also be a more useful definition for scientific purposes: if we want to find out something about the effects of exposure to pornography, it is useful to have a working definition which is relatively uncontroversial; and it is probably a lot easier for people to agree on what counts as sexually explicit and intended to be titillating than for them to agree on what counts as degrading to women.

It's also important to note, however, that there is really no such thing as a *purely* descriptive or neutral definition or strategy. By working from a definition of porn as 'sexually explicit material with the primary purpose of arousal', one makes a statement to the effect that it is appropriate to keep a particular question – the question of whether there is anything wrong or damaging about porn – *open*. Now, arguably this is perfectly reasonable, at least in some contexts – in the laboratory context already mentioned, for instance. But the point here is that this judgement of appropriateness is a partly *evaluative* and *political* judgement. All it takes to see this is to look at some of the questions which we don't normally – or ever – think it permissible to keep open: e.g. the question of whether black people are as intelligent as white people.[13] Likewise, there are some cases where a 'neutral' definition seems out of place. Suppose we are interested in studying and analysing sexual harassment. It is difficult to see how we can define 'sexual harassment' in a way which does not build in the idea that this term refers in particular to sexual advance or attention *which is inappropriate* – and it's not clear that this 'normative loading' is a problem, but rather an indispensable aspect of

---

[13] It would be naïve to claim that *no one* thinks that this question should remain open. A significant number still do (including members of the scientific establishment – examples are discussed by Anthony Kwame Appiah in his article, 'Race, culture, identity: misunderstood connections'; see Appiah & Gutmann (1998)). My claim is just that more or less everybody within the liberal mainstream (and to the left) agrees that this position is unacceptable.

a concept which has enabled us better to recognise and articulate a problem which previously had no name.[14]

When we keep a question open, or define something in such a way as to say nothing about its moral status or desirability, we make a judgement about what is *appropriate* in the context in question. And this judgement cannot be a 'purely descriptive', 'neutral' or politically uncontroversial one. In refusing to treat the question of the relative intelligence of blacks and whites as open, we are making a statement about the *obviousness* of the falsehood of claims of black inferiority, or about the political dangerousness of taking such claims sufficiently seriously as to debate them, or both. In the case of sexual harassment, the thought goes: 'here is something bad that is continually happening to women; let's give it a name'. From the point of view of having seen that the phenomenon is real and that it has an especially deleterious effect on women, it doesn't really make sense to ask whether sexual harassment is bad or harmful, any more than it makes sense to ask that question about child abuse or cancer.[15] We have seen that it is real and harmful, named the harm, and now are interested in analysing how it happens, why it happens and how we might best fight it. In adopting a pejorative definition such as that employed by Dworkin and MacKinnon, radical feminists *pass a verdict* on porn, understood as a real phenomenon under patriarchy and as a major industry under capitalism: the verdict that pornography wreaks violence and damage on women that is both *extreme* and *obvious*.[16]

We may draw two main points from what has been said so far. First, there is no simple and stable answer to the question of what definition of 'pornography' is appropriate, since the sort of definition that is appropriate

---

[14] See MacKinnon (1979), one of the first to use and offer a definition of the term 'sexual harassment' (see also MAKERS (2013) for a short clip of MacKinnon speaking about her dealings with this issue).

[15] Medical categories, like 'health' and 'disease', are a very interesting case, since they belong to purportedly descriptive science, but also often seem to carry evaluative content – see Cooper (2002).

[16] That verdict could, at least in theory, be passed in a different way, as the conclusion of an investigation undertaken on the basis of a non-pejorative definition of pornography. Similarly, a scientific investigation could easily result in a decisive rejection of the claim that blacks are less intelligent than whites. But we might still think that – at least in some contexts – one makes a different and perhaps stronger statement by refusing to contemplate such research than by conducting it and getting the results one would desire and predict.

will depend on what we are trying to do with it – e.g. conduct a laboratory study, or highlight an industry and its practices. Second, the way in which it is appropriate to define porn ultimately depends on our politics – *including* the matter of what kind of feminists we are (if we are feminists at all), and including the significance we attach to the phenomenon of pornography. If that is right, then the idea of proceeding from a 'neutral' definition of porn has got things backwards. There may on occasion be advantages to the use of a more descriptively couched definition – and it may be that such definitions reflect the right view of porn in general. But that is just the point: they reflect a particular view of porn. We cannot decide how to conceive of pornography in a way that is completely independent of what we think of pornography as a phenomenon – including the question of what, if anything, is wrong with it. That is the next question to ask.

9.2 What's the problem?

Feminists have criticised porn on various grounds, but all have wanted to distance themselves from a traditionally conservative allergy to 'lewdness' and to the violation of the dictates of conventional morality and taste.[17] After all, feminists are interested not in preserving current attitudes and practices but in transforming them – and as we have seen, an important part of the motivation for this is the recognition of the importance and positive value of sexuality.

Feminist critiques focus instead on what pornography does to (and says about) women. Almost all feminists have held that at least a substantial amount of porn projects degrading views of women:[18] in some sense, porn 'says' that women are inferior, mere objects for men's sexual pleasure, deserving of subjection and abuse. Many have also wanted to draw a link between

---

[17] Some feminists – though not by any means all – have argued that we should reject the idea of a *moral* criticism of porn altogether. See MacKinnon's 'Not a moral issue' (MacKinnon (1987)).

[18] At the same time, some have emphasised the positive aspects or potential of pornography for feminist purposes. McElroy (1995, p. vii) claims: 'Pornography is good for women, both personally and politically.' Similarly, Palac's (1995) stance on pornography reflects her own experience of pornography as sexually empowering, despite having previously opposed it on feminist grounds.

what porn says about women and what happens to them as a result – i.e. what porn *does* to women.

This link appears as a more or less intimate one, depending on the underlying approach. Liberal feminists tend to present their critique as a worry that the message about women conveyed by pornography may have harmful effects further down the line, in terms of the way in which men who have consumed pornography go on to treat women – in particular, the charge is that pornography causally contributes to the incidence of rape and other sexual violence. Radical feminists, too, emphasise the link between pornography and sexual violence and abuse, but have urged that we should view porn not primarily as something 'said' about women – which may or may not be causally related to later doings – but as *itself* an act of violence and discrimination committed both against women as a group and, in particular, against the women involved in the making of pornography: as MacKinnon puts it, pornography is not 'only words';[19] rather, it is 'a form of sex discrimination with some visual and verbal moving parts'.[20]

So, pornography is criticised by feminists on the grounds that it harms women in general, and those directly involved in the porn industry in particular. I don't attempt a comprehensive survey of the evidence here, but I'll indicate some of the main concerns that have been raised in each case.

9.2.1 Harm to workers

Contrary to an image sometimes promoted in the media – where relatively privileged, educated young women find confidence, high pay and sexual liberation in this stigmatised line of work – women who work in the pornography and sex industries are especially likely to be both vulnerable and to have suffered trauma. They are in general far more likely to be in economically precarious situations, and to be (or have been) in violent and abusive relationships with men. Many are subject to (sexualised) racial oppression.[21] They are also much more likely to have been victims of rape and other violence. Perhaps most strikingly, studies suggest that between 60 and 80 per cent of women

---

[19] See especially MacKinnon (1994).   [20] MacKinnon (2012, p. xi).

[21] Forna (1992) describes the prostitution and porn trades in South-East Asian women, as well as the use of Latin American women and children in untraceable 'snuff' films (i.e. films which depict actual murder).

involved in the porn industry are survivors of childhood sexual abuse.[22] There are, of course, many exceptions to all of these generalisations, just as there are plenty of real-life Billy Elliot stories, and tales of next-door neighbours who smoked sixty a day well into their nineties. That is why the lazy parading of exceptions to the rule is one of the lowest forms of social commentary and not the 'myth-busting' service it often presents itself as being.

It is not just the backgrounds of women in the porn industry that are relevant here, but also the industry's typical practices and working conditions. In her 2010 book, *Pornland*, Gail Dines describes the physical damage to women's bodies and health that is becoming increasingly common as a result of a combination of low standards of safety and hygiene – the condom is a notoriously rare sight in porn – and a demand for ever more 'extreme' and adventurous practices.[23]

Not only do the situations and personal histories of many women in porn cast doubt upon the degree to which their choice of work can be regarded as truly voluntary, in many cases the production of pornography involves coercion, rape and other violence.[24] The most high-profile example of this is perhaps the case of Linda Marchiano (aka 'Linda Lovelace'), the star of the movie *Deep Throat*, which in 1972 became one of the first porn films to be a box office hit.[25] Marchiano later published a memoir, *Ordeal*, in which she recounts being repeatedly raped and forced to perform at gunpoint. 'When you watch *Deep Throat*,' she writes, 'you are watching me being raped.'[26] As is generally the case with acts that are illegal, it is extremely difficult to know with any precision how much of this sort of thing goes on. In the view of some radical feminists, most notably Andrea Dworkin and Catharine MacKinnon, the case of *Deep Throat* is a particularly stark illustration of a phenomenon which is the rule rather than the exception in pornography.[27] Many are unconvinced. Whatever the exact truth, it seems highly likely that the reality of pornography is worse than most people think. Of course, criminals in general have a strong motive to conceal their crimes.[28] Often, they make

---

[22] See Corcoran (1987).   [23] Dines (2010).
[24] See MacKinnon (1987, 1989, 1994); A. Dworkin (1989); Itzin (1992); Russell (1993).
[25] See Gloria Steinem's essay 'The real Linda Lovelace', in Steinem (1984).
[26] Lovelace (1980).   [27] Dworkin (1989); MacKinnon (1994).
[28] I am not suggesting, by the way, that the problem with these acts is that they are criminal. Feminists need not necessarily have anything against crime. The point is

sure that this is true of their victims as well.[29] At least, victims often lack strong motives to *disclose* what is done to them, given the low conviction rates for domestic and sexual violence. We know that rape is underreported in general (around one in ten instances are reported to the police), and the factors which might explain this – (justified) mistrust of the police, feelings of shame or worthlessness, fear of retribution, etc. – are present in an exacerbated form in the case of women in the porn and sex industries. We also know that porn is a multibillion-dollar industry in which – as in the fashion business – mostly white men make fortunes out of women's bodies. To recall once again the notion of ideology, there is every reason to expect perceptions of an institution underwritten by such powerful interests to be distorted in the service of those interests.

What happens to the women who are employed in the making of porn is either denied or else justified as 'free choice'. But there are some harms of pornography which cannot be excused on the grounds that they are chosen by those who suffer from them. To the extent that pornography harms not only workers in the porn industry but women *in general*, appeals to freedom are unavailable – or at least have to take a different form: the form of appeals to the 'free speech' of the pornographer. Women as a class do *not* choose the ways in which they are affected by pornography. I'll now outline some of those ways.

9.2.2 Harm to all women

As I noted above, a common thread in feminist critiques of porn is the identification of a link between pornography and rape or other sexual violence. Partly because of a liberal reluctance to criticise what are seen as the free choices of women, liberal feminists have tended to focus their attention on the question of how pornography affects women in general – in particular, the question of whether pornography increases the incidence of rape. Let us start with that question.

---

just that those who break the law will usually make some effort to conceal it, for obvious reasons.

[29] The use of threats or blackmail in the porn and prostitution industries often involves the exploitation of women's debts, children, immigration status, drug addiction or other points of vulnerability.

What is uncontested is that a large proportion of rape and sexual abuse *involves* porn: abusers often use or imitate pornography while they abuse, showing it to victims and pressuring them to enact what is depicted. Just as sexual abuse occurs in the making of pornography, pornography is used in the making of sexual abuse. Coupled with the tendency for porn workers to be survivors of abuse, this suggests a cyclical reinforcing or facilitating relationship between abuse and porn.[30] Corinne Sweet compares the porn with the tobacco industry, suggesting that the functioning of porn as part of a cycle of sexual abuse owes in part to its addictive quality: pornography provides temporary satisfaction, she argues, but reinforces emotional vulnerabilities in the long term, allowing it to serve as an effective agent of social control.[31]

This, of course, does not prove that porn causes rape – not that this is the sort of thing that is amenable to strict proof, anyway. It conclusively shows only that porn *figures in* rape and sexual abuse, and shapes some of the abuse that happens. But feminists have also argued that such abuse *happens more* because of porn – both within the industry and in society at large.[32] Now, as is noted ad nauseum, a correlation is not sufficient to demonstrate a relationship of cause and effect – nor is it necessary, for that matter.[33] On the whole, feminists haven't argued on the basis of correlations anyway.[34] Besides

---

[30] See Corcoran (1987).

[31] As Sweet (1992, p. 183) argues, 'The use of addictions by the majority is, in fact, central to the maintenance of the "status quo" in capitalist society as it provides the basis for industries creating much-needed employment; it maintains industries which create excess profit; it pacifies and moulds willing and adaptable employees; it develops people as consumers (i.e. creating more and more "goals" for conspicuous consumption); it continually refines new goods to meet consumer "needs"; and, in each case, perpetuates conformity and compliance within the class structure.'

[32] See e.g. Russell's (1992) 'causal model' of pornography and rape.

[33] It is less often pointed out that it isn't *necessary*. But this is quite important for the sorts of causal claims made in the social sciences and political theory. The question of whether the availability of porn is positively correlated with the incidence of sexual violence is not straightforward, and must in any case depend on inevitably controversial definitional decisions (as discussed earlier in this chapter). But since it's impossible to eliminate extraneous variables – e.g. there might be more porn available in Scandinavian countries, and less sexual violence, than in the UK, but there are also all sorts of political, social and legal differences between those societies – this is quite compatible with the claim that porn is a cause of rape.

[34] This may be because there isn't a clear correlation (although as I suggested in note 33 above, this need not undermine the causal claim). According to James

pointing to the use and imitation of porn in acts of rape, and to the testimony of the victims of those acts,[35] one way in which they have argued is by referring to the testimony of rapists themselves.[36] Rapists and murderers often cite their use of pornography – sometimes what they describe as an 'addiction' to it[37] – as an influence and even a cause of their actions.[38] Further indicators come from the laboratory studies which have been proliferating in the last thirty years. These studies expose people to various kinds of pornographic material, and then question or observe them, comparing their revealed attitudes and behaviour with those expressed beforehand, or with those of a control group. Unlike the identification of correlations, and the analysis of the testimony of victims and perpetrators of rape, this approach has the potential to yield direct evidence of a specifically *causal* relationship between porn and (attitudes to) sexual violence.

What many studies suggest is that certain kinds of pornographic material[39] make their consumers – at least in the short term – more likely to accept 'rape myths', such as the belief that women enjoy rape or are responsible for the rapes that happen to them. For example, studies have found increased agreement with statements like, 'A woman doesn't mean "no" until she slaps you' expressed by participants[40] after viewing pornography,[41] less sympathetic attitudes to rape victims and greater leniency toward rapists in 'mock' rape trials,[42] greater likelihood among men of self-reporting willingness to rape if they could get away with it,[43] and decreased recognition of rape as

---

Weaver, though, the pattern of results indicates a strong correlation between exposure to sexually explicit material and occurrence of sexual offences (Weaver 1992, p. 303).

[35] For testimony from victims of sexual assault, see Dworkin & MacKinnon's *In Harm's Way* (1998).

[36] For testimony from rapists, see Beneke (1982).

[37] One recent example is the case of Ariel Castro, who kidnapped, imprisoned and abused three women between 2002 and 2013.

[38] MacKinnon (1987, pp. 184–6; 1994, p. 13).

[39] For material that is sexually explicit but non-violent, results are more mixed. Experimenters suggest that it depends on whether the material is 'degrading' (e.g. bestiality) or not (e.g. mild erotica, nudes), and there is some evidence of beneficial or neutral effects from 'mild erotica' (see Einsiedel 1992, p. 282).

[40] Whilst most studies focus on men, Weaver (1992) finds that pornography encourages attitudes of what he terms 'sex callousness' in both men and women.

[41] Donnerstein *et al.* (1987, pp. 75–6); cf. Einsiedel (1992).

[42] Einsiedel (1992, p. 254), Zillman (1989).   [43] Weaver (1992, p. 298).

rape.[44] Some studies have even reported higher levels of aggression *in experimental settings* after exposure to pornography, especially towards female confederates.[45]

These findings are well confirmed, including by more recent studies – the bulk of the evidence to which anti-pornography feminists have referred was conducted in the 1980s and 1990s, but it is amply reinforced by later research. A comprehensive review of the empirical literature summarised the state of knowledge in 2000 as follows: 'experimental research shows that exposure to nonviolent or violent pornography results in increases in both attitudes supporting sexual aggression and in actual sexual aggression.'[46] And the same conclusion is supported by the results of non-experimental studies.[47] Of course, there are some findings which seem to contradict this consensus,[48] and any individual study may be attacked as flawed, accused of skewing or misrepresenting its results – as is always the case in the social sciences and in psychology. But the overall picture is difficult to refute (which is not to deny that many commentators try to do so, usually by moving from one or two recalcitrant findings to the verdict that the evidence on porn and sexual violence is 'inconclusive').[49]

So, feminists have drawn on correlations, testimony, experimental and non-experimental data on the relationship between pornography and sexual violence in order to support their critiques. But perhaps most of all, they have examined and analysed pornographic material itself, made it their subject matter, in much the same way as a literary critic might examine a piece of writing. If you read the works of Andrea Dworkin and Catharine MacKinnon, the pages are not filled with statistics and experimental data, but with descriptions and interpretations of what happens to women in pornography – what really happens to them, what is depicted as happening, and the relationship, the tensions and continuities between the two.[50] What it makes sense

[44] Everywoman (1988, p. 21).   [45] Zillman (1989); Einsiedel (1992); cf. Allen (1995).

[46] Malamuth *et al.* (2000); cf. Kingston *et al.* (2009), Vega & Malamuth (2007).

[47] Hald *et al.* (2010).

[48] See e.g. Segal (1990, p. 33), who reports that male sex offenders have had on average *less* exposure to pornography than other men.

[49] It's striking that the claim that the evidence is inconclusive is presented as though it were not itself a controversial empirical claim. As MacKinnon puts it: 'There is no evidence that pornography does no harm' (1994, p. 26).

[50] Andrea Dworkin's *Woman Hating* is a particularly clear example of this, as she seamlessly interprets pornographic material, documents real abuse and analyses traditional fairy tales (Dworkin 1974).

to expect pornography to *do* depends on what we think pornography is *like*. Going out and testing the hypothesis that porn harms women is not the only legitimate way to proceed – and findings will always fall short of proof. We can also approach the issue from the other end: look at porn, interpret its message and form from this a fairly good sense of what sort of role this sort of material is liable to play in the lives of men and of women. This is not to say, of course, that we are warranted in expecting everything that is depicted in porn to be straightforwardly and reliably replicated in the subsequent behaviour of its consumers. That would be clearly naïve. But it is surely equally naïve to think that what we see and read will have no effect on who we are and how we behave, remaining hermetically sealed off in the 'fantasy' compartments of our lives. Everything we consume has an effect, and it doesn't seem overly audacious to expect that the sort of material MacKinnon describes – images of women brutalised, beaten and humiliated for the pleasure of men, and also depicted as enjoying this injury and humiliation – will have an effect which in some way reflects the character of that material.

Approaching the question of porn's role and effects through an examination of the material also allows feminist critics of porn to press claims about some more subtle forms of harm, which may not be amenable to being made the subject of laboratory study. An important component of the critique made by many feminists is that porn not only contributes to rape and sexual violence – the incidence of which is to at least some degree measurable – but that it also inflicts less tangible harms on women as a group, their social respect and civic equality, through changing men's attitudes and behaviour towards women, as well as through changing *women's* attitudes towards each other and to themselves. The reduction of women to sex objects in pornography, it is argued, has a detrimental effect on women in every sphere of their lives: a porn-saturated society is not just a society in which a woman is at a higher risk of being raped, it is also a society in which she is less likely to be employed in certain roles, to be listened to when she speaks,[51] and generally to be understood as a full human being with interests, views and projects as well as a body.[52]

At this point, of course, we are well outside the territory where neat proofs or empirical demonstrations are possible. But what is really important to

[51] MacKinnon (1994); cf. Langton (1993).
[52] See e.g. MacKinnon (1987, 1994); Dworkin (1989); Itzin (1992); Russell (1993).

emphasise is that this alone cannot be taken as grounds to throw out the sort of feminist claim just outlined. It is simply neither possible nor desirable to eliminate from our analysis of the social world all claims which do not admit of logical proof or experimental verification. We make and argue all the time over statements like, 'The Government's anti-immigration rhetoric is playing into the hands of racists', or 'Young children are becoming increasingly sexualised' or 'The inhabitants of advanced capitalist societies suffer from an extreme form of alienation.' Not everyone will agree with any of these statements, and they are statements which are complex, ambiguous, partially value-laden, and which only make sense against a rich and vast background of further claims and assumptions. But they are not thereby inadmissible – and in fact, all three seem to me to be plausible and important. When we want to convince one another (or ourselves) of truths like this, we have to play a long game. We are not moving in an area in which there is a straightforward means of assessing the key claims, one by one, accepting or finding them wanting. Instead, it is a matter of keeping our eyes open, and through continual more-or-less-drastic adjustments and overhauls, trying to arrive at the outlook that makes best overall sense of the world as we experience it.

That is why theorists like MacKinnon and Dworkin proceed by relentlessly confronting us with their observations and stories and interpretations and analyses. It is an effort to bring about a kind of *Gestalt* shift in the way we see the world – and to offer us an outlook that might allow us to make better sense of what we see. The effort may or may not ultimately be successful, but efforts of that form are, it seems to me, not only legitimate but indispensable in thinking about politics. What is illegitimate is to dismiss them for failing to be the kind of narrow and manageable critiques that they never for a moment claimed (or never should have claimed) to be.

One of the most striking things about this debate, in fact, is the way in which the *response* to the feminist critique of porn – from fellow feminists as well as from opponents of feminism – exhibits a whole series of the sorts of double-standards and ideological twists and turns to which feminists should be well attuned. Under the guise of 'rigour' and 'caution', a barrage of doubts and objections is raised about each and every suggestion to the effect that porn causes harm. It is of course quite proper to counsel against jumping to conclusions too hastily and without adequate evidence. But it can also be instructive to ask: would an objection or doubt of this sort seem ridiculous, even desperate, in another area? Take something like the 'self-fulfilling prophecy': the idea that people, and especially children, respond to the expectations placed on them by tending to fulfil those expectations – so that children who are told that they are capable and who are expected to do well tend to be much more successful (at least in a narrow sense) than children who are told that they are untalented and bound to fail. It would be quite possible to meet this familiar observation – which is also supported by a substantial body of social-scientific research – by saying things like: 'Well, *some* children might respond to low expectations by being highly motivated to confound them. And I knew someone once who had such pushy parents who put so much pressure on her to succeed that she couldn't take the pressure and ended up flunking out of school . . . And anyway, even if there is a correlation between low expectations and poor performance and low well-being, how can we know that this is a relationship of cause and effect? It might be that some children are told that they are no good because they *are* no good (and *that's* why they perform badly) . . . '

We might be justified in having some concerns or suspicions about someone who talked like this – even though they might not be saying anything strictly false. We couldn't absolutely rule out their being right, but we could and should ask ourselves: what would you have to believe about the world – or *want* to believe – in order to uphold such scepticism in this case? What might such a person be trying to prove?

In the last couple of years, several millions of pounds were spent in the UK on two scientific studies: one which established that the taste of beer makes you want to drink more beer; and another, conducted by researchers at Oxford University, which found that ducks like water.[53] With some justification, the media reaction to these studies was one of mild ridicule: we kind of knew these things already. It is interesting to hold these cases in mind as a contrast, when considering a comment by MacKinnon on the issue of empirical research into the effects of porn:

> You know, it is fairly frustrating that it takes studies by men in laboratories to predict that viewing pornography makes men be sexually more violent and makes them believe we are sexual things, before women are believed when we say that this does happen.[54]

She might have added: . . . and even then they are not believed.

[53] Morris (2009).   [54] MacKinnon (1987, p. 202).

9.3 What is to be done?

I've outlined what, for feminists, are the main problems with pornography. There is no shortage of evidence for the harm it does to women: porn is a feminist issue. There is a large gap, however, between an acknowledgement of this and the endorsement of any particular view as to the appropriate remedy or reaction. It's usually assumed that feminists – or at least, the 'extreme' or 'radical' ones – are hell-bent on censoring pornography (and also, perhaps, a lot of the more mildly titillating or suggestive stuff which we would *not* normally class as 'porn').

In fact, one of the striking things about the feminist literature on pornography is how few writers actually recommend censorship in the usual sense of that term.[55] Somewhat surprisingly, given the traditional stance of liberals on 'freedom of expression', the thinkers most likely to countenance censorship (and to call it by that name) are *liberal* feminists – but few of these are prepared to defend it decisively.[56] Radical feminists, it is important to

[55] It's also worth noting that contemporary high-profile feminist campaigns outside academia are mostly not calling for censorship either. 'Object' and the 'No more page 3' campaign headed by Lucy-Anne Holmes, as well as the campaigns against lads' mags, frame themselves in terms of an opposition to the objectification of women, particularly in widely available and visible soft-core porn such as *FHM* or *Nuts*, but they do not call for such material to be banned. Rather, they ask for certain institutions – Tesco, the magazine producers, the owners of the *Sun* – to agree to change their practices (mostly so as to avoid sexually explicit material being inflicted on children and on those who do not wish to see it). In short, we are dealing here with largely mild-mannered lobbying and 'public education' drives with quite limited and modest objectives. To note this is not to imply that these campaigns are or should be uncontroversial: they certainly *are* controversial, and have also been the subject of critiques which should at least give feminists pause for thought (for example, some women – including some who work as glamour models – have argued that this kind of action is hypocritical, stigmatising, distracting and ineffectual). As the blogger Zoe 'stavvers' Stavri pointed out, when the 'No more page 3' campaign achieved its stated goal, *The Sun* replaced the offending nipples with something much worse: 'candid' photos of celebrities taken without their consent (see Stravri 2015). My only point here is that these campaigns are not campaigns for censorship, but merely a kind of 'ethical consumerism'.

[56] For instance, Rae Langton and other liberal proponents of the 'silencing argument' against pornography claim only that there *might* be respectable liberal reasons for restricting pornography (i.e. to protect women's freedom of speech), but stop short of actually recommending it (see Langton 1993). I discuss the silencing argument in Finlayson (2014a).

remember, are distinguishable by a conception of themselves as *revolutionaries*: they are feminists who want to destroy patriarchy at its root, and who believe that this requires a fundamental transformation of existing societies. They are not primarily interested in the question of what the liberal state should and should not censor. At best, the censorship of some pornographic material might be one of a whole range of possible weapons in the struggle against patriarchy – although many radical feminists would be highly suspicious of placing *more* power over thought and ideas in the hands of a male-dominated patriarchal state. The most famous anti-pornography feminists of all, Dworkin and MacKinnon, have repeatedly emphasised that their proposed measure – the adopted and subsequently abandoned Minneapolis Ordinance – is a piece of *civil* (not criminal) legislation: its aim is to empower women who have been harmed and abused in ways that have centrally involved pornography to sue those responsible for its production and distribution. Plenty of objections can and have been raised against this proposal – some of them better than others (as we'll shortly see) – and it has in fact been repeatedly struck down on grounds of violation of the First Amendment. But the point here, which seems to be lost on many commentators, is that neither Dworkin nor MacKinnon has *ever* advocated censorship in the traditional sense of state prohibition of the production of certain kinds of material, precisely because they want to put more power into the hands of women – particularly those who have been abused – as opposed to already-powerful states which are distinctly lacking in feminist (or, indeed, humanitarian) credentials.

As a rule, feminists aren't nearly as interested in censorship as the popular image of them suggests. Partly this is due to a recognition of its dangers, and of the ample historical evidence that it is no friend of radical politics. Partly it is because even if safeguards could protect against well-recognised dangers of abuse and unintended consequences, censorship just isn't a very radical measure. It is so un-radical, in fact, that it is what we already have. Violent pornography, pornography featuring children and pornography involving the rape or coercion of adults – the sort of porn on which many radical feminist critics focus most – is already illegal in the UK (which of course does not stop people from consuming it).

So what *have* feminists proposed should be done about porn? Their sugges-tions have ranged from 'feminist porn', to education programmes, through the lobbying or boycotts of publications and other businesses, to civil remedies such as the Dworkin–MacKinnon Ordinance. As with the empirical evidence

that porn harms, what is perhaps the most striking thing here is not the proposals themselves – each of which may well be subject to compelling worries –
but how *uncompelling*, and often contradictory, many of the most common
actual responses to the anti-porn position appear to be.

Take the mainstream commentary on the Dworkin–MacKinnon Ordinance.
The latter is usually objected to on grounds of 'freedom of speech': although it
may not be censorship in the narrow sense, the consequences of the attempt
to implement the Ordinance are widely held to illustrate the dangers of mess-
ing with the free expression of ideas. Much of this focuses on alleged events in
Canada – not the same country in which the (failed) attempt was made to introduce the Ordinance. Nevertheless, it is argued that feminist critiques of porn
such as that developed by Dworkin and MacKinnon influenced the interpretation of 'obscenity' adopted by the Canadian Supreme Court in 1992, which
refers to 'the harm [the material] inflicts, particularly harm to women'.[57] So
far, so tenuous. It is then reported – although I have never seen a source
for this claim – that the Canadian law has been misapplied, and that even
MacKinnon's and Dworkin's own works have been seized at the Canadian border (whether more than once is not specified).[58] From this, it is quickly concluded that anti-porn measures such as the proposed Ordinance – which, as a
piece of civil legislation aimed at allowing women to sue for damages, presumably would *not* sanction the seizing of materials at borders anyway[59] – tend
to hit the wrong targets: since it is not radical feminists who enforce the laws
they have inspired, those laws will tend to be used not against the harmful

[57] See Scales (2000, p. 324).
[58] See e.g. Strossen (1996, p. 159). In a 1994 press release, Dworkin and MacKinnon
explicitly deny the charge that their work has contributed to repressive or discrimi-
natory legal practices. In particular, they point out that Canadian customs' practice
of seizing 'obscene' material is long-standing, and has not in any way been modified
as a result of the *Butler* decision (on which Andrea Dworkin was consulted), in which
the 'court held that the obscenity law was unconstitutional if used to restrict materials on a moral basis, but constitutional if used to promote sex equality' (Dworkin
& MacKinnnon 1994). They also make clear that the law which Canada has adopted
is not the one they advocate, and not one which they can fully endorse: 'Although
we recognize that the equality test adopted by *Butler* is an improvement on Canada's
criminal obscenity law, we still do not advocate criminal obscenity approaches to
pornography. They empower the state rather than the victims, with the result that
little is done against the pornography industry.'
[59] Saul (2003, p. 93, fn. 14) seems to forget this when she suggests that Dworkin and
MacKinnon might be happy with the seizure of *sadomasochistic* lesbian porn.

materials that feminists had in mind, but instead against stigmatised groups such as homosexuals,[60] trans people, and feminists.

Much, much more would need to be said in order to show that this sort of worry is as decisive as it has often been taken to be. It certainly cannot be claimed that misapplication of this sort is a danger specific to *feminist*-inspired legal measures against pornography. Under traditional anti-obscenity laws, too, there were absurd misapplications – such as the seizure of the geological study *Rape of Our Coasts* by customs officials in 1957.[61] To some extent, incidents like this are inevitable even for laws which we think are as sensible as any, and we would do well to guard against ideologically motivated exaggerations (and even fabrications) here. As Saul points out, many of the horror stories used to discredit the recognition of 'sexual harassment' as a criminal offence turn out, on investigation, to be highly misleading – and yet she is quite uncritical of what may well be parallel argumentative manoeuvres in the case of anti-pornography legislation.[62] Some discussion of the case of university lecturer Donald Silva, for example, gives the impression that he was suspended for a few off-colour jokes,[63] and for conducting a spelling test which included 'sexual' sentences – exactly the sort of context in which otherwise unacceptable sentences might be rendered perfectly innocent. Cue cries of 'Political correctness gone mad!' As Saul points out, however, the fuller details of the case paint a different picture: Silva had repeatedly made female students uncomfortable by standing too close to them, asking for their home addresses and phone numbers, and backing one woman up against a table. In the particular incident of the spelling test, what had happened was that a female student was waiting to see Silva while he administered the test to a male student; Silva looked the female student fixedly in the eye as he delivered the sentence, 'It may or may not be appropriate for a

---

[60] Califia (1994, pp. 108–9) recounts that the *The Joy of Gay Sex* has been targeted by anti-porn laws proposed and defended on feminist grounds.

[61] The work, dealing with soil erosion, was seized under the Obscene Publications Act of one hundred years before (1857). See Hyde (1964).

[62] Saul (2003, pp. 92–5). Referencing Califia (1994, p. 124), Saul further suggests that MacKinnon's definition of 'pornography' must be flawed, because terms such as 'postures of display' are open to interpretation. Whilst this is certainly true, the same may be said for descriptions like 'unreasonable sexual advance' in sexual harassment law – and yet Saul does not call for the overturning of the criminalisation of sexual harassment.

[63] See Bernstein (2001).

student to earn her "A" by sleeping with her professor.'[64] In reality, courts have consistently required that behaviour be pervasive and severe before they are willing to convict anyone of sexual harassment[65] – and the cases in which they have been too *reluctant* to convict easily overshadow the cases in which they were allegedly over-zealous.[66] It is hardly surprising to find a reliably misogynistic media giving the opposite impression. Just as the reactionary right are always complaining of a 'liberal bias' or 'left-wing takeover', whether in the Government or in the BBC, anti-feminists can be relied upon to present us with an entirely fictional world in which men are in constant danger of being imprisoned for rape if a lying sexual partner turns against them, in which (white) boys in particular are being failed by schools, and in which women generally exert a sexual, social and economic tyranny over men.

Admittedly, the comparison is imperfect. In the case of sexual harassment law, the reactionary claim is that 'feminazis' are responsible for generating paranoia in the workplace, persecuting the innocent and generally ruining everyone's fun. In the case of measures against porn (including some inspired by feminist ideas, or at least given a feminist pretext), the claim being considered is not that the authorities will be too feminist but that they will not be feminist *enough* – and, moreover, will be generally bigoted and homophobic – in their implementation of laws. That is a much more plausible claim – although it too has the potential to function as a convenient piece of patriarchal ideology. But even if we accept that there is a more real and systemic problem of this kind with attempts to counter porn through legislation, it's not clear that this should be taken as a condemnation of such attempts, rather than as a condemnation of the (patriarchal) *world*. The acquittal in 2013 of George Zimmerman, the killer of unarmed African American teenager Trayvon Martin, brought to the fore the problems of racism endemic in the United States (as did the thirty-five-year sentence handed to a black woman in the same state of Florida, for firing one warning shot into

---

[64] Clark (2001, p. 198).   [65] See Zalesne (1999a, 1999b).

[66] In one 1990 case, a technician held a knife to a colleague's throat, forced her into a filing cabinet, threatened to bang her head on the floor, and grabbed her breasts and crotch. The court ruled that she could not have found this unacceptable, on the grounds that she had been heard using 'abusive and vulgar' language on the phone to her boyfriend (*Weinsheimer* v. *Rockwell International Corp.*, discussed in Schultz (1998, p. 1731); see also Saul (2003, pp. 60–1)).

the air in an attempt to deter an attack from her violent partner, although this case was virtually ignored by the media). These cases illustrate something deeply wrong with US society, and many would also take them to illustrate flaws in its legal system, but we don't normally take them to show that laws against violence are dangerous and unworkable, even though they often enough function (in the US and UK alike) to criminalise young black men, without adequately protecting *them* from violence.

The same point applies to another common objection to legal measures designed to counter the harms of porn and prostitution, raised by feminists such as Gayle Rubin: that they criminalise, stigmatise and thereby cause further harm to the people whom these measures are supposed to help.[67] In many cases, perhaps, an objection of this form should prevail – *how many* cases depends, I suppose, on what view we take of the potential of the state and the law to be used as tools to counter oppression. But we also have to guard against a kind of double-think whereby any recognition of a problem is condemned on the grounds that it 'problematises'. Saul, for example, treats Rubin's point as a compelling objection to anti-pornography legislation in general, having seemingly forgotten (again) that the Dworkin–MacKinnon Ordinance is a piece of civil legislation: it's not at all obvious why enabling women to sue for damages, when damaged, harms porn workers and others thus empowered by 'stigmatising' them.[68]

In general, what emerges from many discussions of porn, legislation and empirical evidence is a series of double standards. Why are claims about the dangers of legislation taken so seriously, whilst far better-grounded claims about the effects of porn are brushed off? Why are Dworkin and MacKinnon held responsible for seizures of materials by Canadian border guards, whereas we are told (usually on the basis of some anecdote about 'Helter Skelter' or *The Brothers Karamazov*) that *porn* cannot be held responsible even for acts of sexual violence in which that porn is explicitly aped or referenced or used?

None of this, of course, yet vindicates any practical response, legislative or otherwise, to the problems posed by pornography. I'm not going to try to argue for any particular answer to the question of what should be done about porn, but instead I will make two points about the status of that question. The first is obvious, though at the same time often overlooked: to ask what we

---

[67] See e.g. Rubin (1993, p. 33).   [68] Saul (2003, pp. 97–8).

should do about pornography is to ask the much bigger question of what kind of feminists we should be. From a radical feminist point of view, for instance, the fundamental answer to the question of what we need to do in order to get rid of the problems associated with porn is not any of the measures just mentioned, but is basically the same as what we should do about most things: *smash the patriarchy!* This in turn, of course, raises a whole series of fraught and controversial questions as to how best to do that. We cannot treat the issue of porn as an isolated module, such that we can debate what to do about it without also debating our wider political commitments. To pretend the contrary, very often, is merely equivalent to an assumption that our wider political commitments are all the same: that we are all interested in the question of what the liberal state may justly censor, in the light of its feminist and other commitments.[69]

The second point is perhaps equally obvious (and equally overlooked). To the extent that we do say something more specific in answer to the question, 'What is to be done about pornography?' – more specific and targeted an answer than, 'End patriarchy!' – we confront a real-political issue, not an abstract issue of justice. Political philosophy in the twentieth century, largely under the influence of John Rawls, has turned its back on concrete political realities and distanced itself from history. The full absurdity of this approach comes out most clearly when attempts are made to apply it to issues like pornography, which is not an abstract value or principle but above all a real industry and historically evolving institution – in one particularly spectacular example, the liberal feminist Susan Moller Okin argues for the restriction of pornography on the grounds that the hypothetical parties in the 'Original Position' would surely agree to this, from their perches behind the 'veil of ignorance'.[70]

Porn is not an abstract issue, and nor can it adequately be addressed within the framework of what I have called 'static theory': e.g. by asking how porn would be regulated in the 'correct' or 'ideal' state or, even, how the current

---

[69] As MacKinnon (2012, p. xvii) observes: 'Why all these topics must be considered within the confines of liberalism is not broached even sideways, leaving liberalism assumed rather than interrogated.'

[70] Okin (1989, pp. 104–5). According to Okin, parties behind the veil would be 'highly motivated . . . to find a means of regulating pornography, that did not seriously compromise freedom of speech' (p. 105).

Government should act with regard to it.[71] In an *ideal* society, there wouldn't be a problem of pornography, since nothing like porn as we know it would exist – sexual expression might well abound, perhaps more than ever, but it would no longer be tied up with the systematic subordination and brutalisation of women.[72] Under the current 'non-ideal' conditions, on the other hand – the term 'non-ideal' is pretty horrific when you think about it – it's not at all clear why we would think that there is any point in feminists arguing about what the Government 'should' do: on virtually any issue one cares to mention, we can be confident that it *won't* do what it should; so if we are going to think beyond the limits of what that sort of regime is likely to offer us, then we will have to think in terms of acting *on our own behalves*, of forcing the Government's hand and ultimately getting rid of it, or of effecting change without it.

So, what action (if any), should feminists take (or demand) against the harm of porn? *Because* this is a question of real politics, and not of abstract political theory, what counts as an appropriate answer must be sensitive to the time, place and context, and to the sorts of social change we are aiming at: in other words, it is a question of dynamic, not static theory. There is a world of difference between the 'pornographic' material traditionally defended by liberals and leftists alike when it fell foul of 'obscenity' law in the first half of the twentieth century,[73] on the one hand, and the multi-billion dollar industry that confronted feminists by the 1980s, on the other. And there is arguably another world of difference in the practical possibilities available to opponents of pornography before and after the rise of the internet. A political issue like pornography, then, is fluid at the same time as it is concrete. It makes more sense – in the context of this book, at least[74] – to emphasise this

---

[71] There is something seriously perverse, for example, in expecting British feminists to busy themselves in arguing for or against David Cameron's proposed 'default-on' internet filters, when we are talking here about a prime minister who not only has no shred of genuine concern for the sexual objectification of women, but has also overseen a range of 'austerity' measures which have disproportionately punished women (and poor and working-class women in particular).

[72] MacKinnon (1994) expresses this view, indicating once again the distance between her approach and (a) 'anti-sex' purism or traditional conservative prudery, and (b) the liberal 'ideal-theoretic' project of designing 'just institutions' (for MacKinnon, the problems associated with porn would not arise in a remotely 'just' society).

[73] The case of *Lady Chatterley's Lover* is one of the most notable examples.

[74] The context of a political meeting might be another matter.

concreteness and fluidity than to press for a particular strategy on porn. I will, however, finish off this section by identifying a strand in some practical and theoretical responses to porn, which, I suggest, is to be avoided.

We can call this strand 'atomism'. The term applies in two senses – or in two places. On the one hand, what I mean to pick out is a tendency to treat porn as something which requires a *personal* (or at most, interpersonal) response, which may be couched in terms of individuals and how they manage their lives. The second sense of 'atomism' I have in mind is a tendency to single out pornography as something exceptional, relative to the rest of culture, and as something which may be addressed separately from the way in which we deal with that culture as a whole. As we'll see, these two kinds of atomism go hand in hand.

It's common to assume that the feminist critique of porn implies a great deal about personal morality and habits: that we should never look at porn (except maybe 'egalitarian' or 'feminist' porn), that we should not have friends or partners who use porn, or that we should lobby hard against their use of it. There is an element of pissing in the wind here. As MacKinnon says: 'try arguing with an orgasm'.[75]

Now, there is nothing necessarily wrong with fighting against the odds, or even fighting losing battles – often it seems the only acceptable course. But what I want to suggest is that there is something misguided about this way of interpreting the issue of porn, something which goes beyond the worry about unfeasibility. We might think back, at this point, to Andrea Dworkin's words against the practice of distinguishing 'erotica' from 'pornography'. It's very easy for the mostly white, Western, middle-class women who populate academic feminism to blame or pity others whom they take to be in the grip of misogynist thinking and practices: working-class girls wearing almost nothing on cold winter evenings; sun-bed addicts and those who opt for breast-enlargement surgery; Muslim women who wear religious dress (whatever the reasons behind what is often a careful and conscious, personal and political decision to wear a headscarf or veil); more or less anybody's underage daughter who wants to wear sexy clothing, and who idolises musicians who could pass for porn stars; *Sun* readers; parents who dress their little girls in pink and their little boys in blue, etc., etc.

---

[75] MacKinnon (1994, p. 17).

This is part of a general tendency for feminism to become a matter of the policing of our own and others' lifestyles. As we have seen, the second-wave slogan 'The personal is political' drew attention to something crucial: that the tendency to dismiss issues that affect women – issues of childcare, reproductive health, beauty norms and so on – as 'merely personal' is an ideological device which serves to make women's oppression invisible. But from the recognition that the personal is political, we should not draw the lesson that the political is (only or mainly) personal.[76] We have to resist the reduction of feminism to an issue of personal grooming: feminism is not primarily about the decision whether or not to shave our legs, whether or not to conform to 'feminine' norms of appearance, whether or not to get married (and so on). The tendency to pretend otherwise only serves to trivialise feminist politics, to divert our attention from collective action in pursuit of more radical change, and to pit women against themselves and each other.

It is of course true that these 'personal' decisions have a political dimension. And it may be that few (if any) lifestyles are entirely innocent, from a feminist point of view. In fact, one way of understanding the radical feminist position is as maintaining that *nothing* is innocent.[77] As writers like Andrea Dworkin are well aware, patriarchy pervades and moulds the identities and sexualities of all of us. Many of the same women who tut at Essex girls for making sex-objects of themselves would not give up the upper-middle-class equivalents of white stilettos, the things on which *they* rely in order to secure and keep the approval of the men around them. Bourgeois feminist women have not transcended stereotypical norms of conduct and beauty and patriarchal prejudices. They just talk differently and shop in different shops. Many would not date a man shorter than themselves, and few would be happy to go around with unshaved armpits or legs. Their critiques, above all their choices of target, often reek of condescension, hypocrisy and worse: condescending feminist critique can act as a veil for – among other things – class hatred, racism, misandry, misogyny, and an easy disrespect for (and lack of empathy with) children and teenagers.

---

[76] I owe this way of thinking of it to Katharine Jenkins.

[77] This marks another important point of connection between radical feminism and critical theory. See, in particular, the work of Theodor Adorno and Max Horkheimer, which exhibits a commitment to 'negative' criticism as a response to a 'radically evil' world.

Focusing on the level of individual dos and don'ts, when asking how feminists should react to porn, is not only connected with the various kinds of condescension mentioned above, but also with the idea of a world divided into the 'cool' and the 'not-cool': being a feminist is a matter of making the right individual choices; we do that by involving ourselves in only those bits of social reality which are 'cool' (whether by buying them, liking them, wearing them, watching them, etc.). If porn has been consigned to the 'not-cool', then it looks like being a good feminist means having nothing to do with it, and with converting others around us to the same lifestyle decision.

This is the standard but, I suggest, also the wrong way to look at it. It picks out a class of material called 'pornography', and calls on individuals to renounce it and to eradicate it from their lives and those of others around them. Now, that *might* be an appropriate practical intervention to make – in some cases, and for some kinds of porn – although my own view is that there can be no hard and fast rules in this area. (I certainly do not mean to imply that no lifestyle is any better, in feminist terms, than any other.) But it is certainly not the heart of the radical feminist critique of porn, and nor does it necessarily follow from that critique. According to this approach, patriarchal culture cannot usefully be divided up into the bits that are 'OK' and the bits that are 'problematic'. That policy has the effect of limiting the scope of our critique and committing us to too affirmative an attitude towards the social world as a whole, and it also tends to involve ideologically driven decisions as to where to draw the lines.

Whilst the contemporary porn industry can hardly be described as the poor scapegoat or underdog – an interpretation that made some sense in the 1950s – it is in another sense an easy target. Porn's very identity is caught up with the perception of it as naughty, dirty, sordid – and as the feminist's bête noire. We also know well enough the kind of stuff we mean by 'porn'; and it is not practically difficult for most feminists to boycott that class of material (though they do, of course, have to walk past the softer forms of it in supermarket aisles and corner shops). The status of this industry and the material it produces relative to feminism is comparable to the status of certain big, 'nasty' companies relative to critics of capitalism: MacDonald's, Wal-Mart, Starbucks or Gap. No anti-capitalist should be an apologist for these companies, for the ways in which they treat workers, consumers and the environment; but this does not make it clever or even accurate to point out the 'irony' of a Marxist eating a Big Mac (unless you think that the mere fact that some of us are immersed in a world whose structure we oppose is enough to count as 'ironic'). There *may* be some companies that an anti-capitalist simply can't stomach buying from, at a given time; and there are certainly contexts, such as the context of an organised boycott, where she might well alter her patterns of consumption on political grounds. But anti-capitalism is not reducible to a commitment to 'ethical consumerism'; nor does the latter follow from the former; and in fact, there are often clear tensions between the two, as approaches to politics. Marxists, for instance, do not believe (as many liberals seem to) that capitalism can be tamed by responsible consumer or lifestyle choices, but that collective political struggle is required in order to change the system – and that fixating on (often illusory) 'green' and 'fair-trade' products distracts from and often denies this necessity. Nor do genuine anti-capitalists hold that certain companies are peculiarly bad or evil – or at least, if they do hold this, this is not their main point. What distinguishes the anti-capitalist from the liberal who is merely unable to deny the undeniable is the vehement rejection of a dominant 'bad apples' rhetoric, according to which our task is to root out the corrupt and poisonous so as to preserve the purity of the capitalist crop. The whole point about companies like Wal-Mart and Gap is that they are *not* exceptional – except perhaps insofar as they illustrate more general features of capitalism with particular clarity.

A feminist attitude to porn could run along parallel lines. Critics of the anti-porn strand in feminism often point out that what is said about porn might also be said about many other things: mainstream films, popular music, novels, visual art. Do we have to renounce all that, they ask? Assuming that we *don't* accept such a drastic, unattractive and unfeasible conclusion, they suggest, the feminist critique of porn must fall as well – as some contemporary philosophers might put it, the critique 'proves too much'. The premise of this objection is correct, but the wrong inference is drawn. From a feminist point of view, porn both is and is not special. The radical feminists who have attacked it have been motivated by a recognition that there is something especially powerful about expression which pairs inequality and misogyny with sexual arousal: as MacKinnon puts it, porn 'makes hierarchy sexy'. In that respect, the analogy which some draw between porn and racial hate speech is imperfect:[78]

---

[78] I'm not criticising the use of the analogy, nor the conclusions some have drawn from it about the relationship between porn and free speech. The additional feature of porn seems to strengthen their case against it, if anything.

porn does not just express misogyny or convey a message that women are sex objects; it sexualises misogyny by misogynising sexuality.[79] Porn is also special in the same sort of sense in which certain big corporations might be of particular interest to anti-capitalists: it exhibits the character and reality of patriarchy particularly vividly and in a particularly concentrated form, *telling us something about what our society is like.*

And this gives us the sense in which porn is not special, but rather typical. If it were completely anomalous, unlike anything else in our society, then we wouldn't need to talk about overthrowing an entrenched system of patriarchy, but just about eradicating a rogue industry – and that is how people often understand the feminist position. But on the most plausible reconstruction, the feminist critique of porn is in important part a diagnostic device that is supposed to lead us into and reinforce a critique that is more radical and wider in scope. In one sense, porn is a recognisable subclass of material for consumption, which we can distinguish from other kinds of material like music videos or 18-rated films. But in another sense, we might think of porn as an *element* or *aspect* which runs through the culture of patriarchal societies (including some of the bits that respectable academic feminists like): an element which presents women as subordinated or objectified in such a way as to make that subordination or objectification sexy.[80]

To criticise and unmask 'porn' in this sense is unworkable – or apt to 'prove too much' – if we assume that our primary project is that of deciding what should be censored. But this neither is nor should be feminists' primary project (probably, it should not be their or anybody's project at all). Such an understanding of 'porn' will also be unattractively broad if we have bought into the idea that what feminists should be doing is telling us how to purge our individual lives – the products we consume and the areas of culture we partake in – of traces of patriarchy. If that is what we assume, then the realisation that porn-in-the-pejorative-sense is all around us, not neatly contained in its paper bag, threatens to set us on a slippery slope, at the bottom of which we will

---

[79] In one of the studies collated in Itzin (1992), participants were conditioned to become aroused at the sight of a woman's boot. It's not plausible, in my view, to say that the things presented in porn etc. are just a response to what people antecedently find sexy – a line that is quite transparent when applied to the relationship between mainstream media coverage or advertising and the attitudes, interests and tastes of viewers and consumers.

[80] For a defence of this approach, see Kappeler (1992).

not be allowed to like Beyoncé anymore; and that, of course, is intolerable. But if we shake off these constraints – do not assume that the issue of porn is mainly a matter of censorship or of personal habits – the fact that the feminist critique of porn has wide implications is not a refutation; on the contrary, it constitutes the very strength and interest of that critique.

10 Among sisters: anarchism, socialism and feminism

The last chapter examined the issue of pornography, an issue that divides liberal and radical feminists, and tried to show how we might resist the misrepresentations, double standards and the attempts at 'de-radicalisation' which characterise the usual discussions of that issue. In the process, surprisingly strong affinities emerged once again between the emphases and habits associated with 'radical feminism' and with the Marxist-influenced tradition of 'critical theory' respectively. The quick-yet-convoluted dismissals of the empirical case against porn in the dominant liberal discourse, as ingenious as they are seemingly inevitable, cry out for a critique in terms of the notion of (patriarchal) ideology – and that is exactly what they get, in effect, from figures like Catharine MacKinnon. In the attempt to resist what I regarded as the reduction of the critique of porn to a matter of lifestyle-policing, I also stressed another point that is of central importance to critical theorists: the need to critique society as a totality,[1] recognising the interconnectedness of social life and the pervasiveness of its oppressive character, rather

---

I take this title from a chant published in the radical feminist newspaper *It Ain't Me Babe* (1 December 1970, p. 11; cited in Ehrlich 1977, p. 4):

We build autonomy
The process of ever growing synthesis
For every living creature.
We spread
Spontaneity and creation
We learn the joys of equality
Of relationships
Without dominance
Among sisters.
We destroy domination

In all its forms.
[1] Cf. Horkheimer (1999).

than attempting to break it up into isolated fragments, patches of light and dark. I stressed the links and parallels between the critique of porn and the critique of capitalism, the limitations of 'atomistic' approaches centred on doomed attempts to live individual lives that are politically unproblematic and morally squeaky-clean under a system which is anything but. As Adorno puts it, 'Wrong life cannot be lived rightly.'[2]

So whilst the issue of porn is most usually regarded as a battlefield between 'liberal' and 'radical' feminists, central themes from socialist and Marxist feminism hover unavoidably in the background. What I want to do next is to drag those themes into the foreground, and focus more closely on the relationship between feminist ideas and left-wing critiques of capitalism. I already said a little, in Chapter 6, about the historical clashes and affinities between Marxists (or other socialists) and feminists. In this chapter, I take a different tack, and consider a face of feminism that is very rarely seen or acknowledged: anarchist (or 'anarcho-'/'anarcha'-) feminism. By giving anarchist ideas the consideration they deserve, I suggest, we can get a clearer view of the vexed question of the relationship between feminist and socialist ideas: we may better see where there is a war, and where there isn't.

10.1 What is anarchism?

The first thing to note about anarchism is that it is a body of thought and practice which (much like the category of 'critical theory') is made more difficult to pin down and define by the fact that it is a position that is *inherently uneasy with the whole project of fixing definitions*. As one prominent early twentieth-century anarchist thinker, Emma Goldman, puts it: 'Anarchism urges man to think, to investigate, to analyze every proposition.'[3] Or, to take the words of the Italian anarchist Errico Malatesta:

> We do not boast that we possess absolute truth, on the contrary, we believe that social truth is not a fixed quantity, good for all times, universally applicable or determinable in advance . . .[4]

It should become clearer, in the course of this chapter, why anarchists have tended to take this line. But in any case, their reticence with regard to

---

[2] 'Es gibt kein richtiges Leben im falschen'. Translated in Adorno (1974, p. 39, §18).
[3] Goldman (1969, p. 50).   [4] Malatesta (1965, p. 21).

definitions and absolute statements, their reluctance to 'pin anything down', has not removed the practical necessity for anarchists to issue concise and digestible statements of their philosophy, although these have sometimes been offered rather grudgingly. Goldman, having just stated anarchism's inherent hostility to fixed definitions, nevertheless relents ('but that the brain capacity of the average reader be not taxed too much . . .'):

> ANARCHISM: – the philosophy of a new social order based on liberty unrestricted by man-made law; the theory that all forms of government rest on violence, and are therefore wrong and harmful, as well as unnecessary.[5]

This, I suggest, is as good a starting point as any, if we want to get a general overview of what the anarchist approach to politics and to political philosophy is. By elaborating on Goldman's definition, we may identify the main hallmarks of anarchist thought.

First, and most obviously, anarchists have voiced their commitments in the language of 'freedom' or 'liberty' – and have often insisted that this freedom be full, absolute or 'unrestricted' (Goldman). 'Freedom' is, of course, a notoriously vexed concept, and so there is a large and urgent question to be asked as to what anarchists mean by it. The answer, inevitably, will vary from one anarchist thinker to another, but a couple of general observations may be made. For one thing, when anarchists talk about 'freedom' or 'liberty', they are ultimately interested – like those who identify themselves as 'liberals' – in the freedom of the *individual*. This freedom does also have a collective dimension, as will become clearer later, and anarchists also talk in terms of the self-regulation of *communities*; but it is clear that what is being advocated is not some system in which groups may be 'free' or 'self-determining' in a way that comes at the cost of the freedom of the individual members of those groups – those groups must be *internally* free, not just free of external constraints. As the Russian anarchist Peter Kropotkin (1842–1921) insisted, the 'communes of the next revolution will not only break down the state and substitute free federation for parliamentary rule; they will part with parliamentary rule within the commune itself . . . They will be anarchist within the commune as they will be anarchist outside it.'[6]

This is not yet to say exactly what this individual freedom is, or how it is possible for it to be fully and universally realised. The stance on that will

---

[5] Goldman (1969, p. 51).   [6] Kropotkin (1970, p. 132).

vary from anarchist to anarchist – and in any case, we cannot adequately understand what anarchists (even in general) mean by 'freedom' without looking at this in the context of their other distinctive commitments (to be discussed shortly). Here, I will merely strike a note of caution. It is tempting to assume that anarchists are concerned with what is now often called 'negative' liberty. According to a distinction famously articulated by the liberal political theorist Isaiah Berlin in his 1958 essay,[7] 'negative' liberty is the state of being unconstrained by external agency: I am free if no one ties my hands, stands in my way, locks me in prison or holds a gun to my head. It is notoriously more difficult to say what 'positive' liberty is – and Berlin's own account of it has been justly accused of conflating more than one thing[8] – but the usual understanding is that it connotes a state of *self-authorship* or *self-mastery*: I am positively free if I am meaningfully in control of my own life – and as we all know, it's quite possible to fall short of that condition without being locked up in prison (conversely, it has sometimes been claimed, it is possible to achieve a state of self-mastery even while our negative freedom is denied us).

In one sense, it must be true that anarchists are interested in 'negative' freedom, or 'negative' liberty: they see the freedom of the individual as requiring the *absence* of restrictions, force or domination by others – as witnessed by Goldman's 'liberty unrestricted by man-made law' – although as we'll see, they have a distinctive, *socialist* view of the conditions that are necessary to realise this. But it is clear from the writings of prominent anarchists that they are also interested in freedom in a more positive sense – in what has sometimes been called 'freedom-*to*'[9] – and that, like many socialists (including Marxists), they tie this closely to an ideal of flourishing, self-realisation or fulfilment. As Goldman puts it: 'Only in freedom can man grow to his full stature. Only in freedom will he learn to think and move, and give the very best in him.'[10]

As anarchism centrally involves a commitment to individual freedom, equally central is the corresponding opposition to whatever is seen as incompatible with such a commitment, i.e. the threats or impediments to individual

[7] Berlin (1970 [1958]).

[8] See Raymond Geuss's talk on freedom of speech, addressed to a student occupation in Cambridge (Geuss 2011).

[9] As opposed to freedom-*from*.

[10] Goldman (1969, p. 61). Cf. Bakunin's statement that everyone 'should have the material and moral means to develop his humanity' (1964, p. 409).

freedom. The main enemy or antithesis of freedom is variously identified by anarchists as 'law' or 'government' (e.g. Goldman), 'power' or 'domination' or 'hierarchy' (e.g. Carol Ehrlich),[11] 'authority' (e.g. Kornegger,[12] R. P. Wolff)[13] and – perhaps most obviously – 'the State'. Anarchists often analyse these phenomena not only as *violations* of individual freedom, but as (literally) vio*lence* (albeit often in a covert or unacknowledged form): recall Goldman's statement, above, that 'all forms of government rest on violence'.

We may understand the point here as twofold. First, there is a point associated with the liberal political theorist Max Weber, that government, no matter how 'legitimate', no matter how 'democratic' or apparently peaceful and benign, always rests ultimately on the threat of brute physical force: sooner or later – and often, sooner – dissent will be met with nothing more subtle than the policeman's bodily strength and assorted weaponry. Second, though, we might understand anarchists as making the point that the existence and operation of various forms of government, law and domination, even when things do not come to the point of a physical confrontation, not only *rest on the threat* of violence, but are themselves *already instances of* violence: for anarchists, these wreak an everyday (but very real) violence on the individuals that live under them, by constraining their freedom, their powers and even their thought[14] (we might think of this as comparable to the invisible but constant 'violence' that some would say is inflicted on a child by an excessively constraining or otherwise psychologically abusive upbringing).

In addition to being viewed as forms of violence, government and state, power or authority, domination and hierarchy are described by many anarchists (though certainly not *only* by anarchists) as having a 'corrupting' effect,

---

[11] See Ehrlich (1977).   [12] See Kornegger (1975).   [13] See Wolff (1970).

[14] Many anarchists have espoused something reminiscent of the Marxist theory of ideology: they have argued that our forms of thought are distorted by the inhuman societies in which we live and which have produced us, and that our thought and powers of imagination would be profoundly different (and better) under conditions of freedom. For instance, the anarchist political theorist William Godwin (also husband of Mary Wollstonecraft and father of Mary Shelley) argued that wage labour creates a 'sense of dependence' and a 'servile and truckling spirit', thus ensuring that the 'feudal spirit still survives that reduced the great mass of mankind to the rank of slaves and cattle for the service of the few' (see Godwin 1986, pp. 125–6). Arguably, though, Godwin took this a bit far when he claimed that the mental powers unleashed by an anarchist revolution would allow human beings to cure all disease and to live forever.

on those in privileged as well as in subordinate positions within the structures in question. As Marx's main anarchist adversary Mikhail Bakunin explains, anarchists 'realise that power and authority corrupt those who exercise them as much as those who are compelled to submit to them'.[15]

For all these reasons, anarchists stress that they are interested not in acquiring control for themselves, or in raising themselves or even the 'masses' to higher positions within the systems of domination that exist. As Ehrlich puts it: 'The goal, then, is not to "seize" power, as the socialists are fond of urging, but to abolish power.'[16]

It is not that anarchists are opposed to 'power' in every sense of that word – even when they declare their intent to abolish it, and even to abolish it 'in all its forms'. How could they coherently be opposed to what philosophers have called 'power-to', i.e. power as a capability or creative capacity?[17] As noted above, this is precisely something that anarchists say they want to unleash, nurture and expand. What they are against, then, is something more akin to what philosophers have termed 'power-over' – according to one influential definition, 'A has power over B to the extent that he can get B to do something that B would not otherwise do.'[18] What they are against is a kind of power that is exercised by some *over others*, a power which suppresses and restricts those others.

Of course, even this is not going to be straightforward to articulate and defend. The problem is not necessarily 'power-over' per se. Given their focus on open discussion and dialogue and collective decision making, anarchists presumably are not interested in eliminating all *influence* of some persons over others – what would be the point of such discussion, if nobody ever changed the way they think as the result of anybody else's contribution? And it's unlikely that the anarchist will even be interested in eliminating *unequal* influence, as such, since it seems both inevitable and harmless that some individuals will be more persuasive than others (perhaps by being more charismatic, or simply more *right*), at least in some contexts.

---

[15] Bakunin (1964, p. 249). See also Bakunin (1867).   [16] Ehrlich (1977, p. 7).

[17] A classic articulation of power as power-to comes from Hobbes: power is a person's 'present means . . . to obtain some future apparent Good' (Hobbes 1985 [1641], p. 150). A more recent example is Hannah Arendt, who understands power as 'the human ability not just to act but to act in concert' (Arendt 1970, p. 44).

[18] Dahl (1957, pp. 202–3).

It may be instructive, at this point, to think of the anarchist position alongside a favourite liberal value that is also prized by anarchists: *equality*. The advocacy of 'equality' can easily be interpreted in such a way as to make it absurd: if the proposal is that all human beings should be rendered the same in all ways, or equal in all their capacities and traits, or treated as strictly equal in their needs, then it's just stupid – and everyone knows it. But almost nobody takes this to be a refutation of liberal egalitarianism.[19] This owes to a recognition that liberals have much more to say on the matter. And the same should go for anarchists.

When we ask what more anarchists have to say, as it happens, the favourite liberal notion of equality comes back into view – but not as we know it. Anarchists are interested not only in freedom, but in equal freedom for *all* individuals – some extend this beyond adult human beings, to children or to non-human animals.[20] But for anarchists, the commitments to freedom and to equality are not really distinct, let alone competing: it is not a matter of placing a value on a good ('freedom') and then adding that this good is to be distributed equally among persons. Contrary to a common idea among liberals, whereby freedom and equality are inherently in tension – two competing considerations which need to be 'balanced' – anarchists understand freedom in such a way that it is *conceptually bound up with* equality so that the one value implies the other. Freedom is not some good to be parcelled out, so that some may enjoy it whilst others are denied it. For anarchists, human beings are free when their relationships with one another are non-hierarchical, and not otherwise (since to be dominated is to be un-free).

What is important to recognise here is how closely linked are the three hallmarks of anarchism I've been describing: the commitment to freedom is one side of a coin which has the opposition to domination or hierarchy as its other side, and therefore there is an equation in anarchist thought between freedom, and conditions of *non-*domination or social equality. Anarchists have varied in their willingness to specify more positively what such conditions should look like, and where they have been willing, their suggestions have

---

[19] Actually, it is an element – but only an element – of Marx's critique of egalitarianism (see his *Critique of the Gotha Programme*, written in 1875).

[20] E.g. Kropotkin (1897): 'Civilised man . . . will extend his principles of solidarity to the whole human race and even animals.'

naturally differed. But all, I think, are united by a commitment to 'bottom-up' or 'de-centralised' and 'horizontal' forms of organisation, as opposed to the 'top-down', 'centralised' or 'vertical' form of control epitomised by the state. As the anarchist feminist Penny Kornegger puts it, what is envisaged is a system of 'overlapping circles rather than a pyramid'.[21]

This vision of a horizontal as opposed to a vertical mode of organisation has informed – and been interpreted in the light of – existing political movements such as trade unionism and feminism. The fusion of anarchist ideas with industrial trade unionism occurred most notably in Spain in the first half of the twentieth century, giving rise to an 'anarcho-syndicalist' movement which became the largest political force during the Civil War of 1936–9 (in the form of the anarcho-syndicalist union *Confederación Nacional del Trabajo* (CNT) and the closely related militant anarchist organisation, *Federación Anarquista Ibérica* (FAI)). During this period, 60 per cent of the land was worked collectively, with large-scale organisation taking the form of federations linking hundreds of small collectives – the most successful examples being the Peasant Federation of Levant (which included 900 collectives) and the Aragon Federation of Collectives (composed of about 500 collectives).[22] Like some trade unionists, many feminists have had an automatic affinity with anarchism, insofar as both movements have shared an 'emphasis on the small group as a basic organizational unit'.[23] Describing the feminist movement of the second half of the twentieth century – and pointing in particular to phenomena such as consciousness-raising groups, rape crisis centres and women's health collectives – Kornegger writes: 'Our impulses toward collective work and small leaderless groups have been anarchistic, but in most cases we haven't *called* them by that name.'[24] In a similar vein, Carol Ehrlich identifies 'small, leaderless groups where tasks are rotated and skills and knowledge shared' as a common element of the approach of anarchists and of many feminists.[25]

Although the details vary, then, the positive commitment of anarchists to horizontal or 'bottom-up' organisational forms can be understood in terms of the following cluster of elements: large-scale networks of small groups (where the network is connected 'horizontally' rather than being held together by

---

[21] Kornegger (1975, p. 5).   [22] See Kornegger (1975); Dolgoff (1974).
[23] Kornegger (1975, p. 15); cf. Ehrlich (1977, p. 8).   [24] Kornegger (1975, p. 14).
[25] Ehrlich (1977, p. 8). Cf. also Allen (1970).

any central authority); within the small groups, a kind of 'direct-democratic' participation (facilitated by the groups' small size),[26] an emphasis on discussion, and an avoidance of privileged leadership in favour of 'task rotation' – as Ehrlich underlines, anarchists are not necessarily against leadership per se ('provided that it carries no reward or privilege, and is temporary and specific to a particular task').[27]

This ideal of horizontal forms of organisation is not only relevant to the way in which anarchists characterise the kind of society they prescribe and aim for – as we'll see, anarchists have sometimes been rather wary of the whole project of mapping out their favoured sort of social world. To put it in terms of my earlier distinction, anarchists apply their preference for horizontal modes of co-operation not only in their contributions to 'static' theory, but also in their approach to 'dynamic' theories and processes of social transformation. This is sometimes expressed in terms of a need to match means to ends: the strategies used to bring about social change must live up to the anarchist values (freedom, non-domination etc.) that motivate that social change in the first place.[28] As Ehrlich insists: 'You cannot liberate yourself by non-liberatory means.'[29] Anarchists therefore have opposed hierarchical organisations and parliamentarianism as means of bringing about a better society – a policy which has frequently brought them into conflict with Marxist and other socialist approaches as well as with liberals.[30] This is closely tied up with anarchists' insistence – noted earlier – against seizing power or mimicking or exploiting hierarchy, even where the apparent and avowed purpose is to abolish those very things. Against the strategy of those who seek feminist change through involvement in electoral politics, for example, Ehrlich writes:

---

[26] 'the key concept underlying both the social/political and the economic structure of libertarian socialism is "self-management", a term that implies not only workers' control of their workplaces but also citizens' control of their communities (where it becomes "self-government"), through direct democracy and voluntary federation' (Anarchist Editorial Collective 2009, p. 9).

[27] Ehrlich (1977, p. 11).

[28] 'For example, the anarchist collectives in Spain were organised in a bottom-up manner, similar to the way the C.N.T. (the anarcho-syndicalist labour union) was organised *before* the revolution' (Anarchist Editorial Collective 2009, p. 10; emphasis mine).

[29] Ehrlich (1977, p. 4).

[30] Cf. Lenin's 1919 letter to 'Comrade Sylvia Pankhurst' (Lenin 1972).

'they will all drown in the depths of things as they are'.[31] Like many whose politics are closer to the political mainstream, anarchists have warned of the dangers of seeking power in order to liberate others. Instead, anarchists have placed an emphasis on *self*-liberation. In Malatesta's words: 'We do not want to emancipate the people. We want the people to emancipate themselves.'[32]

* * *

The above is certainly not intended as a comprehensive account of anarchist thought, and there is undoubtedly great variation between different anarchist positions. But one thing should by now be absolutely clear: *anarchy ≠ chaos!!* Commenting on a right-wing author who conflated the two, George Orwell once remarked that it is 'a hardly more correct use of words than saying that a Conservative is one who makes jam'.[33] No anarchist theorist (as far as I am aware) opposes structure or organisation per se – as Ehrlich points out, anarchists are not opposed to structure, but to *a particular kind* of structure (the rigid, hierarchical kind).[34] In practice, too, we have seen that anarchists are capable of impressive feats of large-scale co-operative endeavour.

Nothing, however, could be further from the fiction, which constantly depicts anarchism as terminally haphazard.[35] Of course, anarchists are well used to being attacked on this and other grounds – when they are not ignored altogether, that is (as Ehrlich notes, 'anarchism has veered between a bad press and none at all').[36] It is worth now considering a couple of the most common charges levelled against anarchism, in order to show that they are not nearly so decisive as often assumed. Anarchists are not idiots: they have heard these charges (repeatedly), thought about them and responded; whether or not we think that their responses are ultimately adequate, they are at least compelling enough to show that we are not dealing here with knockdown objections; the responses, too, demand a response.

* * *

---

[31] Ehrlich (1977, p. 4).

[32] This statement first appeared in the Italian magazine *l'Agitazione* (18 June 1897), and is reprinted in Malatesta (1965, p. 90). Cf. Bakunin: 'revolution should not only be made for the people's sake; it should also be made by the people' (Guérin 1997, vol. 1, p. 141).

[33] Orwell (2001, p. 298).   [34] Ehrlich (1977).

[35] As Ehrlich notes: 'Unfortunately, the picture of a gaggle of disorganized, chaotic anarchist women, drifting without direction, caught on' (ibid., p. 11).

[36] Ibid., p. 6.

In her essay 'Anarchism', Emma Goldman notes and counters two of the most common and predictable criticisms that anarchists face:[37] first, that anarchism is 'impractical' (though a nice idea 'in theory'); and second, that anarchism is violent or destructive.[38] Goldman meets both objections with characteristic verve. I'll consider each objection, and Goldman's reply, in turn.

10.2 Be realistic!

Responding first to charges of 'impracticality', Goldman retorts:

> A practical scheme, says Oscar Wilde, is either one already in existence, or a scheme that could be carried out under the existing conditions; but it is exactly the existing conditions that one objects to, and any scheme that could accept these conditions is wrong and foolish. The true criterion of the practical, therefore, is not whether the latter can keep intact the wrong or foolish; rather it is whether the scheme has vitality enough to leave the stagnant waters of the old, and build, as well as sustain, new life.[39]

Here, Goldman is drawing attention to a kind of (small-'c') conservative bias inherent in many familiar demands for us to be 'realistic', or to make proposals that are 'practical' or 'feasible'. Those who are strongly critical of the social and political status quo have always been met with accusations of being 'unrealistic'; and, particularly in the world after the fall of many of the regimes inspired by communist and socialist ideas, we are invariably asked

---

[37] It's worth pointing out that these objections, and many of the possible responses I'll mention, are also applicable to the case of non-anarchist socialist and Marxist views.

[38] Goldman's impression of the most common objections facing anarchists is one shared by later theorists. As self-described 'anarca-feminist' [sic] Penny Kornegger notes: 'Anarchism has been maligned and misinterpreted for so long that maybe the most important thing to begin with is an explanation of what it is and isn't. Probably the most prevalent stereotype of the anarchist is a malevolent-looking man hiding a lighted bomb beneath a black cape, ready to destroy or assassinate everything and everybody in his path. This image engenders fear and revulsion in most people, regardless of their politics; consequently, anarchism is dismissed as ugly, violent, and extreme. Another misconception is the anarchist as impractical idealist, dealing in useless, Utopian abstractions and out of touch with concrete reality. The result: anarchism is once again dismissed, this time as an "impossible dream"' (Kornegger 1975, p. 4).

[39] Goldman (1969, p. 49).

the question, 'But what would you put in its place?' Since our answers to that question – if we are able to furnish any at all – are always considered either too vague or too pie-in-the-sky, those answers *and also our criticisms of the existing state of things*, are often dismissed on the grounds of a failure to be 'constructive'.[40]

The problem is that these sorts of demands, expectations and reactions often presuppose exactly the things that the radical critic is calling into question (that is to say, they are 'question-begging'). People often talk as though it is obvious what it means to be 'practical' or 'realistic', as though we all know what those words mean, and mean the same thing by them. But the matter is about as far from obvious as you can get. Does 'realistic' mean 'similar to what we already have' (in much the same way as a naturalistic sketch or painting might be 'realistic')? If so, then only small-scale, modest criticisms and suggestions can ever be realistic (so much the worse for 'realism', the radical critic might say). Or does 'realistic' or 'practical' mean 'possible'? Possible in what sense? Logically, physically, economically, psychologically? Or, does it mean 'likely to happen'? Likely to happen under what conditions? Isn't what is (and is not) likely to happen partly *up to us* – partly, even, a function of the political criticisms we choose to take seriously or to dismiss? Suppose we think that the Government is ruling in a way that is insensitive to the wishes of the people and highly detrimental to their interests, and that it should therefore be kicked out as soon as possible. Suppose also that we are required to be 'realistic' and 'practical', where these concepts are understood in terms of what is possible or likely *under the present Government*. Then, surely, those who impose that expectation on us have *already* dismissed our point of view: they do not reject our position on the grounds that it is impractical; they find it impractical because they reject our position.

Anarchists, as Goldman emphasises, are radically opposed to 'the existing conditions'. And yet they are held to a standard of 'practicality' which seeks to tether them to those conditions by rejecting as 'impractical' any proposal that is incompatible with them. When conceptions of the 'realistic', the 'practical' (etc.) are loaded in this way, the decks are stacked against the anarchist, and against any radical critic of the status quo, from the very beginning.

---

[40] I discuss the conservative (and ideological) force of prevailing notions of 'constructiveness' in Finlayson (2015, chapter 1).

None of this means that anarchists themselves (and other radical critics of the status quo) see no value in being practical or realistic – they only reject dominant conceptions of what these things mean. This comes out very clearly in Goldman's reply, when she identifies 'the true criterion of the practical' as being whether some idea or scheme 'has vitality enough to leave the stagnant waters of the old, and build, as well as sustain, new life'. Of course, it will not always be easy to say exactly what *this* means, nor to determine which schemes do and do not satisfy the criterion. But what is clear is that practicality cannot be equated with keeping things (more or less) as they are – or as Goldman puts it, 'keep[ing] intact the wrong or foolish'.

Many radical critics of social life as we know it – and anarchists are no exception – take the view that the status quo is 'realistic' only in an extremely unimpressive and uninteresting sense: it is the status quo; it is 'realistic' qua 'real' qua 'actual' (and again, we knew that already). But capitalism is not realistic, say Marxists, in the sense of being stable – it is crisis-prone and ultimately doomed. And it is not realistic in the sense of being honest about itself – it relies on ideological forms of thought which paper over social contradictions.[41] Many anarchists, too, have suggested that far from being the criterion of the practical, there is something crucially *un*real about prevailing social reality.

This emphasis on inauthenticity is one that is shared by some critical theorists and twentieth-century anarchists – in particular, the strand of anarchism known as 'situationism'. The core ideas of situationism are those of the 'commodity' and of the 'spectacle'.[42] Situationists identify a particularly radical form of 'commodification' as characteristic of modern societies: not only is the capitalist economy arranged around the production, sale and consumption of commodities; in capitalist societies, *everything* is progressively transformed into a commodity – ideas, culture and even people.[43] The idea

---

[41] See (especially) Marx and Engels's *The German Ideology* (1987; written 1845–6, first published 1932).

[42] See Debord (1994).

[43] 'The individual does not own himself, and is not permitted to be his true self. He has become a mere market commodity, an instrument for the accumulation of property – for others... Individuality is stretched on the Procrustes bed of business... If our individuality were to be made the price of breathing, what ado there would be about the violence done to the personality! And yet our very right to food, drink and shelter is only too often conditioned upon our loss of individuality. These things

of people as commodities conveys the sense that they become objects rather than subjects: just one more thing to be churned out and consumed by the social machine, and not agents with either a meaningful inner life or control over their own destiny. And this connects with the second core idea: the 'spectacle', an idea which is meant to convey *passivity*, on the one hand (people are presented as passive spectators rather than as actors in the great social performance), and *inauthenticity*, on the other (what the spectators are passively taking in is not real life, but something acted out – no more or less than a spectacle). According to this view, it is not anarchism that is unrealistic, but the social world as we know it – a fundamentally *un*real world, which – as long as it persists – supresses the possibility of a truly liberated collective life. Hence the situationist slogan: *Be realistic, demand the impossible!*

None of this is meant to suggest that it would always and everywhere be illegitimate to accuse anarchists of being impractical – maybe (some of) the forms of organisation that they (or some of them) have championed wouldn't work on the scale and in the manner that they have claimed; maybe 'human nature' is indeed such that hierarchies of the kind anarchists want to eliminate will always emerge (a claim that is frequently asserted, but which is much more difficult to establish);[44] maybe anarchists and other radical critics really do lack proposals with enough 'vitality' to give us any hope of actually being able to overthrow the existing state of things. Maybe. There are endless, involved discussions to be had over these and many other questions. But we would actually have to *have* these discussions. It is not good enough just to declare relatively more radical criticisms and proposals 'impractical'; very

are granted to the propertyless millions (and how scantily!) only in exchange for their individuality – they become the mere instruments of industry' (Baginski 1907, p. 150).

[44] Goldman (1969, pp. 61–2) has an equally brisk response to this objection: 'Poor human nature, what horrible crimes have been committed in thy name! Every fool, from king to policeman, from the flatheaded parson to the visionless dabbler in science, presumes to speak authoritatively of human nature. The greater the mental charlatan, the more definite his insistence on the wickedness and weaknesses of human nature. Yet, how can any one speak of it today, with every soul in a prison, with every heart fettered, wounded, and maimed? [...The] experimental study of animals in captivity is absolutely useless. Their character, their habits, their appetites undergo a complete transformation when torn from their soil in field and forest. With human nature caged in a narrow space, whipped daily into submission, how can we speak of its potentialities?'

often, such declarations turn out to mean little more than that the criticisms and proposals in question are radical ones – when we knew *that* already.

It is worth saying something about the terms 'utopian' and 'anti-utopian', since part of the issue under discussion here has to do with the degree of willingness and ability of anarchists – and others who aim at far-reaching criticisms of current society, such as Marxists and radical feminists – to describe the form of society they envisage. In general, it should be noted that the 'objection from impracticality', levelled against anarchists and socialists alike, is two-pronged: either the anarchist or socialist says something about what she wants to see (in which case she is told it is impractical); *or* she doesn't – in which case she criticised for not saying anything 'positive' (either way, she is seen as failing to be sufficiently 'practical' or 'constructive'). The strand of 'anti-utopianism' present in both anarchist and socialist (and, especially, Marxist)[45] thought may be seen as a stance of resistance against the second prong. 'Anti-utopianism', simply put, is *not* – as is often assumed – the rejection of ambitious or radical proposals for change; rather, it is *the principled reluctance to specify in detail a 'correct' or acceptable form of society.* To say that this reluctance is 'principled' is to say that it is not a mere sign of laziness, or culpable failure of insight, but is thought to follow from key features of the theorist's view of the world. I'll mention two important motivations for anti-utopianism now.

First, there is the realisation that our forms of thought are shaped by the societies in which we live, and that they may, moreover, tend to take on the ideological function of supporting the interests of those occupying positions of dominance within the system that prevails at a given time: being the products of a particular social system, our imaginations may be constrained by its bounds – some social possibilities are likely just to be *too* distant from what we have so far experienced for them to occur to us, or even to be comprehensible to us. For example, Kropotkin predicts that, under conditions of freedom, human beings will arrive at a system of collective living that 'will be a lot more attuned to popular aspirations and the requirements of co-existence and mutual relations than any theory, however splendid, devised by the thinking and imagination of reformers'.[46]

---

[45] For a statement of the Marxist opposition to 'utopianism', see Engels's *Socialism: utopian and scientific* (Engels 1993).

[46] Kropotkin in Guérin (1997, vol. 1, p. 232).

A second motivation – present in both socialist and anarchist thought, but emphasised particularly strongly by anarchists – has to do with the particular value of *freedom*: if freedom is really what we're interested in, the thought goes, then we have no business trying to specify the contours of a future that will be shaped by free individuals – we simply can't know what such a future will be like; and if we think we can, this is indicative of (at best) arrogance, or (worse) an intent to impose our own will upon that future in an inappropriate way. The anarchist Charlotte M. Wilson (1854–1944) states simply that, 'when [the workers] find themselves their own masters, they will modify the old system to suit their convenience in a variety of ways . . . as common sense is likely to suggest to free men'.[47] Marx, more famously, maintains that it is not his (or our) business to write 'recipes for the cook-shops of the future'.[48] Ironically, perhaps the best motto for anarchist anti-utopianism comes from Lenin, who for many anarchists represents the point at which the authoritarian elements in Marxism triumph over the more truly socialist and egalitarian. Lenin identified the central question in politics as 'Who whom?' – i.e. 'Who does what to whom, and for what purpose?'[49] Anarchism is above all a view not about *what is to be done* – to allude to another of Lenin's questions[50] – but about *who should decide* what is to be done. Anarchism is the view that people should decide for themselves what to do, and not have it dictated to them from above.

At the same time, there is a clear 'utopian' strain in anarchist thought (as there is in socialism too): attempts to describe the world that is to be brought into existence by anarchist struggle. What else could be going on, when (for example) Goldman describes anarchism as 'the liberation of the human mind from the dominion of religion; the liberation of the human body from the dominion of property; liberation from the shackles and restraint of government . . . a social order based on the free grouping of individuals for the purpose of producing real social wealth, an order that will guarantee to every human being free access to the earth and full enjoyment of the necessities of life, according to individual desires, tastes, and inclinations'?[51] The

---

[47] Wilson (2000, p. 23).

[48] See Marx's 1873 'Afterword' to the second German edition of *Capital*, vol. I.

[49] See Geuss (2008), who suggests that this might represent a promising central question around which to structure political philosophy (as opposed to currently prevalent approaches which prioritise questions of ideal 'justice').

[50] See Lenin (1969).   [51] Goldman (1969, p. 62).

anarcho-syndicalist Rudolf Rocker affirms the anarchist commitment to some form of utopianism quite unapologetically:

> People may … call us dreamers … They fail to see that dreams are also a part of the reality of life, that life without dreams would be unbearable. No change in our way of life would be possible without dreams and dreamers. The only people who are never disappointed are those who never hope and never try to realise their hope.[52]

There is more going on here than confusion or in-fighting, I think. On the one hand, we have to resist the tendency to dismiss radical political positions unless they can provide us with detailed proposals, for several reasons: first, it paves the way for these to be thrown out on ideologically driven charges of 'impracticality'; second, it makes some sense to expect that we will not have full epistemic access to utopia; third, a commitment to human *freedom* seems to imply a commitment to a certain *open-endedness* in our proposals (we are not primarily proposing any particular set of arrangements, but demanding that people be able to determine for themselves the sorts of arrangements they are to live under). But a recognition of all these points, it seems to me, is quite compatible with continuing to reach for and offer 'utopian' glimpses of possible worlds unlike this one. As Malatesta argues, discussions over the shape of an alternative society are indispensable, for it is 'absurd to believe that, once government has been destroyed and the capitalists expropriated, "things will look after themselves" without the intervention of those who already have an idea on what has to be done and who immediately set about doing it'; 'social life,' he adds, 'as the life of individuals, does not permit of interruption'.[53]

Perhaps the problem is not with offering utopian sketches, then, but with (a) automatically treating the omission to do so as a refutation of radical politics (and as a vindication of the status quo), and (b) making a mistake about the status of the enterprise we are engaged in when we do make positive suggestions – namely, convincing ourselves that we are in the business of producing permanently valid, non-negotiable blueprints for the future, rather than stimulating one another's imaginations and impulses towards social

---

[52] Rocker (2005, p. 95).   [53] Malatesta (1995, p. 121).

change.[54] Above all, anarchists are concerned not so much to sketch utopia, but to ease the movement towards it: to propose practical measures which, by evoking a different form of society, might help bring us closer to it. As Malatesta says, to 'neglect all the problems of reconstruction or to pre-arrange complete and uniform plans are both errors, excesses which, by different routes, would lead to our defeat as anarchists and to the victory of new or old authoritarian regimes. The truth lies in the middle.'[55] The answer, on this view, is not to be either a 'utopian' or an 'anti-utopian', but to understand these terms so as to realise the possibility of being proudly both.

10.3 The passion for destruction

As with the charge of impracticality, Goldman responds to the claim that anarchism is 'destructive' or violent by turning the accusation back against the status quo:

> Destruction and violence! How is the ordinary man to know that the most violent element in society is ignorance; that its power of destruction is the very thing Anarchism is combating? Nor is he aware that Anarchism, whose roots . . . are part of nature's forces, destroys, not healthful tissue, but parasitic growths that feed on the life's essence of society. It is merely clearing the soil from weeds and sagebrush, that it may eventually bear healthy fruit.[56]

Once again, this response turns the accusation on its head by attacking the understanding of the concepts that are used to discredit anarchism: in this case, the concepts of 'violence' and of 'destruction'. Anarchists can agree that violence and at least some kinds of destruction are bad things – just as they can agree that it is important to be 'realistic' or 'practical' *in the right sense of those terms*. But this, they believe, is a reason to destroy the destructive forms of social life that now exist, not to preserve them. Just as anarchists might say that it is *reality* that is unreal and impractical, not anarchism, Goldman

---

[54] This is something which many radical feminists have understood (although their interpreters very often have not). Referring to the contrast between the intent and the reception of Shulamith Firestone's best-known work, the *Dialectic of Sex*, Faludi writes: 'In one of the later chapters, Firestone floated a "sketchy" futuristic notion that she intended only "to stimulate thinking in fresh areas rather than to dictate the action"' (Faludi 2013, p. 54).

[55] Malatesta (1995, p. 121).   [56] Goldman (1969, pp. 49–50).

is saying that it is not anarchism but the status quo – and in particular the 'ignorance' that pervades and underpins it – that is violent and destructive.

As with the case of 'practicality', then, the problem is that the notions of 'violence' and 'destruction' tend to get understood in a way that already tacitly reflects an allegiance to the status quo and an antipathy towards positions that seek to overturn it. What we choose to call 'violent', or 'destructive' in a pejorative sense, is neither a straightforward matter nor an apolitical one. The dominant tendency is to call 'violent' and 'destructive' all and only those things which upset or disrupt everyday life, conventional morality and the continuance of existing social structures. That is why, when we think of violence, we are likely to think of the mugger or bank robber or terrorist. Slavoj Žižek suggests that this 'subjective' violence – so termed because, on Žižek's picture, this kind of violence will also have a clearly identifiable *subject* who is the perpetrator – is often the only kind which gets recognised as violence. Against this, he juxtaposes 'subjective' with what he calls 'systemic' violence: the violence inherent in the 'smooth' running of everyday life – in oppressive political structures and exploitative economic relations.[57]

To understand 'violence' in a way that effectively identifies it with disruptions of 'business as usual' has a twofold function: it renders the violence inherent in the 'business as usual' of capitalist societies invisible-as-violence; and it potentially taints any serious attempt at social change by associating such attempts with violence and destruction. As Goldman points out, there are plenty of things which are in some sense 'destructive', but which we find not only permissible but vital: surgery, many forms of medicine and hygiene, the removal of 'parasitic growths' or the 'clearing [of] the soil from weeds and sagebrush'.[58] Or, as the nineteenth-century anarchist Mikhail Bakunin famously put it: 'The passion for destruction is a creative passion too!'[59]

The quick-and-easy dismissal of anarchism as violent, then, is just as illegitimate and confused as the quick-and-easy rejection on grounds of 'impracticality' – and just as misleading as the kneejerk equation of anarchy with chaos. At the same time, there are genuine questions to be asked about the stance of anarchists towards violence. In view of the anarchist commitment to the employment of *only those means which they see as living up to anarchist ideals* (e.g. the ideal of non-hierarchy), it would make some sense to expect that anarchists must be automatic pacifists. We have seen that anarchists view

[57] See Žižek (2009).   [58] Goldman (1969, p. 50).   [59] Bakunin (1971, p. 55).

domination and hierarchy as forms of violence, and oppose them as such. It also seems plausible that the narrower class of acts which we normally designate with the terms 'violent' or 'violence' – acts of physical coercion, force and the infliction of injury – would count, for anarchists, as acts of domination (and hence violence) of the sort to be opposed, even while it is also emphasised that these more obvious forms of violence are not the only ones to be found in unfree societies. If anarchist organisations must be non-hierarchical in order to be fit to usher in a non-hierarchical future, then must they not also be committed to non-violence?

On the whole, however, anarchists have *not* identified themselves as pacifists. The Christian pacifist (and, some have suggested, a perpetrator of sexual violence)[60] Leo Tolstoy stated that '[t]he Anarchists are right in everything; in the negation of the existing order and in the assertion that, without Authority there could not be worse violence than that of Authority under existing conditions. *They are mistaken only in thinking that anarchy can be instituted by a violent revolution.*'[61] Tolstoy clearly regards pacifism as the logical consequence of anarchist principles; but as his statement makes clear, anarchists have in general not drawn this conclusion – and some, most notoriously the Russian anarchist Sergey Nechayev, seem to have been full subscribers to the doctrine of 'by any means necessary' and apologists for the most bloodthirsty violence.[62] In reality, the attitudes of anarchists towards violence in the pursuit of social change have covered an extremely wide spectrum.

Is Tolstoy right in seeing this as a failure on the part of many anarchists to live up to their own principles? I won't try to settle this question here. But what is clear is that we have to approach it with a constant and lively appreciation of Goldman's insight: that the way in which we understand concepts like 'violence' – as with understandings of 'the political', discussed in Chapter 8 – is never a politically neutral matter. What is at issue here is no simple question of whether violence is acceptable or not, but also the question of what should *count* as 'violence' – a point of which pacifists have been acutely aware. Goldman's warning is against being blind to the forms

---

[60] See A. Dworkin (1987, chapter 1).   [61] Tolstoy (1900; original emphasis).

[62] See Nechayev's 'Revolutionary Catechism' (1869), which includes such openly terroristic statements as: 'Above all, those who are especially inimical to the revolutionary organization must be destroyed; their violent and sudden deaths will produce the utmost panic in the government, depriving it of its will to action by removing the cleverest and most energetic supporters.'

of violence enshrined in the status quo, and of hypocritically tolerating and defending that violence under the guise of a principle of 'anti-violence' which rules out in advance practical efforts towards real social change. On the other hand, just as it is crucial to be critical of dominant understandings of the concept of violence, it is also crucial to guard against precisely the sorts of dangerous self-deception and excuse-making that anarchists detect and condemn in certain 'authoritarian' strands of socialism. If the Leninist is guilty of confusing a vanguard with 'the people', tyranny with democracy, of thinking that a stateless and classless society can be brought about by the seizure of state power by (the self-appointed representatives of) the working class, the anarchist might fall into a parallel delusion when she begins to say of the actions she wants to perform or encourage, 'That's not *really* violence; it's surgery!'

However real this danger is, it must not be used as an excuse to slip back into the sort of mistake that Goldman uncovers: the uncritical acceptance of a dominant understanding of 'violence', which presents itself as politically neutral and uncontested – something which it can never be. The point is that the need for criticism extends to a need for *self*-criticism; not that it is somehow permissible, when this turns out to be more difficult than expected, to give up. This sentiment should not be an unfamiliar one to any anarchist. The emphasis on reflexive self-criticism, I noted earlier, is one of the core commitments of 'critical theory', but it is also definitive of anarchism's resistance to definition. To return to the statement from Goldman from which we started out: 'Anarchism urges man to *think*, to *investigate*, to analyze *every* proposition.'[63]

* * *

Perhaps even more so than with Marxism and socialism, there are historically close connections between anarchist ideas and feminism. With some exceptions – in particular, Proudhon[64] – the anarchist tradition has been

---

[63] Goldman (1969, p. 51; emphasis added).

[64] Nochlin (2007, p. 220, fn. 34) observes that, alongside his early articulations of anarchism, Proudhon also wrote 'the most consistent anti-feminist tract of its time, or perhaps, any other', *La Pornocratie ou les femmes dans les temps modernes*, which 'raises all the main issues about woman's position in society and her sexuality with a paranoid intensity unmatched in any other text'. On the other hand, Proudhon's contemporary Joseph Déjacque apparently recognised the inconsistency of patriarchy with anarchist principles, and called on Proudhon to either 'speak out

committed to the ideal of equality between the sexes.[65] Emma Goldman, sometimes regarded as the founder of anarcha-feminism, identified patriarchy as one of the major structures to be opposed by anarchists (along with the state, religion and property), advocated women's education about contraception, and was one of a handful of feminists of the late nineteenth and early twentieth centuries to speak out in favour of 'free love' – an idea often assumed to be distinctive of 'second-wave' feminism. Goldman wrote, in 1897:

> I demand the independence of woman, her right to support herself; to live for herself; to love whomever she pleases, or as many as she pleases. I demand freedom for both sexes, freedom of action, freedom in love and freedom in motherhood.[66]

Alongside the theoretical commitment of many anarchists to feminist principles, the early twentieth century has seen striking examples of the fusion of anarchist and feminist ideas in practice. The *mujeres libres* ('free women') – although they did not describe themselves as 'feminist' (on grounds of the term's 'bourgeois' connotations) – were a formidable presence during the Spanish Civil War, committed equally to anarcho-syndicalism and to the empowerment (*capacitación*) of women.[67]

Beyond the fact that anarchists have been feminists (and that many of them have also been women), though, what does anarchism have to do with feminism? Whilst Marxism and feminism are regarded by some as going hand-in-hand,[68] and by others as in essential tension,[69] my sense is that – today at least – anarchism and feminism are most often regarded as unconnected. The moniker 'anarchist-feminist' is thus looked on as a mildly comical curiosity, an inventive (even perverse) amalgamation of 'right-on' affiliations.

It is pretty clear, however, that the alliance of anarchism and feminism is *not* simply an aggregation of two unrelated commitments – and anarchist

---

against man's exploitation of woman' or 'do not describe yourself as an anarchist' (see Cohn 2009).

[65] See e.g. Bakunin, in his 1866 'Revolutionary catechism': 'Equal political, social, and economic rights, as well as equal obligations for women' (Bakunin 1971, p. 93).

[66] Goldman (1897).   [67] See Ackelsberg (2005).

[68] And not just by Marxist feminists: in my own experience, many liberals and those to the right of liberalism assume that a woman who is 'on the left' will inevitably be a feminist too.

[69] Mainly by non-Marxist feminists, including some categorised (by themselves or by others) as 'radical feminists'.

feminists themselves have certainly not seen it that way. Anarchists have often taken feminist ideals to be *already implicit in* anarchist ones. More clearly than with Marxism and socialism – commitments which are often initially stated in terms of class, ownership of the means of production, or material equality (not, by themselves, enough to satisfy all the concerns of feminists) – anarchism is based on an explicit commitment to human *freedom*: on the assumption that women are human, anarchism is interested in their freedom as much as anybody's. As Goldman emphasises: 'all human-beings, irrespective of race, colour, or sex, are born with the equal right to share at the table of life'.[70]

It seems that the *generality or open-endedness* of anarchism – more often looked upon as culpable vagueness – is its strength here. Unlike Marxism (at least on some readings of the latter), anarchism is not first and foremost a theory of how society is structured and develops – or at least, it is not a theory which gives primacy to any particular element of social life (such as class) in its depiction of societal development. Rather than 'class' or 'the commodity', the fundamental phenomenon for many anarchists is something extremely general: the relationship and interplay between the *individual* and the *collective* in social life. Goldman makes this explicit:

> A thorough perusal of the history of human development will disclose two elements in bitter conflict with each other; elements that are only now beginning to be understood, not as foreign to each other, but as closely related and truly harmonious, if only placed in proper environment: the individual and social instincts. The individual and society have waged a relentless and bloody battle for ages, each striving for supremacy, because each was blind to the value and importance of the other.[71]

Whilst we might designate this, i.e. the idea of a profound but soluble tension between individual and collective, as the 'descriptive core'[72] of anarchism – much as anarchists like Goldman would probably hate this formulation – the 'normative' core is clearly the central commitment to *freedom* (and the corresponding opposition to domination), which is seen as capturing something vital for the flourishing of human beings. Recall Goldman's statement,

[70] Goldman (2003, vol. 2, p. 450).   [71] Goldman (1969, p. 51).
[72] See my earlier discussion of the 'descriptive-normative' core of feminism in Chapter 2.

quoted earlier (putting its abundant use of the 'generic' male pronoun aside): 'Only in freedom can man grow to his full stature. Only in freedom will he learn to think and move, and give the very best in him.' As we have seen, this attachment to freedom comes with a (sometimes more visible) *hostility* to whatever is perceived as a threat to such freedom, and it is significant for feminists that this hostility is consistently described by anarchists in terms of a hostility towards *all* forms of domination.[73] Freedom is what anarchism is for; un-freedom or domination is what it is against. There is no specification of the *type* or *source* of domination, of the person or group that imposes or suffers it, and no suggestion that any one form of domination (e.g. *class* domination) is inherently privileged in importance over any other (although there is surely room for the acknowledgement that some forms will be more salient than others at any given historical moment).

It is not just that anarchism has a fluidity and open-endedness, which might lend it affinities with *any* movement against oppression – anti-racism or anti-colonialism, for example. Anarchists have shared a concern, characteristic of 'radical' feminists in particular, with the personal and the everyday,[74] a recognition of oppression and domination within those spheres, and an 'emphasis upon transforming the whole of public and private life'[75] – even if this commonality is often unacknowledged by both sides (as Kornegger puts it, 'feminists have been *unconscious* anarchists in both theory and practice for years').[76] This is Ehrlich's thesis in her 1977 essay, 'Anarchism, socialism, and feminism' (from which I've quoted several times already in the course of this chapter). Ehrlich argues that situationism, in particular, can provide a framework well suited to radical feminists' concerns:

> All radical feminists and all social anarchist feminists are concerned with a set of common issues: control over one's own body; alternatives to the nuclear family and to heterosexuality; new methods of child care that will liberate parents and children; economic self-determination; ending sex stereotyping in education, in the media, and in the workplace; the abolition of repressive

[73] See, once again, Ehrlich (1977, p. 17).

[74] By the same stroke, it might be argued that there are important affinities between anarchism and 'progressive' philosophies of childhood and education, since children, like women, mainly inhabit what has traditionally been called the 'private sphere'.

[75] Ehrlich (1977, p. 12).   [76] Kornegger (1975, p. 13; emphasis added).

laws; an end to male authority, ownership, and control over women; providing women with the means to develop skills and positive self-attitudes; an end to oppressive emotional relationships; and what the Situationists have called 'the reinvention of everyday life'.[77]

In the remainder of this chapter, I'll use Ehrlich's argument to explore the relationship between anarchism, feminism, and socialism. We have already seen some of the reasons for seeing affinities between anarchism and feminism. But what about the relationship between each of these – or the synthesis of the two implied in the position of 'anarchist feminism' – and socialism? Is there a war? If so, who are the adversaries?

The interesting thing about Ehrlich's thesis, as we'll see, is that she is saying *both* that there is a war *and* that there isn't. On the one hand, all paths lead to the same 'social anarchist' (and feminist) destination: there is a sense, then, in which anarchists, socialists and feminists only need to make themselves aware of the fundamental agreement that already exists between them. But Ehrlich's message is not the (either naïve or sinister) 'can't-we-all-get-along' line, discussed earlier:[78] there is an equally important sense in which the disagreements are all too real. Her point is that the usual division into rival camps or 'isms' does not reflect deep-seated and intractable disagreements between the philosophies of anarchism, feminism and socialism, but owes instead to their adherents' failure to be faithful to what they claim are their own core principles.

* * *

Given the affinities between anarchism and feminism, it is no surprise to find that the criticisms which anarchists have made against some forms of socialism – in particular, Marxism – echo some of the main criticisms made by radical feminists. Above all, anarchists have argued that 'authoritarian socialism' – a term sometimes used to pick out the *forms* of socialism that are being opposed without tarring the whole of socialism with the same brush – re-enacts and entrenches forms of domination, exploitation and oppression which the overthrow of capitalism should aim to eliminate. Because of this, it is also argued, authoritarian socialism is doomed to failure, relative to its own ultimate objectives – such as the goal of realising a classless society.

---

[77] Ehrlich (1977, p. 7).   [78] See Chapter 6 above.

It is important to note that this disagreement overwhelmingly manifests itself as a difference within what I've called 'dynamic' theory: anarchists and Marxists both state a commitment to a future society that is both classless and stateless; but whilst Marx famously holds that the state will 'wither away' at some point after its seizure by the proletariat, anarchists regard this as hopelessly naïve, and argue that new power elites will emerge and that those who have found themselves in control of the state will cling on to it at any cost.[79] It is, sometimes, much easier to agree on distant visions than on immediate courses of action. Thus, the disagreements between anarchists and socialists often belong to a kind I described in Chapter 6: invisible or near-invisible at the level of theory, but unmistakable in practice.

Ehrlich is well aware of the tensions between anarchist or radical feminists, on the one hand, and those described as 'socialist feminists', on the other: 'The newer socialist feminists', she observes, 'have been trying in all manner of inventive ways to keep a core of Marxist-Leninist thought, update it, and graft it to contemporary radical feminism. The results are sometimes peculiar.'[80] What Ehrlich suggests is that such attempts produce only a comforting-but-empty rhetoric that obscures a deeper tension: 'an incredible smorgasbord of tasty principles – a menu designed to appeal to practically everyone'.[81] She sees as implicit in feminism – and, more strongly, *radical* feminism – the view that 'non-hierarchical structures are essential to feminist practice', and adds: 'This, of course, is too much for any socialist to take.'[82]

From this, she concludes that feminism is 'far more compatible' with a certain kind of anarchism than with most kinds of socialism. Whilst '[b]oth [anarchists and radical feminists] work to build alternative institutions, and both take the politics of the personal very seriously', she observes, '[s]ocialist feminists are less inclined to think either is particularly vital to revolutionary practice'.[83] The latter are, of course, quite capable of lip-service – Ehrlich refers to socialist-feminist statements such as, 'We agree that all oppression, whether based on race, class, sex, or lesbianism, is interrelated and the fights for liberation from oppression must be simultaneous and cooperative'[84] (one

---

[79] As Kornegger (1975, p. 4) puts it: 'the means create the ends, . . . a strong State becomes self-perpetuating'.

[80] Ehrlich (1977, p. 5).   [81] Ibid., p. 5.   [82] Ibid., p. 6.

[83] Ibid., p. 7.   [84] Ibid., p. 5.

of the principles agreed by the first national conference of socialist feminism, held in Ohio in 1975). But the suggestion is that the clash between the commitments and priorities of radical or anarchist feminists and self-described 'socialist feminists' always makes itself felt in practice (and perhaps in theory, too, once we look beyond the reassuring slogans).

At the same time, Ehrlich is adamant that anarchism and socialism are *not* in tension. Rather, the 'social anarchism' that she espouses is itself a form of socialism:

> Contrary to popular belief, all social anarchists are socialists. That is, they want to take wealth out of the hands of the few and redistribute it among all members of the community. And they believe that people need to co-operate with each other as a community, instead of living as isolated individuals.[85]

Here, Ehrlich's line is in keeping with the anarchist tradition in general. Just as Tolstoy regarded pacifism as the logical conclusion of anarchist principles (whether anarchists realised it or not), so anarchists have consistently claimed that their position is not only *a* form of socialism, but that it is the 'truest' form – the one which most faithfully and correctly draws out the consequences of central socialist principles. As John Most and Emma Goldman once argued, the 'system of communism logically excludes any and every relation between master and servant, and means really Anarchism'.[86] In a similar vein, Malatesta and Hamon, reacting to the expulsion of anarchists from the Second International, reflected:

> It could be argued with much more reason that we are the most logical and most complete socialists, since we demand for every person not just his entire measure of the wealth of society but also his portion of social power, which is to say, the real ability to make his influence felt, along with that of everybody else, in the administration of public affairs.[87]

Summing up these sentiments, Rudolf Rocker famously declared: 'Socialism will be free, or it will not be at all.'[88]

If socialism implies anarchism, the implication is also held to work the other way around: anarchism implies socialism. (It is worth noting, at this point, that the term 'libertarian' was being used as a self-description for

---

[85] Ibid., p. 7.   [86] Goldman & Most (2008/2009, p. 28).
[87] In Guérin (1997, vol. 2, p. 20).   [88] Rocker (1938, p. 28).

around one hundred years before its appropriation by the American right in the 1970s.)[89] Although anarchism is now often thought of as having more in common with right-wing 'free-market' politics than with socialism – due to a shared hostility to state control – anarchists have traditionally regarded their position as incompatible with the 'propertarian' system of power and domination associated with the capitalist mode of production. As the editorial collective of the online 'Anarchist Library' points out:

> It has always struck anarchists as somewhat strange and paradoxical (to say the least) that a system of 'natural' liberty (Adam Smith's term, misappropriated by supporters of capitalism) involves the vast majority having to sell that liberty in order to survive. Thus to be consistently libertarian is, logically, to advocate self-management, and so socialism.[90]

And, developing this connection:

> To be a true libertarian requires you to support workers' control otherwise you support authoritarian social relationships. To support workers' control, by necessity, means that you must ensure that the producers own (and so control) the means of producing and distributing the goods they create. Without ownership, they cannot truly control their own activity or the product of their labour. The situation where workers possess the means of producing and distributing goods is socialism. Thus to be a true libertarian requires you to be a socialist.[91]

Summing up both directions of implication, Bakunin states: 'we are convinced that liberty without socialism is privilege, injustice; and that socialism without liberty is slavery and brutality'.[92]

So what is going on here? On the one hand, we hear that there are profound tensions between anarchism and socialism (and between feminism and socialism): Ehrlich tells us that anarchism and feminism are much more compatible with one another than either is with socialism (although even the anarchism-and-feminism pair may sometimes need a little help recognising

---

[89] 'In fact, anarchists have been using it as a synonym for anarchist for over 150 years, since 1858. In comparison, widespread use of the term by the so-called "libertarian" right dates from the 1970s in America (with, from the 1940s onwards, limited use by a few individuals)' (Anarchist Editorial Collective 2009, p. 15).

[90] Anarchist Editorial Collective (2009, p. 18).   [91] Ibid., p. 19.

[92] Dolgoff (1974, p. 127).

the fundamental agreement that exists between them). On the other hand, we are told that anarchism stands to socialism not as an opponent or rival but as its truest expression.

There's actually no particular mystery about this, I think. In the first place, we can say that what we have here is a war between those who say there is a war and those who say that there isn't. And one thing we have to recognise is that this still counts as a *war*. In many of the cases where this line is most applicable, there will be a deep division – a fundamental clash of interests or perspectives – and also a secondary clash between those who are trying to unmask that division and those who are trying to protect and conceal it (those who are concerned to 'paper over social contradictions', as Marx would have it). But there are also cases where the reverse is true: i.e. there is a fundamental *unity* or agreement, and then a secondary clash between those who assert that unity and those who deny it – and this secondary clash is still a clash, and may have real effects.[93] Even if anarchists are right to say that the most logical conclusion to draw from socialist principles is anarchism, there remains a very real practical conflict between those who say that we must seize the state, through means which mimic its structure, and those who say that we must abolish it, through means which more closely resemble the sort of society we would like to bring about.[94]

* * *

By this point, it may strike readers as though this has been the chapter in which, after a lengthy build-up, I finally 'come out' as an anarchist. That is not how I see it. Although I am, as it happens, beginning to think that this is the position which most closely corresponds to my own way of thinking about politics, my point has not been to try to vindicate or make the case for anarchist feminism. The most I hope to have done here is to have given some

---

[93] It is worth noting that Marx believes in the importance of this second case as much as in the first: since he holds that *everyone*, not only the proletariat, would fundamentally be better off in a classless society than in one riven by class divisions and an alienation that affects all classes, he must be seen as trying to counter the dominant denial of this correspondence of interests as well as dominant denials of the points at which interests diverge.

[94] For that matter, there also remains a real conflict between those who theorise and act in the light of the unity of anarchist and feminist principles, and those (sometimes termed 'manarchists') who carry on as though it were possible to be an anarchist whilst trampling over women.

sense of what anarchism and anarchist feminism have meant to their proponents, and why the usual grounds on which they are dismissed are highly
dodgy: above all, I have tried to emphasise some of the things anarchism is *not*.
Anarchism does not simply romanticise chaos. It does not oppose structure
or organisation outright. It is not merely destructive, and what it proposes is
not so obviously impractical as is almost universally assumed – partly this is
because 'practicality' is not a straightforward or politically neutral concept;
but it is also because, although individual anarchists may make plenty of concrete political proposals, it would be a 'category error' to identify anarchism
with any particular one or set of these.

The most important point to come out of this discussion, I think, is a point
about the significance of the taxonomy between anarchism, socialism and
feminism: that we should abandon the habit of thinking of these as if they
were rival teams or products, and as if we were faced with a choice as to which
one to support or buy. Instead, 'anarchism', 'socialism' and 'feminism' emerge
as rough-and-ready labels for different habits of thought, priorities and ways
of looking at the world. Throughout this book, I've tried to show what is
right and important in certain habits of thought and perception associated
with feminism, Marxism and critical theory. In this chapter, I've tried to do
the same for the insights and habits associated with the label 'anarchism':
a distrust of hierarchy and domination, wherever it might appear; a corre-
spondingly broad conception of the 'political'; a fluidity and open-endedness
as to political vision; and a commitment to universal interrogation, including
(equally) the relentless interrogation *of ourselves*.

I want to end this chapter, however, by returning to the point from which
we began: the anarchist discomfort with labels and definitions. In politics,
labels swarm around us like flies. Part of the reason for my being so cagy
about the affiliation 'anarchist' (or any other, for that matter)[95] comes from
the fact that many people simply cannot rest until they have selected and
attached a label to any political position or proposal they come across. One of
the many disadvantages of the fetish for labels is that the latter often serve
to obscure the very content that they are supposed to represent. Labels such
as 'anarchist', 'feminist' and 'socialist' – as we've seen – are continually used

---

[95] I make an exception for 'feminist', much as I would make an exception for 'anti-
racist' or 'anti-fascist', and perhaps 'anti-capitalist'. Maybe the problem is with *positive* labels, then, rather than labels per se.

with either an inadequate or a positively inaccurate sense of what they mean. It is much more rare to come across cases where people feel able, confident and permitted to *explain* themselves and what they actually think, without recourse to labels.

For that reason, it seems apt to end with some exemplary words from an article by Angela Davis, in which she does not label herself (or 'the tradition of feminism with which I have always identified'), but instead states what that tradition *does*: it 'emphasizes not only strategies of criticism and strategies of transformation but also a sustained critique of the tools we use to stage criticism and to enact transformation'.[96]

[96] Davis (2008, p. 20).

11 Not in our name: colonialism, capitalism and the co-option of feminism

In the chapters so far, I've had more to say about now-unfashionable political and philosophical traditions, and about movements (such as anarcho-syndicalism) which might now appear to be dead or dormant, than about the situation of feminists in the twenty-first century. The decision to focus on these things was deliberate, since my view is that we have much more to learn from anarchist and socialist ideas and practice or even from Suffragette militancy than we do from anything that contemporary liberal political philosophy has to offer – and yet these themes are almost entirely absent from mainstream introductions to feminist thought. In this last main chapter, however, I want to turn to consider the current state of things, what feminism means today, and some of the main obstacles it faces. Obviously, what is up-to-date very quickly becomes *out*-of-date, but my aim here is to look at some contemporary themes with the aid of concepts that are of more enduring significance. In fact, although my examples are current, the main phenomenon under consideration here is far from new. This is the phenomenon of 'co-option'. To ask about the co-option of feminism, as we'll see, is to ask about the ways in which feminist theory and practice is absorbed, hijacked, twisted and betrayed by the world it seeks to change.

* * *

The first thing to say about the question of 'where feminism stands now' is that, yes, it *is* still relevant – for the reasons I listed at the close of Chapter 2, and more: it is still a response to something real, i.e. the fact of patriarchy. But of course patriarchy takes vastly different forms across different times and across cultures. The sort of patriarchy feminists are confronting now is obviously not the same as that confronted by feminists in the eighteenth and nineteenth centuries, for example – and it is not adequate to express this just by saying that things are *less bad* than they used to be ('we've come a long way...'). It is certainly true that formal legal inequalities between men and women have dramatically diminished, in some cases as a result of feminist struggle. One of the most recent instances of this, widely celebrated as a triumph for 'feminism', is the decision to allow women to fight alongside men in the 'front line' (a rather misleading term, given the realities of modern warfare) in the US Armed Forces. In some ways, it is also true that sexist or misogynistic attitudes have had to become more subtle, at least in 'enlightened' social circles: it's generally not 'OK' to say publicly that women are less intelligent than men – although the frequency with which it is still said (or implied) is striking, as is the relative lack of repercussions.[1]

But in many cases, it is not obvious that forms of patriarchy have got better rather than merely more subtle – and it's not even obvious that they have got more *subtle* in every respect. For instance, the treatment and construction of women as sex objects, as objects to be bought and sold, and as consumers of endless products regarded as necessary in order to make them 'beautiful', has arguably intensified over the last decades. Any adequate understanding of the development of patriarchy, I suggest, will see this as a simultaneous process of 'getting better' *and* 'getting worse', increasingly subtle *and also* increasingly crude. How do feminists fight this enemy, which is sometimes so hard even to see?

Obviously enough, it would be foolish to try to give even an overview of an area as vast as twenty-first-century feminism. We also have to be careful not to confuse the reality of any 'time-slice' of the feminist movement with its facing surface. That was one problem feminists have had with the 'waves' picture of their history: it identifies periods of feminist activity with periods in which feminist activity briefly became eye-catching, fashionable or notorious, ignoring the steady and tireless work which is always going on beneath the surface.[2] bell hooks, for example, frequently draws attention to the disconnect

---

[1] Of course, we only know about the cases where there *have* been (some) repercussions. The other incidents are often too ambiguous or simply too ordinary to be of public interest, but that doesn't mean they don't happen (see, for example, the blog 'What is it like to be a woman in philosophy?' https://beingawomaninphilosophy.wordpress.com/). Even in high-profile cases, it has been rare for those who make these comments to suffer much as a result, e.g. in terms of their careers. It is also noticeable that cases of such sexist remarks are often seen as much less sinister than comparable comments made about race – but even in the latter case, it's amazing how people seem to bounce back (as historian David Starkey appears to have done, for example, after his racist tirade on the BBC's *Newsnight*).

[2] Cott (1987).

between the feminist movement that she as a young woman knew 'from the inside', and the (elite, white, academic) feminism that was the movement's sole representation in the mainstream media.[3]

Today, too, there may be a world of difference between the feminism that exists and the feminism that is visible to large numbers of people, or between feminism and what *calls itself* 'feminism'. Plenty of people who recognise the oppression of women and the need to end it would be unwilling to describe themselves as 'feminists'. Plenty of people who describe themselves as 'feminists' properly recognise neither.

The surface appearance or 'public face' of feminism is still an object of interest, however, and is far easier to sketch than the richer and more diverse reality that it may serve to mask.

Actually, it's not *all that* easy. The public face of feminism is patchy, fickle and changeable in its expressions – which is, after all, to be expected in a capitalist, mass-media society characterised by a cult of novelty and by incessant and restless competition for the attention of consumers. Feminism continually blinks in and out of the public consciousness. We are told, one minute, that feminism is dead; then that it is reborn; then that it is alive and kicking – usually in some glamorous but relatively unthreatening guise – then that it is dead again.[4] Since we all know about the first and second waves, it stands to reason that there must by now be a third one, and so commentators have raced each other to catch it and to note its defining features. Tiring of this, some now even claim to have spotted a fourth or fifth wave.[5]

Unfortunately, however, it seems that nobody really has any clear idea what the 'third wave' of feminism is (let alone the 'fourth wave').[6] Some identify the 'third wave' as 'post-feminism', the view that women are liberated now (and just need to adjust to their new freedoms and learn to enjoy them

---

[3] hooks (2000b).

[4] There are far too many examples in the mainstream media to mention here. Feminist academic philosophy, by contrast, has struck a more consistently self-congratulatory tone in its self-assessments over the past few years.

[5] In fact, the idea of a 'fourth wave' goes back at least to 2009, to a *New York Times* interview with Jessica Valenti (and probably, sporadic mentions go back much further than that) – see Solomon (2009). But the term did not really catch on – even Valenti had the sense to distance herself from it – and there is some hope that the new wave of 'fourth wave' talk will not be permanent either.

[6] I am grateful to Katharine Jenkins for pointing this out to me – that is, for letting me know that I was not alone in my utter confusion.

like men) – in which case, it is not a wave *of feminism* at all.[7] Others have associated it with what Ariel Levy has termed 'raunch culture': the embrace of a highly sexualised, 'daring' lifestyle of unrestrained consumption.[8] In fact, the attachment to raunch culture as a source or instance of liberation may also be seen as a branch of 'post-feminism': the idea, quite often, is that men and women are now equal, and all that remains is for women to cast away their inhibitions and join in with men in activities such as frequenting strip clubs and, of course, heavy drinking – activities which were previously supposed to be male monopolies. A third interpretation of the 'third wave' associates it with the quest to get more women in 'high places' (such as the boardrooms of corporations). Like the 'raunch culture' variant, this doesn't have to indicate an attitude of (pure) 'post-feminism': proponents may agree that we still 'have a long way to go', but regard lap-dancing (or, as the case may be, executive power) as the route to a more complete liberation. Perhaps yet another interpretation is bound up with the philosophy of 'having it all', or the cult of the 'superwoman': we are told that as modern women, we either do or should aspire to a holy trinity of sexiness, high-powered career success and motherhood. A fifth, more sympathetic use of the term 'third wave' – especially prominent in the US – equates this with a feminism that is more inclusive of queer identities and more accommodating of 'intersectional' perspectives, as well as of certain groups (such as sex workers) which have found themselves alienated by the traditional feminist tendency to problematize their activities and occupations.[9]

As for what the 'fourth wave' is, that is even less clear. But as far as I can tell, it refers to a kind of upbeat campaigning to improve the public image of women: to resist the cruder forms of objectification, whilst finding ways to 'celebrate' women – and, especially, 'great' women. This 'wave', in fact, seemed for a time to be more or less identical with an episode in 2013, where a small group of women campaigned against the planned replacement of the only woman (other than the Queen) to appear on the UK's paper currency, Elizabeth Fry, with former prime minister and symbol-of-bullish-Britishness

---

[7] See Chapter 2 above.

[8] Levy (2005). I suppose 'raunch culture' is actually fundamentally ambiguous between acting 'like a lad' – including joining in the objectification of women – and acting 'like a porn star'.

[9] See my discussion in Chapter 8 above.

Winston Churchill; in response, the Bank of England agreed that the face of Jane Austen would appear on the new British £10 note. What was most interesting about this episode, for those of us who could not care less either about Jane Austen or about the way in which the current incarnation of capitalist patriarchy chooses to design its currency,[10] is that this was a case of a huge backlash without very much 'lash'. It really is hard to think of a more modest proposal – which is probably why the Bank of England capitulated a 'mere' two years into the struggle. And yet the reaction was vicious, prompting a public debate over the problem of 'trolling' on internet media such as Facebook and Twitter: one of the campaign's organisers, Caroline Criado-Perez, was subjected to rape and death threats, as were several of the high-profile women who stepped in to defend her and to condemn her treatment.[11] This cannot have come as much of a surprise to many women who have any kind of public profile, and who are therefore used to being subjected to various kinds of harassment and threats of sexual violence as a countermove against any hint of criticism of patriarchy (and of sexual objectification especially).[12] It did, however, apparently come as a surprise to some, and sent the media into a short-lived spate of handwringing – which might have been more convincing had it not been coupled in many publications with their routine practice of objectification and misogyny. What the whole episode actually illustrates is an undercurrent of sexual violence that is always present, but which usually takes forms that are slightly subtler and easier to ignore. The campaign over the £10 note – a reformist gesture apparently so tiny as to be barely detectable – brought that undercurrent to the surface in a particularly striking way.

Once again, the talk of 'waves' turns out to mean very little, but the 'feminism' that is most visible in the early twenty-first century seems to fall into three main categories. First, there is the 'Let's get more women into X' variety, where 'X' stands for 'the boardroom', 'Parliament', 'the armed forces', 'the

---

[10] For once, I found myself sympathising with the reaction of a 'comment-is-free'-er: 'I wish I had a £10 note for every time the *Guardian* has printed this story. I wouldn't care what was on them.'

[11] The women included MP Stella Creasy and Cambridge academic Mary Beard.

[12] Note on the fact that this strategy – of meeting attacks on patriarchy with derogatory personal, physical and often sexual comments – is age-old: think of the famous description of Mary Wollstonecraft as a 'hyena in petticoats', or the traditional stereotype of feminists as unattractive and embittered.

police', 'the top earners', or whatever other existing compartment of the Establishment. In terms of the distinction discussed earlier in this book, between 'reformist' and 'revolutionary' feminism, this strand is paradigmatically reformist: it leaves existing institutions and social structures unaltered, calling only for an equal gender balance within those institutions and structures. Second, there are various forms of 'empowerment'[13] – many of which turn out to involve (a) embracing and participating in practices that have traditionally been criticised by feminists at least since the 'second wave', such as pole- and lap-dancing, and (b) buying things. Third, there is the kind of feminism which focuses on the need to rescue brown women from the tyranny of brown men.[14]

In order to make sense of this 'feminism', I suggest, we need to refer to a concept which was once common currency amongst social critics but which, like many things popular in the 1960s and 1970s, has now fallen out of fashion. This is the concept of 'co-option'.[15]

The term 'co-option' (sometimes also referred to as 'co-optation') comes from the Latin *cooptare*, meaning 'to select, or incorporate into (one's group or tribe)', and can now also indicate a more abstract process of taking something over or absorbing it – particularly where the absorbing body is seen as somehow opposed or hostile or at least indifferent to the thing absorbed. It would be slightly odd to speak of a social climber, who has always revered hierarchy, as being 'co-opted' into the middle class. But we *might* speak that way of someone who had previously been proud of their working-class affiliation and critical of class privilege. The process of co-option converts something which stands against or apart from a system *into something which is a functional component of that system*. We might think of it as analogous to the action of an amoeba, engulfing whatever stands in its way, converting it into nourishment – or a white blood cell in a human body, neutralising pathogens which pose a threat to that body's healthy functioning.

The idea of co-option may be thought of as the inverse of another political category, which has been of central importance to Marxists: the notion of

---

[13] As Nina Power observes: 'Books like *Manifesta: Young Women, Feminism and the Future* and *Full-Frontal Feminism* aim to capture the youth feminist market with seemingly endless amounts of 'sass' and breathless confidence-building' (Power 2009, p. 27).

[14] See Abu-Lughod (2002) for a critique of the Western obsession with 'saving' Muslim women.

[15] See, for example, Marcuse (1965, 1968).

'alienation'.[16] Alienation occurs when something which should be a part of me – or should belong to me or be somehow 'with' me – comes to stand *apart* from me, as either indifferent to my interests or actively hostile to them. For Marxists, the most significant form of alienation is the alienation of labour: our work is our creative expression, deeply bound up with our identities; it *should* be a part of us, our own; but under capitalism (and, in different ways, in *any* class society) our labour is sold to another in such a way that it becomes something alien, meaningless, even hostile.[17] For Marx, alienation from labour also means both estrangement from other human beings and a kind of enslavement, self-loss or *dehumanisation*:

> in work [the worker] does not belong to himself but to someone else ... The activity of the worker is not his own spontaneous activity. It belongs to another. It is the loss of his own self ... The result, therefore, is that man (the worker) feels that he is acting freely only in his animal functions – eating, drinking, and procreating, or at most in his shelter and finery – while in his human functions he feels only like an animal. The animalistic becomes the human and the human the animalistic.[18]

Thus Marxists and many anarchists agree that wage labour must be abolished in order to bring about the conditions of freedom that will allow human beings to become truly human. It's worth noting that, although Marx has no interest in attaching the words 'wrong' or 'unjust' to the phenomenon of alienation (and, indeed, is consistently critical of 'moralistic' approaches), it makes some sense to think of the revulsion against alienation as the moral 'core' of Marxism: there is something that class societies do to people which is dehumanising, and capitalist alienation dehumanises in a particularly profound way; it is from this that the human need for revolution arises. It seems beside the point to say that dehumanisation is morally bad or wrong: it is *dehumanising*, and that is enough.[19]

---

[16] See Swain (2012) for a helpful introduction to the notion of alienation and its place in Marxist thought and politics.

[17] 'The *externalization* of the worker in his product means not only that his work becomes an object, an *external* existence, but also that it exists *outside him* independently, alien, an autonomous power, opposed to him. The life he has given to the object confronts him as hostile and alien' (Marx 1967, p. 290).

[18] Marx (1967, p. 292).

[19] For an in-depth discussion of the relationship between Marxism and morality, see Lukes (1987).

What interests me here, though, is the symmetry between the notions of alienation and co-option: to alienate is to take something that is or should be a part of or belong to someone or something, and to make that something alien, indifferent or hostile; to *co-opt* is to take something that stands apart (or wants to or ought to stand apart), separate from or opposed to something else, and *make it a part of that thing*. All political criticism, perhaps, ultimately rests on one or other of these twin notions. Politics – indeed, all of human life, art and action – is at the most basic level about deciding what to put together, and what to take or keep apart. Political philosophy and critique, including feminist critique, is in important measure about pulling apart – if only momentarily – appearance from reality, actuality from possibility, ideology from what it simultaneously conceals and holds in place. It is about identifying points in both social forms *and forms of thought* where things are put together, or kept apart, when to do so is in some way inappropriate, inauthentic or artificial.[20]

The importance of the more specific phenomenon of co-option in politics is clear. Whilst we may disagree about what does and does not count as an instance of it, we can all recognise the existence of a syndrome whereby what starts out as opposition or dissent ceases to be this, apparently through gaining a kind of status or acceptance that might easily be mistaken for success. We use the related term 'tokenism' to describe cases where a small number of a minority, oppressed or disadvantaged group are admitted into institutions or positions of privilege. By co-opting a few black people into an overwhelmingly white political class, for example, the system of white supremacy can partially defuse the threat posed to it by black anger. A black president in the White House can act as a decoy, helping to project a false impression of racial equality whilst distracting from the reality of an America in which a young black man is more likely to be in jail than in university. The same phenomenon occurs in the case of gender, with the allocation of a few women to positions of highly visible power or status within institutions which remain male-dominated in their composition and patriarchal

---

[20] This insight informs Angela Davis's view of 'feminist methodologies' as 'methods of thought and action that urge us to think things together that appear to be entirely separate and to disaggregate things that seem to naturally belong together' (Davis 2008, p. 22).

in both their internal structures and external effects.[21] As Zillah Eisenstein argues:

> US Secretary of State Condoleezza Rice wields power, but not as a woman – whatever this might really mean today – and not for women and their rights – but for an imperial democracy that destroys women's equality and racial justice. Imperial democracy uses racial diversity and gender fluidity to disguise itself – and females and people of color become its decoys. Condi's black skin and female body operate to cloud and obfuscate.[22]

Tokenism is one form of co-option, an instance of a broader strategy of neutralising threats *by absorbing them*, of exploiting opposition, of extracting value from those whose interests are otherwise a matter of indifference.

It's crucial to look at this phenomenon in connection with the notion of ideology that has been our touchstone throughout this book. Not only can the co-option of flesh-and-blood individuals into certain institutions be a way of creating and fostering forms of false consciousness, but practices, ideas, forms of thought and language may also be co-opted – and this process may be seen not just as a cause but also as a key *instance* of the ideological distortion of thought.

The remainder of this final chapter outlines some of the main ways in which this happens in the case of contemporary feminism.

* * *

What does it mean for a body of thought and practice like feminism to be co-opted? What does this look like?

What it means is for feminism – its name, or the ideas and practices associated with it – to be pressed into the service of something which stands to a *true* feminist consciousness and deportment in a relationship of (mutual) indifference or active hostility. We have *seen* what it looks like, in this book

---

[21] It's useful to understand this notion and phenomenon of co-option in connection with the notion and phenomenon of *reformism*, discussed at several points in this book. The objection that some have had against what they see as 'reformism', recall, was that it is a way of allowing the status quo to concede little or nothing in the way of fundamental structural change – where the structures in question may oppress and embody violence against women (or non-whites) – whilst shoring up those oppressive structures against the pressure of criticism and opposition. Co-option, then, is an important way of doing the same thing.

[22] Eisenstein (2008, p. 27).

as well as out of it. I've emphasised throughout that the way feminist ideas are treated and presented, and feminism's history interpreted, has a political dimension – that there are often features of this treatment which embody a bias towards the status quo which all feminists, to a smaller or larger extent, seek to overturn. When this phenomenon takes a sufficiently *positive* form – in a sense I'm about to explain – we may call it 'co-option'. I mean, when it is not just a matter of feminism being interpreted in a way that narrows the scope of critique, blunts its force or makes it appear absurd and hence easy to dismiss, but a matter of feminist ideas being more positively turned to the *advantage* of elements within the status quo which seem either to have nothing to do with women and feminism, or to represent interests actively opposed to ours: feminism is put to use.

Since there are multiple power structures embodied in the social status quo (white supremacy, capitalism, imperialism, patriarchy) – and in my view, a true feminism must see these as closely intertwined and attack them together – so there are multiple possible forms of the co-option of feminism. Since the power structures in question are so intimately bound up with one another, so too are the forms of co-option I'll mention here: there is no 'pure' capitalist co-option of feminism, for example, since the capitalism in question is capitalist *patriarchy*. With that caveat, it makes sense to discuss this phenomenon of the co-option of feminism under two main headings: there is 'feminism' that kills; and there is 'feminism' that sells – although, as the scare quotes are meant to indicate, neither brand deserves the label.

11.1 A 'feminism' that kills

> Unless the complexities of sex, gender and racial formations are understood for their urgency, females can present a kinder and softer face to militaristic global capitalism. It is more urgent than ever that women's rights, along with their female bodies, are not used to obfuscate the moves toward fascistic democracy. Not in our name. (Zillah Eisenstein)[23]

In January 2013, it was announced that women would for the first time be allowed to be frontline soldiers in the US army. This news was greeted with evident satisfaction in all quarters of the mass media, from the *Guardian* and

---

[23] Eisenstein (2008, p. 44).

Independent in the UK to the *New York Times* and Fox News. Commentators focused on the 'sacrifices' made by women in the armed forces, and on the number of jobs that this move promised to open up to women.[24] Often, there was a clear suggestion that this development was a measure of the progress of feminism. Perhaps most theatrically, Gail Collins's op-ed for the *New York Times* concluded: 'We've come a long, sometimes tragic, heroic way.'[25] The only possible objections that were usually mentioned were (a) that women might lack the necessary strength and stamina (the view of Rick Santorum), (b) that the public might not tolerate it and (c) that women in the military are at high risk of being raped[26] (overwhelmingly, however, it was judged that this should not count against the inclusion of women in combat roles, but rather in favour of more effective management and surveillance).[27] What united virtually every mainstream commentary was the complete absence of any criticism based on concerns about the actual role played by the US military. The assumption was that everyone – certainly, all feminists – should join in celebrating this latest step towards equality.

If any feminist were to object to all this on grounds of an opposition to the recent and ongoing wars waged by the United States, the probable response would be that this is a separate issue: we can argue about whether America is fighting just or unjust wars (or even, conceivably, about whether *any* wars are just); but if an army exists – whatever kind of wars it fights – then, surely, feminists should hold that women should be able to participate in it on equal terms with men. As Eleanor Smeal, president of the liberal National Organization for Women (NOW) famously declared: 'Peace is not a feminist issue.'[28]

The disingenuousness of this line becomes clear as soon as we ask, hypothetically, whether feminists should have welcomed equal opportunities for women to become concentration camp guards – or, to bring it up to date, whether feminists should celebrate the fact that women, too, have exercised the opportunity to torture prisoners at Abu Ghraib. Not that feminists should say that torture is for the boys, not fit work for the delicate hands of women.

---

[24] See the 2013 report by Fox News: 'Military leaders lift ban on women in combat roles' (Fox News 2013). Cf. Harris (2013).

[25] Collins (2013).   [26] See e.g. Dowell (2008).

[27] See e.g. the coverage in *The Independent*, 'About time US military allowed women to fight on the front lines', 24 January 2013, and cf. Collins (2013).

[28] Cited in Elshtain & Tobias (1990, p. xi).

The point is nothing to do with any alleged differences between men and women. It is just that it seems obviously and offensively beside the point to call for equal participation in practices which it has become routine to condemn. Which goes to show what should have been obvious in the first place: that the issues here are *not* separate; that the unabashed enthusiasm with which media and political circles reacted to the extension of combat roles to women depends upon a degree of apologism as regards the function of the US military.

Historically, feminists have been neither consistently pro-war, nor of the view that violence, women and patriarchy were issues that could be kept separate. There have been strong alliances between feminist and anti-war movements, and the opposition to the Vietnam War (for example) was to a large extent organised and participated in by women (although they did not usually occupy the most public or visible roles). Whilst liberal feminists have tended to focus on making sure that women and men participate on an equal basis in existing institutions, including the military, many radical feminists have understood *their* feminism to imply a rejection of the violence wreaked by patriarchal states. After the military draft was reinstituted in 1980, certain elements within NOW insisted that the women's movement commit itself to stopping the draft and opposing the Cold War, precipitating a split between liberals and radicals in the organisation.

A common assumption seems to be that the anti-war strain in feminism was a reflection of the idea that, whilst men are naturally aggressive, women are fundamentally nurturing and gentle. Since we have begun to move on from that now, the thought then goes, we can cheer on the troops without hesitation or conflicted feelings. In a revealing blog post for the right-wing British newspaper *The Telegraph*, Tim Stanley writes:

> It would seem that, in the long run, the liberals won the argument.
> Contemporary political feminism has become more detached from pacifism,
> socialism or any other Left-wing movement that seeks to overhaul society as
> well as gender relations. It is far more focused on narrow single-issue policy
> goals: abortion, contraception, hiring, equal pay. And the concept of
> 'difference' – that women bring a unique perspective to policy that's more
> peaceful and compassionate – is something of an anathema. The idea that
> putting women on to the General Staff might make war obsolete nowadays
> reads like chauvinist stereotyping. Likewise, the campaign to have more
> women in the boardroom isn't predicated on the hope that they will make

their companies operate more fairly and honestly. The single, overriding concern is simply that women will have the freedom to make as much money as men. And who would deny them that? Similarly, the modern model of a political woman is Hillary Clinton: tough, brilliant and committed to pursuing a military policy that an older generation of feminists would have regarded as the product of a chauvinist and unequal society. The suffragists would regard the drone strikes with horror.[29]

How far we've come. Stanley's article is of interest for its poisonous blend of truth and falsity. In descriptive terms, he may be right about the direction that contemporary feminism has taken – at least in its most visible, mainstream manifestations. It is also true that some strands within feminism have suggested that women might contribute a different perspective and set of qualities to public life, if allowed to participate in it more fully, and even that their fuller participation might produce a shift away from violence and towards dialogue and diplomacy. But it is not necessary to assume that the differences between women and men are fixed or 'natural' in order to hold to this point: all you have to think is that women and men under patriarchy have importantly different experiences, and develop importantly different points of view, vices and virtues, as a result of those experiences, and that it is a mistake to identify the male-under-patriarchy with the human.[30] If you think that, then this suggests that including women in roles and areas of society where they traditionally have *not* been included is one of the things that is necessary in order to bring about a better and more truly human world. It does not have to suggest, however, that posting women – even substantial numbers of them – in such roles is *sufficient* to bring about the kind of change feminists and other radical social critics want to see.

The most compelling forms of feminism have been clear that we have to fundamentally change existing social structures, and that this cannot be done by a 'just add women' approach which simply inserts more women

[29] See Stanley (2013).

[30] It is worth noting here that Carol Gilligan's position, associated with her hugely influential book *In a Different Voice* (1982), is widely interpreted as an essentialist view of sex/gender differences, which reinforces the stereotype that women are soft and empathetic whilst men are calculating and rule-based in their thinking (an interpretation which, in my view, is mistaken – see the interview with Gilligan by MAKERS at www.makers.com/carol-gilligan; accessed 04/03/2015).

into those structures.[31] It is true that feminists have sometimes fallen into this trap – although, contrary to what Stanley suggests, these feminists have arguably been more likely to be the liberals than the radicals (or socialists or anarchists, for that matter). As Stanley himself observes, the (largely liberal) suffrage movement of the nineteenth and early twentieth centuries 'argued that if women got the vote then war would become less likely because they would rarely vote for politicians who wanted it. Not only would women not have to fight on the front line, but neither would men.'[32] This, as it stands, is a pretty damn naïve suggestion – as post-suffrage history has abundantly confirmed.[33] But feminism has always been diverse, and there were always those who recognised the limitations of the narrow focus on the suffrage as the solution to all of the problems facing women and the world, just as there are now plenty of feminists who reject the 'boardroom approach'[34] that has become so visible in recent years. Emma Goldman, in her 1910 essay 'Woman suffrage', warned of the dangers of the 'fetish' of universal suffrage, and of the illusion that extending the vote to women would make any significant difference to politics while the system of parliamentary democracy remained in place.[35] Woman, Goldman argued, 'can give suffrage

[31] Even if we were to assume an old-fashioned essentialist view of men's and women's characteristic virtues and vices, this 'just add women' view of social change wouldn't follow, since there will still presumably be plenty of women who deviate from the feminine norm – easily enough to fill the limited number of spaces in positions of power at the tops of existing governments and of corporations – and it makes sense to expect a traditionally patriarchal and male-dominated system to attract these 'manly' women to a disproportionate extent.

[32] Stanley (2013). Stanley continues: 'In 1915, 3,000 women gathered in Washington DC to discuss "a practical solution of a means to end war." To quote the *Washington Post*: "Prepared after lengthy deliberation by a committee headed by Mrs Carrie Chapman Catt, president of the International Alliance for Suffrage, . . . this program sets forth in its preamble that, as women with 'a peculiar moral passion of revolt against both the cruelty and the waste of war, and as custodians of life of the ages,' they have preeminently the right to protest its ravages and spoils."'

[33] We should also bear in mind that these arguments were made in the context of an ongoing campaign, a context in which it may have seemed appropriate to employ a scattergun approach, finding as many reasons in favour of votes for women as might conceivably be found persuasive by somebody.

[34] Mary Buffett (2013), writing in the online *Huffington Post*, uses the term 'a boardroom approach to feminism' to describe (approvingly) the contribution of entrepreneur Sheryl Sandberg, multi-millionaire and author of the best-selling 2013 book *Lean in: women, work and the will to lead*.

[35] Goldman (1969).

or the ballot no new quality, nor can she receive anything from it that will enhance her own quality'.[36]

We are not justified in equating feminist critiques of war with their most naïve expressions. Crude essentialism is hardly the only possible reason for being an anti-war feminist. For example, contemporary feminists frequently point to the disproportionately destructive impact that war has upon women. They have pointed out that, contrary to the common association of war with male sacrifice – above all, the 'heroic' self-sacrifice of young male soldiers – most of the victims of modern wars are civilians, and most of them are women and children.[37] They have analysed the role of rape in war and colonialism.[38] They have opposed war as a major form of (predominantly male) violence. In recent years, however, these voices have tended to be drowned out by louder ones (i.e. better-amplified ones), which have cheered on the wars waged by the US and its allies – and all in the name of 'feminism'. It is no surprise if these voices have been louder, since the 'feminism' in whose name they speak is one which aligns itself with the interests of the powerful (mostly, powerful white men). These voices are heard not only when they are raised in applause at the inclusion of more women in the military. Still more often, they are heard – whether in jubilant or apologetic tones – speaking in justification of military action itself, and specifically of the wars of invasion waged by 'liberal' states in other parts of the world (the US–UK presence in Afghanistan being the most obvious example. Introducing a recent collection on feminism and war, Robin Riley, Chandra Mohanty and Minnie Bruce Pratt note the prevalence of these two themes, and the expectations they create: 'Feminism, it is popularly assumed, supports women in the military and supports the cause of going to war to ensure women's rights in countries where these rights may be restricted.'[39]

---

[36] Ibid., pp. 210–11.

[37] Sivard (1996) estimates that in the twentieth century, 90 per cent of war casualties were civilians, mostly women and children. Similarly, Nadar (2002) claims that 80 per cent of all casualties of contemporary wars are women and children. And as Chew (2008, p. 75) observes: 'Women are disproportionately affected by the economic harms of war, as well. Globally, women make up 70 percent of those starving or on the verge of starvation. Imperialism helps intensify the gender gap in poverty, a situation reflected in indicators from health to literacy.'

[38] Eisenstein (2008, pp. 37–9); see Harding (2004) and Shumway (2004) on the incidence of rape by US and US-trained agents after the 2003 invasion of Iraq.

[39] Riley, Mohanty & Pratt (2008).

What some have dubbed 'colonial feminism'[40] argues that invasions of countries such as Afghanistan and Iraq by Western powers are justified by the overriding good of liberating the women of those countries from a patriarchal oppression which has come to be symbolised by The Burka.[41] In fact, it is rather misleading to think of this as a strand of feminism at all – although there are certainly some self-described 'feminists' who argue along these lines. My point here is not just that 'colonial feminism' is not feminism – although that is true, too, for reasons that have already been raised and will be developed further in a moment. The additional point is that it is not obviously the case that a large section of feminists – i.e. of those with a prior conception of themselves as 'feminist', and a history of theoretical and practical commitment to what they see as the advancement of feminist objectives – have been prepared to be cheerleaders for US wars of occupation. Certainly, there have been some who fit this description. But what is more salient is a process which has effectively created a category of 'feminism' that did not exist before – a process of the co-option of feminism, which, like all such processes, has *changed what feminism is*. 'Colonial feminism' didn't really come from feminism, so much as from colonialism: it represents a much more cynical appropriation of feminist rhetoric on the part of those who, apart from its justificatory convenience at certain moments, have shown and continue to show zero interest in the freedom or equality or dignity of women – people like George W. Bush, for example.

And with that, we come to one of the major reasons why 'colonial feminism' is fraudulent. The main perpetrators and advocates of the recent US and UK

---

[40] Chew (2008, p. 82): 'An "imperialist feminist" standpoint . . . is influential in the self-perceptions of many US women today. Such a view professes a concern for global South, non-white women, without acknowledging the role of racism, colonialism, and economic exploitation in shaping their conditions.' Khan (2008) cites Sally Armstrong's book, *Veiled Threat: the hidden power of the women of Afghanistan*, as an example of 'colonial feminism'.

[41] *Burqa* is the term used by Afghan Muslims for just one of the many forms of veil worn by some Muslim women (Muslim women more commonly refer to the *hijab*). Western discourse tends to ignore this diversity, along with the embeddedness of practices of veiling in their social contexts, in favour of a simplifying rhetoric in which The Burka or The Veil figures as a symbol of backwardness and oppression (see Abu-Lughod 2002, pp. 785–8; and see also Scott's 2010 book-length discussion). As Chew (2008, p. 82) notes: 'Burqas and veils have come to embody the ultimate in gendered persecution.' On the other hand, 'Bikinis equal freedom. Sex is emancipation.'

wars have not been allies of women or feminist struggle, whether abroad or in their own countries. As Katharine Viner points out, in a 2002 article for the *Guardian*, the 'feminist' crusade of George W. Bush in Afghanistan was accompanied by domestic policies which have come be known as the Republican 'War on Women':

> On his very first day in the Oval office, Bush cut off funding to any international family-planning organisations which offer abortion services or counselling (likely to cost the lives of thousands of women and children); this year he renamed January 22 – the anniversary of Roe vs. Wade which permitted abortion on demand – as National Sanctity of Human Life Day and compared abortion to terrorism: 'On September 11, we saw clearly that evil exists in this world, and that it does not value life ... Now we are engaged in a fight against evil and tyranny to preserve and protect life.'[42]

As well as opposing or ignoring current feminist struggles (and reversing the achievements of past ones) at home, pro-war forces in American politics – as also in other Western countries – have been markedly less interested in the plight of oppressed women in countries where (and when) invasion is not so ... *convenient*. The US was not so concerned about the oppression of women in the Arab world when, during the Cold War, it was arming and training theocratic and fundamentalist forces in that region. It was not so concerned about Iraqi women (or men, for that matter) when it was supporting the violently repressive regime of Saddam Hussein in the 1980s. And whilst 'feminist' war is waged on Afghanistan to 'liberate' its women, little is said about the comparable (but significantly worse) situation of women in Saudi Arabia, a major US ally. As critics of US foreign policy – including many feminists – have repeatedly observed, the determination of the US and many other Western states to wage the wars that allegedly rescue women from oppression does not track the condition of either women or men in other countries, but has much more to do with maintaining control in regions such as the Middle East, and with using that control to further the interests of wealthy corporations and elites.

There is a possible reply, at this point, which says something like: 'OK, it may be hypocritical, and it may be cynical – "feminist" military intervention is a policy pursued inconsistently and often for the wrong reasons – but if it helps

---

[42] Viner (2002).

women, then we should support it.' It would certainly alter and complicate things if 'colonial feminism' did help women. However, it is pretty clear that it doesn't – even as an accidental by-product of unrelated and independently malevolent projects. This is not to say that there are *no* benefits at all arising from interventions like the invasions of Afghanistan and Iraq, nor that there are never any benefits *to women*. (It would be extraordinary, in fact, for any large-scale political process to have *absolutely no* positive consequences.) But in a pattern of 'causal attributions' which cognitive psychologists have consistently associated with males (including male children),[43] anything good that happens for women is loudly trumpeted by politicians and the media, and attributed to Western intervention, whilst the same media remains silent on the ongoing problems suffered by women after the occupation of their countries, or else attributes those problems to whoever is the current 'enemy' (sometimes regretfully inferring the need for the continued presence of occupying troops or private security forces).[44] Speaking at the 2004 Republican National Convention, First Lady Laura Bush proclaimed triumphantly:

> After years of being treated as virtual prisoners in their own homes by the Taliban, the women of Afghanistan are going back to work . . . the little girls in Afghanistan are now in school. [applause] . . . wasn't it wonderful to watch the Olympics and see that beautiful Afghan sprinter race in long pants and a t-shirt, exercising her new freedom while respecting the traditions of her country![45]

In a similar vein, Condoleezza Rice was reported as commenting, in 2005, that: 'There could be no better story . . . than Afghanistan's democratic

---

[43] See also Kanazawa & Perina (2009) on 'imposter syndrome' in successful women.

[44] For example, Khan (2008, p. 161) comments on the role of the Canadian media in drumming up support for the continued presence of Canadian troops in Afghanistan, after their deployment in 2002: 'Support for military involvement in the region has also been sustained by a continuous recurrence of visual and textual representations of Afghan women which sensationalize their plight under the Taliban and reiterate that their situation has improved under the current regime. *Such comments also suggest that withdrawal of NATO troops will result in women going back to their harsh lives under the Taliban regime.* While they do contain some truth, these comments do not present the whole story. They do, however, endorse the neocolonial military intervention in Afghanistan and they fuel a desire to rescue Afghan women – or colonial feminism' (emphasis added).

[45] Cited in Chew (2008, p. 81).

development.'[46] Feminist scholars add to the picture some of the 'details' that Bush and Rice do not mention: that although the equality of men and women is now enshrined in the Afghan constitution, poverty still forces many families to sell female children as brides, some as young as seven or nine years old,[47] and that the Karzai government installed by the US upholds a law passed in the mid 1970s which forbids these 'married women' from attending school;[48] or that the Karzai government 'has attempted to resurrect the infamous Department for the Promotion of Virtue and the Prevention of Vice', a department set up by the Taliban and 'known to enforce bans – against, for example, wearing nail polish, laughing out loud, wearing white shoes and going out without being accompanied by a close male relative';[49] that whilst 'life has become harder', 'sex work has become easier' since the invasion of Afghanistan in 2001.[50] Despite this, as Shahnaz Khan observes, media coverage of Afghanistan has been drastically reduced since 2004, and what coverage there has been focuses on 'feel-good' messages such as those propagated by George Bush and Condoleezza Rice.[51]

In Iraq, likewise, female literacy plummeted during the era of US sanctions, and rising unemployment after the 2003 invasion disproportionately affected women.[52] As Huibin Amelia Chew observes:

> Economic hardship and oppressive gender relations combine to fuel sexual commodification. Following a pattern observed across different conflict regions by feminist scholars, Iraqi women have faced increasing pressures to earn their subsistence from men by bartering their sexuality. In Baghdad, prostitution became widespread between the fall of the Hussein administration in April 2003 and November 2003, as women disproportionately suffered growing poverty. By 2005, reports surfaced of Iraqi teens working in Syrian brothels, after being displaced from Fallujah, where US forces had launched brutal offences and chemical weapons attacks on civilians.[53]

'Moreover,' Chew continues, 'since at least 2005 the Pentagon has armed, supported, and trained "death squad"-style militias in Iraq, known to use sexual violence and targeted femicide as tactics for consolidating their power.'[54] Against those who see the wars in Afghanistan and Iraq as having liberated

---

[46] Cited in Khan (2008, p. 170).   [47] Cited in ibid.   [48] Ibid., pp. 168–9.
[49] Ibid., p. 169.   [50] Ibid., p. 169.   [51] Cited in ibid., p. 170.   [52] Chew (2008, p. 76).
[53] Ibid., p. 77. Here, Chew cites Phillips (2005).   [54] Ibid., p. 78.

women and contributed to their quality of life, several feminist scholars have documented the disproportionately negative effects which 'Structural Adjustment Programmes' (SAPs), imposed through the IMF on debt-ridden countries like Iraq, have on women.[55] Besides perpetuating poverty (and the misery and un-freedom it inevitably brings), feminists have drawn attention to the tendency for military occupation to further the deprivation of women's control over their own sexuality and bodies. In addition to the increased pressure on women in both Iraq and Afghanistan to enter the sex trade, the 2003 invasion of Iraq led to an increase in backstreet abortions (due to loss of access to healthcare and contraception).[56] Before this, the 340 tons of depleted uranium dropped on Iraq during the first Gulf War are thought to have given rise to a higher rate of birth defects and maternal mortality.[57]

To sum up: (i) those waging wars on 'feminist' pretexts are not always such impassioned feminists at home; (ii) their priorities, and patterns of military and political intervention and non-intervention, are not plausibly demonstrative of a commitment to the liberation of women (as opposed to, e.g., the pursuit of oil); and (iii) those actions do not, in fact, produce the liberation or advancement of women, but tend to punish women disproportionately. There is not, as is so often suggested, a painful liberal dilemma between rolling in with tanks and standing by and doing nothing. Those who are actually interested in the fate of women in other countries could begin by (a) opposing policies by their own countries which kill, maim, impoverish and prostitute those women under the banner of 'liberation', and (b) extending their support and solidarity to indigenous feminist movements in the Middle East (for example) – which do exist, after all, albeit often in extremely difficult circumstances.[58]

'Colonial feminism' does not begin or end with a pro-war position, it is important to note. The spate of 'feminist' wars on Muslim and Arab countries has been accompanied by a general shift in academic feminism's focus

---

[55] See ibid., p. 76.   [56] McElroy (2003).   [57] Al-Ali (2012).

[58] See Elizabeth Miller's 'An open letter to the editors of *Ms.* magazine' of 20 April 2002, condemning the Feminist Majority Foundation's 'representation of its handiwork as having "a foremost role in 'freeing' Afghan women" while failing to mention RAWA's [Revolutionary Association of the Women of Afghanistan] twenty-five-year presence in Afghanistan (indeed, failing to mention RAWA at all), as if they had "single-handedly freed the women of Afghanistan from an oppression that started and ended with the Taliban"' (quoted in Puar 2008, pp. 49–50).

onto the plight of women in non-Western countries, and also the position of women from 'cultural minorities' within liberal states. This way of understanding feminism continues to have purchase even on those who might not accept the idea of invading other countries in the name of either 'feminism' or 'democracy'.[59] A now-familiar topic in political philosophy addresses the question, 'Is multiculturalism bad for women?' (the title question of the influential essay by liberal feminist Susan Moller Okin).[60] This is a strange and unsettling debate, if approached with the expectation that feminist, multiculturalist and anti-racist politics should go hand-in-hand, since what Okin and some others argue is that there is a tension or dilemma as to how one balances a commitment to women's rights (or freedom, or well-being) with a commitment to multiculturalism. The two come into apparent conflict, Okin suggests, when we recognise that many minority or non-Western cultures are 'more patriarchal' and 'illiberal' than the majority cultures of modern Western 'liberal democracies'.[61] On the one hand, many liberals are committed to 'pluralism', 'diversity' and to what they see as an attitude of 'tolerance' towards cultural difference – arguably extending to certain 'illiberal' practices and values. On the other hand, they see themselves as committed to the 'equal moral worth' of all human beings, whether male or female, and regardless of racial or cultural background. Then the worry is that liberal tolerance comes into conflict with feminist ideals, particularly as to the autonomy of women, their freedom to choose their own lifestyle and style of dress, and so on. Minority cultures, it is argued, tend to contain many elements which are deeply patriarchal and 'illiberal' – such as 'honour killings', forced marriage, veiling, segregated prayers, and a whole host of informal social pressures and expectations for women to be submissive, dependent, uneducated and chaste. Many liberals are terrified of the charge of being 'culturally imperialist', but are in equal measure disgusted by the various illiberal, patriarchal and downright violent practices which they associate with immigrants and foreigners. And the great, sprawling and confused debate over 'feminism and

---

[59] Puar (2008, p. 50) talks about liberal US feminists who have 'already foregrounded Islamic fundamentalism as the single greatest violent threat to women'. Despite the fact that many were opposed to the invasion of Afghanistan, they still bought into an 'exceptionalist' narrative (see Lerner 2001).

[60] Okin (1999).   [61] Ibid.

multiculturalism' is the result – the confusion and animosity heightened by the fact that many liberal-feminist critics of 'multiculturalism' do not seem to have made the effort to gain even a relatively basic factual grasp of the nature of some of the cultures and religions they are criticising.[62]

This is not the place to grapple with this debate in any sustained way – and in fact I think the best response to the debate may be to steer clear of it – but I'll just make a couple of general remarks. The debate over 'multiculturalism' and feminism is made a frustrating, deceptive and dangerous one, I believe, by the fact that it proceeds on the basis of premises that are fundamentally ill-defined. When confronting it, the first thing we should ask (since the answer is often unclear) is: 'Are we doing "ideal theory", or are we arguing about what should happen in the world as we know it?' If this is a question of 'ideal theory', I suggest, we should simply walk away. The project is decadent, and also doesn't make much sense: how can we think usefully about the sorts of cultural minorities and practices that would exist in a 'just' world, when in the real (or 'non-ideal') world they are unmistakably marked and shaped by the legacy and ongoing realities of racism and colonialism? If, on the other hand, we understand this as an issue belonging to 'non-ideal theory', I suggest, we should say something similar to what many feminists are saying about military intervention: that women are harmed by racism and social exclusion, still more than men are, and they are harmed again – not helped or 'rescued' – by any policy or influential theoretical tendency which implicitly feeds into a racist and colonialist mindset. Western patriarchal feminism is what is bad for women, as one of Okin's interlocutors points out.[63] It is bad for minority or non-Western women, for the obvious reason that cultural imperialism is bad for those women. And it is bad for white Western women, too, because it serves to divert feminists' attention from the numerous 'non-ideal' aspects of *their* cultures, aspects which are not always recognised as such, but instead mistaken for 'liberation'.[64]

To conclude, the stance of feminism with respect to war and imperialism is mixed, and has always been mixed – something which should really come as no surprise, given the breadth of 'feminism' as a category. It is not so clear that,

---

[62] See the replies to Okin (Okin 1999); cf. Abu-Lughod (2002).   [63] Al-Hibri (1999).
[64] For a careful overview of the issue of multiculturalism, and some useful leads to work by non-Western feminists, see Saul (2003, chapter 9).

as Stanley claims in the passage discussed above, suffragists would have been against drone strikes (insofar as it is possible even to make sense of that sort of counterfactual): Emmeline and Christabel Pankhurst's Suffragettes, at any rate, were pretty gung-ho about the First World War, suspending their usual campaigning activities in order to get behind the war effort. Moreover, the cynical co-option of feminist ideas for military and imperialist ends is also nothing new – as Viner points out, drawing a comparison between Bush's feminist pretences and the hypocrisy of nineteenth-century colonisers:

> The classic example of such a coloniser was Lord Cromer, British consul general in Egypt from 1883 to 1907, as described in Leila Ahmed's seminal *Women and Gender in Islam*. Cromer was convinced of the inferiority of Islamic religion and society, and had many critical things to say on the 'mind of the Oriental'. But his condemnation was most thunderous on the subject of how Islam treated women. It was Islam's degradation of women, its insistence on veiling and seclusion, which was the 'fatal obstacle' to the Egyptian's 'attainment of that elevation of thought and character which should accompany the introduction of Western civilisation,' he said. The Egyptians should be 'persuaded or forced' to become 'civilised' by disposing of the veil. And what did this forward-thinking, feminist-sounding veil-burner do when he got home to Britain? He founded and presided over the Men's League for Opposing Women's Suffrage, which tried, by any means possible, to stop women getting the vote.[65]

Today, as in the past, there are plenty of feminists who oppose the imperialist wars of the US, UK and other Western states, and who are therefore concerned to unmask and resist the co-option of feminist sentiments for pro-war ends. A key feature of the phenomenon of co-option, however, is that it can take multiple and shifting forms, necessitating an attitude of constant vigilance and self-scrutiny on the part of anyone who is serious about being a feminist. Contemporary feminists, it seems to me, must confront not only the edifice of patriarchy, but also two towering, intersecting co-optative structures: imperialism and capitalism. Colonial feminism, as we've seen, is nothing new. What some have begun to call 'capitalist feminism', on the other hand, arguably is. We are not merely talking here about a feminism which is accepting or

---

[65] Viner (2002).

affirmative of a capitalist framework – a characteristic of most 'liberal' feminism, after all – but a 'feminism' that is capitalist in a more aggressive sense: a 'feminism' to be bought and sold.

11.2 A 'feminism' that sells

There are two main aspects to the form of co-option I want to discuss now. The first is something already touched on, in my earlier discussions of a feminist response to pornography and of the distinction between 'reformist' and 'revolutionary' feminisms. This is the reduction of feminism to a series of personal 'lifestyle' decisions. In this instance, what we are confronting is the reduction of feminism to a series of *purchases*. The second, closely related aspect, which has not yet been mentioned, is the use of feminist sentiments, values and rhetoric in order to sell products. Feminism sells, in a double sense: it sells, in the intransitive sense in which we say that *products* 'sell' – as something which can be picked up off the shelf and bought; and it 'sells' as we say that *sellers* sell – it appears as a force or agency which facilitates the sale of things other than itself. Let us now examine these two aspects more closely, starting with the second, 'transitive' sense: the idea of using 'feminism' to sell things.

This phenomenon may be more or less explicit. The crudest example I've seen is probably an advertisement for Canadian tar sands oil,[66] which features women in burkas and describes the horrific practices inflicted on them by the Saudi Arabian government and society, juxtaposing this with the 'ethical oil' that lies beneath the sands of Canada, just waiting to be extracted and enjoyed with a clear conscience by good feminist motorists – that is, extracted through a 'fracking' process which threatens to contaminate local water supplies, and which has been vehemently opposed by Native Canadian communities (as well as by US activists, who have staged large-scale protests against plans to construct a pipeline stretching from Texas to the tar sands in Canada).[67] But there are also legions of examples where products are sold to women on

[66] Available on YouTube: www.youtube.com/watch?v=1SjZlqbDudI (find by typing in 'ethical oil ad').

[67] See 'Tens of thousands rally to stop Keystone XL pipeline & urge Obama to move "forward on climate"', *Democracy Now!* 18 February 2013 at: www.democracynow .org/2013/2/18/tens_of_thousands_rally_to_stop.

the basis that they will empower and/or liberate them, where the rhetoric used to sell these products is, often quite transparently, borrowed from the language and ideas of twentieth-century ('second-wave') feminism: L'Oréal's famous 'Because you're worth it', Revlon's 'revolution in eyelash technology', the injunction to 'stand up to split ends' and so on.

In these latter examples, the phenomenon of the co-option of feminism in order to sell things comes together with the other aspect I wanted to look at: the *reduction* of feminism to individual purchase and consumption. This is not just a matter of: 'Buy this if you're committed to feminist principles!' (the basic pattern at work in the Canadian tar sands case). The message becomes something more dramatic: 'Being a feminist *just is* buying this, that or the other product. This product will make you free – and being free means buying this product!' Feminism, what it stands for and what it strives for, starts to become something that can be simply picked up off the shelf.

What does feminism look like, when it is a 'feminism' that can be bought? The answer, in a word: *cheerful*. There is a kind of aggressive upbeat-ness – simultaneously coerced and coercive – that has come to be characteristic of 'the new feminism', or the third and fourth 'waves'. This is often expressed as a 'myth-busting' project, an effort to get away from stereotypes of feminism as all seriousness and no glamour – when in reality, it is an attempt to get away not from *stereotypes* of feminism, but from feminism itself: women have fought for the right to be serious or hairy if they want to be, just as they have challenged prevailing views as to what is attractive and what is (and is not) funny. As Nina Power says, in response to the 'full-frontal' feminism of Jessica Valenti:

> Valenti's argument is a desperate bid to sell feminism as the latest must-have accessory. Trotting out the tired old line 'I used to think that all feminists were miserable and hairy', Valenti does her very best to sell us her feminist manifesto, in all its faux-radicality: 'liking your body can be a revolutionary act' she concludes, regarding her navel with a curious kind of joy as centuries of political movements that dared to regard the holy body as secondary to egalitarian and impersonal projects crumble to bits around her. Incidentally, for the disproportionate fear that the statistically and historically minimal group of women who were both angry and had hairy legs have inculcated both in their detractors and in their wannabe-successors, we should salute them as often as possible.[68]

---

[68] Power (2009, p. 30).

For Power and others, then, this brand of 'feminism' is (a) *too* 'nice', altogether too unthreatening, (b) basically vacuous and superficial, but also (c) too *bitchy*:

> Slipping down as easily as a friendly-bacteria yoghurt drink, Valenti's version of feminism, with its total lack of structural analysis, genuine outrage or collective demand, believes it has to compliment capitalism in order to effectively sell its product. When she claims that 'ladies, we have to take individual action', what she really means is that it's every woman for herself, and if it is the Feminist™ woman who gets the nicest shoes and the chocolatiest sex, then that's just too bad for you, sister.[69]

It's worth just noting that this combination of smiling vacuousness and a callous, feral, grasping nastiness – especially in the context of competition with other women (for men, above all) – looks suspiciously like a classic patriarchal stereotype of women. Suddenly, this stereotype is identified with the 'up-to-date' manifestation of feminism. As Power is pointing out, the three strands of this new ethos are closely intertwined. For feminism to be as cheerful as this, for it to be all about 'having fun', seems difficult to square with an awareness of the continuing oppression of women: our heads will *need* to be empty of this – devoid of 'structural analysis, genuine outrage or collective demand', as Power puts it; how else could 'feminism' maintain this happy-go-lucky quality? The emptiness here is more profound, however. It is not just a matter of chucking out the anger and the political analysis, leaving a shell-like 'feminism' that amounts to a set of instructions as to what to buy – vibrators, Playboy bunny pendants, shoes and chocolate, for example. At times, even this meagre content seems to evaporate: what we are left with is a message of 'anything goes' – as satirised in an article in the online magazine *The Onion*, 'Women now empowered by everything a woman does'.[70] As Power observes, there is a connection between the radical vacuity of this 'consumer feminism'[71] and a vicious and distinctly un-sisterly brand of self-assertion: 'If feminism is something you define for yourself, then what's to stop it being pure egotism, pure naked greed? Absolutely nothing.'[72]

There is a further strain of 'capitalist feminism' which deserves comment here. Rather than 'consumer feminism', this strain might be termed 'corporate feminism', or the 'boardroom approach', mentioned earlier in this chapter. This is not so much about getting women to buy things, nor about

---

[69] Ibid., p. 30.   [70] *The Onion* (2003).   [71] See Levy (2005).   [72] Power (2009, p. 35).

selling feminism to women, nor about using feminism to sell things. Instead, this is a kind of feminism which identifies liberation for women with being a successful entrepreneur: emancipation for women is a matter of their becoming, in ever greater numbers, the exploiters rather than the exploited under capitalism. At the time of writing, the most prominent example of this is Sheryl Sandberg, obscenely wealthy COO (Chief Operating Officer) of Facebook, whose best-selling book, *Lean in: women, work, and the will to lead*, calls on women to 'lean in' to their careers (which seems to have a meaning somewhere between 'go girl!' and 'grow a pair!'), in order to reach the top positions in terms of wealth and status. This stance, which Eisenstein dubs 'trickle-down feminism',[73] is an especially aggressive form of reformism: it not only leaves the existing system intact; it enjoins women to trample on anyone who gets in their way (including other women) on their route to the top. Moreover, like the 'pull yourself up by your bootstraps' genre more broadly, it implicitly or explicitly blames the majority of us who are not successful entrepreneurs, CEOs or lawyers: we are obviously not 'leaning in' hard enough! As Eisenstein points out, 'most women in our jobs and lives cannot do what we must do to make a living and care for our loved ones without working beyond our limits – standing firm, and stirring things up. Most women – especially those who live in war-torn countries already *"lean in"* to their lives with no choice but to do so.'[74]

In fact, 'trickle-down' feminism is nothing new. Writing in the late 1970s, Ehrlich discusses the problem of 'capitalism in the guise of feminist economic power'.[75] She goes on to discuss the role of the so-called 'Feminist Economic Network' (FEN), ostensibly 'a network of alternative businesses set up to erode capitalism from within by creating economic self-sufficiency for women' – in contrast to Sandberg's style of feminism, which has no such anti-capitalist pretensions. Ehrlich describes FEN's first major project, which opened in Detroit in April, 1976:

> For an annual membership fee of $100, privileged women could swim in a private pool, drink in a private bar, and get discounts in a cluster of boutiques. FEN paid its female employees $2.50 per hour to work there. Its director, Laura Brown, announced this venture as 'the beginning of the feminist economic revolution'.[76]

---

[73] See Eisenstein (2013).   [74] Ibid.   [75] Ehrlich (1977, p. 4).   [76] Ibid., p. 4.

The obvious differences notwithstanding, there are unmistakable parallels between this and the contemporary case of Sandberg and her 'lean in' movement. Sandberg, who is reported to be worth around $1 billion, attracted a certain amount of criticism when in August 2013 she posted an advertisement for an unpaid intern to work for her Lean In Foundation.[77]

To return to the notion of co-option: this was the notion of hijacking-by-absorption, by a body either indifferent or hostile to the interests of what is absorbed. The kinds of 'feminism' discussed in this section may be considered an instance of the co-option of feminism on a grand scale, to the extent that we view capitalism as a system indifferent or hostile to the interests or advancement of women. In fact, I would suggest, it makes sense to see capitalism as *both* hostile *and* indifferent to women (as it is to human beings in general, for that matter): it is hostile precisely through its indifference. As Power puts it: 'Capitalism, which in a sense knows no morals (or at least can change them easily), couldn't care less about the positive, happy, "feminist" reclaiming of sex so long as it makes a buck out of skimpy nightwear and thongs.'[78] However, just as some feminists have seen war and imperialism as inherently patriarchal phenomena, many feminists – including Marxists, non-Marxist socialists and social anarchists – have seen capitalism as inextricably bound up with the oppression of women in particular. If these feminists are right, it should be no surprise to find that the co-option of feminism by capitalism often looks very much like the co-option of feminism by patriarchy itself.

So much for the false faces of feminism. There is a popular saying, which goes back to the Jewish religious leader of the first century BC, Hillel the Elder:[79] 'If not you, then who? If not now, then when?' At this point in the book, perhaps – having said a lot about what feminists should *not* do, but little about what they should – an inevitable question is: 'If not *that*, then what?'

---

[77] For instance, Dowd (2013) denounced Sandberg as 'tone-deaf to the problems average women face'.

[78] Power (2009, p. 32).

[79] He is also known for 'Hillel's sandwich': a sandwich of lettuce or horseradish, which is meant to facilitate a 'moral migration from wickedness to virtue'.

12 Goodbye to all that . . .

To pre-empt disappointment, I should say now that I really have very little idea what is to be done, and I don't intend to pull some stillborn rabbit out of a hat here. But I suppose I have to say something, by means of a parting shot. These final comments are the best I can do, for now.

In January 1970, during a temporary women's takeover of the magazine *Rat*, Robin Morgan published a statement under the heading 'Goodbye to all that' – a sustained railing against 'the friends, brothers, lovers in the counterfeit male-dominated Left':

> Let's run it down. White males are most responsible for the destruction of human life and environment on the planet today. Yet who is controlling the supposed revolution to change all that? White males (yes, yes, even with their pasty fingers back in black and brown pies again). It could just make one a bit uneasy. It seems obvious that a legitimate revolution must be led by, made by those who have been most oppressed: black, brown, yellow, red, and white *women* – with men relating to that the best they can. A genuine Left doesn't consider anyone's suffering irrelevant or titillating; nor does it function as a microcosm of capitalist economy, with men competing for power and status at the top, and women doing all the work at the bottom (and functioning as objectified prizes or *coin* as well). Goodbye to all that . . .
>
> Goodbye, goodbye forever, counterfeit Left, counterleft, male-dominated cracked-glass mirror reflection of the Amerikan Nightmare. Women are the real Left. We are rising, powerful in our unclean bodies; bright glowing mad in our inferior brains; wild hair flying, wild eyes staring, wild voices keening; undaunted by blood we who hemorrhage every twenty-eight days; laughing at our own beauty we who have lost our sense of humor; mourning for all each precious one of us might have been in this one living time-place had she not been born a woman; stuffing fingers into our mouths to stop the screams of fear and hate and pity for men we have loved and love still; tears in our eyes

and bitterness in our mouths for children we couldn't have, or couldn't not have, or didn't want, or didn't want yet, or wanted and had in this place and this time of horror. We are rising with a fury older and potentially greater than any force in history, and this time we will be free or no one will survive. *Power to all the people or to none.* All the way down, this time.[1]

Of course, that was then, and this is now. It is not 'the Left' (or what remains of it) that is our biggest problem at the moment, in my view, but a mainstream that seeks to make 'feminism' its own, whilst betraying it with everything it says and does.

We could do worse, each of us, than to compose a 'Goodbye' of our own, a statement of what it is that we do *not* want to be and to work with, if we are to be feminists. In a way, that's what I've tried to do in this book. I've tried to identify some of the main threats facing feminism today, and I've suggested that crucial among these are threats of co-option – more important, perhaps, even than explicit opposition. So my Goodbye could run something like this:

> *Goodbye to 'boardroom feminism', to 'consumer feminism', to a feminism that has sold its soul and has nothing more to offer women than the 'liberation' that capitalism already offers them, a 'liberation' through endless consumption fuelled by endless dissatisfaction for all the wrong reasons. Goodbye to a feminism with blood on its hands, a feminism that seeks to 'rescue' women by killing and deforming them and their children. Goodbye, too, to John Stuart Mill – while we are on the subject of colonialism – and goodbye to the burden of endless gratitude we are expected to feel for him, the infinite patience with which we are required to endure his turgid prose. Goodbye to a brainless cerebral feminism that forgets that women have acted as well as spoken, and must act still. Goodbye to the Veil of Ignorance. Goodbye to false friends (and to false enemies, too)...*

It's a shame that our enemies are not so sensitive as to be vanquished by goodbyes alone, but the exercise can be instructive, even so. Saying what feminism should not, cannot be, is already to say quite a lot about what it *should*, *must* be. Skirting the contours of a positive image of feminism by describing what it is *not* to be, Angela Davis calls for

> a feminism that does not capitulate to possessive individualism, a feminism that does not assume that democracy requires capitalism, a feminism that is bold and willing to take risks, a feminism which fights for women's rights

---

[1] Morgan (1971; original emphasis).

while simultaneously recognizing the pitfalls of the formal 'rights' structure
of capitalist democracy... this feminism does not say that we want to fight
for the equal right of women to participate in the military, for the equal right
of women to torture, or for their equal right to be killed in combat.[2]

If we must talk about a 'way forward', then – and I guess we must – it is
a way forward that is best defined negatively, in terms of the places we do
not want to go. But one of the most consistent themes of what has been said
here is that the pitfalls, obstacles and threats to be avoided are not static, but
dynamic and constantly shifting. Not that imperialism or capitalism show
any signs of either going away or releasing their grip on 'feminism'; but the
forms that these systems and their co-optative strategies take are necessarily
and constantly evolving and mutating. The way forward, in that case, can be
nothing more fixed or definite than the ever-changing spaces between the
ever-changing places we have to navigate around; and to navigate effectively,
we need a feminism that is flexible and pluralistic without being empty.

As a kid, I used to pride myself on my 'crowd-dodging', the art of weaving
among moving bodies as fast as possible without collision. As feminists, we
need to move with the agility of a child, constantly readjusting ourselves to the
gaps that open and close before us on our way, steering clear of obstructions
and traps, but also with the critical self-consciousness of a woman. Not exactly
the self-consciousness that has been instilled in us, though – an insatiable
appetite for youth and slimness and desirability and self-hatred – but the kind
of self-consciousness that persists in the face of the greatest efforts to crush it
out of us – a defiant sense of ourselves as agents and centres of consciousness,
as beings restless and resolute in our determination to understand the world,
each other and ourselves.

It is no foregone conclusion that there even *is* a way forward, I should add.
Those who have recently begun to point to a 'plateau' or slowing of the limited
progress that arose from the demands of 'second-wave' feminism may well be
right.[3] But there is something to be said for the tempering of the pessimism
of the intellect by the optimism of the will – at least from the point of view of
individual sanity. And as feminists know better than most, to *say* something
is always also to *do* something. In the context of a feminism understood not
as 'every woman for herself', but as a collective struggle against the status

[2] Davis (2008, p. 21).   [3] See e.g. Porter (2013).

quo, a struggle understood as inseparable from the struggles against the violence inflicted upon human beings (whatever their gender) by an imperialist, white-supremacist capitalism – however threatened, imperfect, dormant, or even largely imaginary those struggles may currently be – a declaration of hopelessness is not only an act of surrender but also of betrayal.

References

Abu-Lughod, Lila. 2002. 'Do Muslim women really need saving? Anthropological reflections on cultural relativism and its others', *American Anthropologist* 104(3), pp. 783–90.

Ackelsberg, Martha. 2005. *Free Women of Spain: Anarchism and the struggle for the emancipation of women*. Oakland, CA, and Edinburgh: AK Press.

Adorno, Theodor. 1974 [1951]. *Minima Moralia*, trans. E. F. N. Jephcott. London: New Left Books.

Al-Ali, Nadje. 2012. 'Why I am here?', in Stellan Vinthagen, Justin Kenrick & Kelvin Mason (eds.), *Tackling Trident: Academics against weapons of mass destruction*, pp. 261–5. London: Irene Publishing.

Al-Hibri, Azizah. 1999. 'Is Western patriarchal feminism bad for third world / minority women?', in Susan Moller Okin, *Is Multiculturalism Bad for Women?*, pp. 41–6. Princeton University Press.

Allen, Mike. 1995. 'A meta-analysis summarizing the effects of pornography II: Aggression after exposure', *Human Communication Research* 22, pp. 258–83.

Allen, Pamela. 1970. *Free Space: A perspective on the small group in women's liberation*. New York: Times Change Press.

Anarchist Editorial Collective (Iain McKay, Gary Elkin, Dave Neal, Ed Boraas). 2009. *An Anarchist FAQ*, version 13.1. Available at: http://theanarchistlibrary.org/library/the-anarchist-faq-editorial-collective-an-anarchist-faq.pdf. Accessed 03/03/2015.

Anger, Jane. 1589. *Her Protection for Women*. London: Printed by Richard Jones and Thomas Orwin. Available at: http://digital.library.upenn.edu/women/anger/protection/protection.html. Accessed 27/02/2015.

Appiah, Kwame Anthony & Gutmann, Amy. 1998. *Color Conscious: The political consciousness of race*. Princeton University Press.

Arendt, Hannah. 1970. *On Violence*. New York: Harcourt Brace & Co.

Baginski, Max. 1907. 'Stirner: "The Ego and His Own"', *Mother Earth* 2(3), pp. 142–51.

Baier, Annette. 1995. *Moral Prejudices*. Harvard University Press.

Bakunin, Mikhail. 1867. 'Power corrupts the best'. Available at: www.marxists
    .org/reference/archive/bakunin/works/1867/power-corrupts.htm.   Accessed
    03/03/2015.
    1964. *The Political Philosophy of Bakunin: Scientific anarchism*, ed. Grigorii Petrovich
    Maksimov. New York: Freedom Press.
    1971. *Bakunin on Anarchy: Selected works by the activist-founder of world anarchism*,
    ed. Sam Dolgoff. New York: Vintage.
Bateson, Gregory. 1972. *Steps to an Ecology of Mind*. University of Chicago Press.
Bebel, August. 1879/1910. *Women and Socialism*. Available at: www.marxists.org/
    archive/bebel/1879/woman-socialism/index.htm?utm_source=lasindias.info.
    Accessed 03/03/2015.
Beneke, Timothy. 1982. *Men on Rape*. New York: St Martin's.
Benston, Margaret. 1969. 'The political economy of women's liberation', *Monthly
    Review* 21(4).
Bergmann, Barbara. 1986. *The Economic Emergence of Women*. New York: Basic Books.
Berlin, Isaiah. 1970 [1958].'Two concepts of liberty', in his *Four Essays on Liberty*.
    Oxford University Press.
Bernstein, R. 2001. 'Guilty if charged', in Linda LeMoncheck & James P. Sterba (eds.),
    Sexual Harassment: Issues and answers, pp. 187–93. Oxford University Press.
Bettcher, Talia Mae. 2009. 'Trans identities and first-person authority', in Laurie J.
    Shrage (ed.), *'You've changed': Sex reassignment and personal identity*, pp. 98–120.
    Oxford University Press.
Bingham, John. 2013. 'Britain's married minority', *The Telegraph*, 12
    October. Available at: www.telegraph.co.uk/women/sex/divorce/10373894/
    Britains-married-minority.html. Accessed 02/03/2015.
Brossard, N., Guilbeault, L. & Wescott, M. 1980. *Some American Feminists*. Available
    at: www.youtube.com/watch?v=8_JjyxPUPfU. Accessed 03/03/2015.
Buffett, Mary. 2013. 'Sheryl Sandberg's *Lean In* and the rise of fourth wave fem-
    inism', *The Huffington Post*, 19 March. Available at: www.huffingtonpost.com/
    mary-buffett/lean-in_b_2902325.html. Accessed 03/03/2015.
Burgess-Jackson, Keith. 1999. *A Most Detestable Crime: New philosophical essays on rape*.
    New York: Oxford University Press.
Butler, Judith. 1990. *Gender Trouble: Feminism and the subversion of identity*. New York:
    Routledge.
    2004. *Undoing Gender*. New York: Routledge.
Califia, Pat. 1994. *Public Sex*. Pittsburgh, PA: Pleis.
Carby, Hazel. 1997. 'White woman listen!', in Rosemary Hennessy & Chrys Ingra-
    ham (eds.), *Materialist Feminism: A reader in class, difference, and women's lives*,
    pp. 110–28. New York: Routledge.

Card, Claudia. 1996. 'Against marriage and motherhood', *Hypatia* 11(3), pp. 1–23.
2007. 'Gay divorce: thoughts on the legal regulation of marriage', *Hypatia*, 22(1), pp. 24–38.

Chalabi, Mona. 2013. 'Single fathers: UK statistics', *The Guardian*, 13 June. Available at: www.theguardian.com/news/datablog/2013/jun/13/single-fathers-uk-statistics. Accessed 02/03/2015.

Chew, Huibin Amelia. 2008. 'What's left? After "imperial feminist" hijackings', in Robin L. Riley, Chandra Talpade Mohanty & Minnie Bruce Pratt (eds.), *Feminism and War: Confronting US imperialism*, pp. 75–90. London: Zed Books.

Chomsky, Noam. 2003. *Hegemony or Survival*. London: Hamish Hamilton.

Clark, M. M. 2001. 'The Silva case at the University of New Hampshire', in Linda LeMoncheck & James P. Sterba (eds.), *Sexual Harassment: Issues and answers*, pp. 194–206. Oxford University Press.

Cohen, G. A. 1978. *Karl Marx's Theory of History: A defence*. Oxford: Clarendon Press.

Cohn, Jesse. 2009. 'Anarchism and gender', in Immanuel Ness (ed.), *The International Encyclopedia of Revolution and Protest*. Hoboken, NJ: Wiley-Blackwell.

Collins, Gail. 2013. 'Arms and the women', in *The New York Times*. Print edition 24 January; available at: www.nytimes.com/2013/01/24/opinion/collins-arms-and-the-women.html?_r=0. Accessed 03/03/2015.

Combahee River Collective. 1983. 'The Combahee River Collective Statement', in Barbara Smith (ed.), *Home Girls: A Black feminist anthology*, pp. 264–74. New York: Kitchen Table/ Women of Color Press.

Cooper, Rachel. 2002. 'Disease', *Studies in History and Philosophy of Biological and Biomedical Sciences* 33(2), pp. 263–82.

Corcoran, Clodagh. 1987. *Take Care! Preventing childhood sexual abuse*. Dublin: Poolbeg Press.

Cott, Nancy. 1987. *The Grounding of Modern Feminism*. New Haven, CT: Yale University Press.

Crenshaw, Kimberlé. 1991. 'Mapping the margins: intersectionality, identity politics, and violence against women of color', *Stanford Law Review* 43(6), pp. 1241–99.

Cronan, Sheila. 1973. 'Marriage', in Anne Koedt, Ellen Levine & Anita Rapone (eds.), *Radical Feminism*, pp. 213–22. New York: Quadrangle Books.

Dahl, Robert. 1957. 'The concept of power', *Behavioral Science* 2, pp. 201–15.

Dalla Costa, Mariarosa & James, Selma. 2012. 'The power of women and the subversion of the community' in Selma James, *Sex, Race, and Class: The perspective of winning: a selection of writings 1952–2011*. Oakland, CA: PM Press/Common Notions.

Davis, Angela. 2008. 'A vocabulary for feminist praxis: on war and radical critique', in Robin L. Riley, Chandra Talpade Mohanty & Minnie Bruce Pratt (eds.), *Feminism and War: Confronting US imperialism*, pp. 19–26. London: Zed Books.

Debord, Guy. 1994. *Society of the Spectacle*. New York: Zone Books.

Dines, Gail. 2010. *Pornland*. Boston: Beacon Press.

Dolgoff, Sam. 1974. *The Anarchist Collectives*. New York: Free Life Editions.

Donnerstein, E., Linz, D. & Penrod, S. 1987. *The Question of Pornography: Research findings and policy implications*. New York: Free Press.

Doughty, Steve. 2012. 'Britain has two million single parent families with majority of children raised by mother alone', *Daily Mail*, 20 January. Available at: www.dailymail.co.uk/news/article-2089144/Britain-million-single-parent-families-majority-children-raised-mother-alone.html. Accessed 02/03/2015.

Douglass, Frederick. 1857. 'If there is no struggle, there is no progress', speech delivered at Canandaigua, New York, on 3 August. Available online at: www.blackpast.org/1857-frederick-douglass-if-there-no-struggle-there-no-progress#sthash.66jc4Su1.dpuf. Accessed 28/02/2015.

Dowd, Maureen. 2013. 'Pompom girl for feminism', *New York Times* (Sunday Review, op-ed pages), 23 February. Available at: www.nytimes.com/2013/02/24/opinion/sunday/dowd-pompom-girl-for-feminism.html. Accessed 03/03/2015.

Dowell, LeiLani. 2008. 'Violence against women: the US war on women', in Robin L. Riley, Chandra Talpade Mohanty & Minnie Bruce Pratt (eds.), *Feminism and War: Confronting US imperialism*, pp. 219–23. London: Zed Books.

Dries, Kate. 2013. 'The many misguided reasons famous ladies say "I'm not a feminist"', *Jezebel* 11/02/13. Available at: http://jezebel.com/the-many-misguided-reasons-famous-ladies-say-im-not-a-1456405014. Accessed 27/02/2015.

Dworkin, Andrea. 1974. *Woman Hating*. New York: Plume (Penguin).

   1987. *Intercourse*. New York: Basic Books.

   1989. *Pornography: Men possessing women*. New York: Plume (Penguin).

Dworkin, Andrea & MacKinnon, Catharine. 1994. 'Statement by Catharine A. MacKinnon and Andrea Dworkin regarding Canadian customs and legal approaches to pornography', press release, 26 August. Available at: www.nostatusquo.com/ACLU/dworkin/OrdinanceCanada.html. Accessed 04/03/2015.

   1998. *In Harm's Way: The pornography civil rights hearings*. Cambridge, MA: Harvard University Press.

Dworkin, Ronald. 2000. *Sovereign Virtue: The theory and practice of equality*. Cambridge, MA: Harvard University Press.

Eagleton, Terry. 2011. *Why Marx Was Right*. Yale University Press.

Ehrlich, Carol. 1977. 'Socialism, anarchism & feminism'. Louisville Anarchist Federation. Available at: http://imaginenoborders.org/pdf/zines/Feminism.pdf. Accessed 02/03/2015.

Einsiedel, Edna. 1992. 'Effects of pornography on the average individual', in Catherine Itzin (ed.), *Pornography: Women, violence, and civil liberties*. New York: Oxford University Press.

Eisenstein, Zillah. 2008. 'Resexing militarism for the globe', in Robin L. Riley, Chandra Talpade Mohanty & Minnie Bruce Pratt (eds.), *Feminism and War: Confronting US imperialism*, pp. 27–46. London: Zed Books.

2013. '"Leaning in" in Iraq: women's rights and war?', *Al Jazeera*, 23 March. Available at: www.aljazeera.com/indepth/opinion/2013/03/2013323141149557391.html. Accessed 03/03/2015.

Elshtain, Jean Bethke & Tobias, Sheila (eds.). 1990. *Women, Militarism, and War: Essays in history, politics, and social theory*. Savage, MD: Rowman & Littlefield.

Elster, Jon. 1986. *An Introduction to Karl Marx*. Cambridge University Press.

Engels, Frederick. 1844. *The Origin of the Family, Private Property and the State*. Available at: www.marxists.org/archive/marx/works/1884/origin-family/. Accessed 02/03/2015.

Engels, Friedrich. 1993. *Socialism: Utopian and scientific*. London: Bookmarks.

Ettelbrick, Paula. 2004 [1989]. 'Since when is marriage a path to liberation?', *Out/look: National Lesbian and Gay Quarterly*, 6(9), pp. 14–17; reprinted in Andrew Sullivan (ed.), *Same-Sex Marriage: Pro and con*, pp. 122–8. New York: Vintage.

Everywoman. 1988. *Pornography and Sexual Violence: evidence of the links: the complete record of public hearings for experts, witnesses and victims of sexual assault involving pornography*. London: Everywoman.

Faludi, Susan. 1993. *Backlash: The undeclared war against women*. London: Vintage.

2013. 'Death of a revolutionary', *The New Yorker*, 15 April. Available at: www.newyorker.com/magazine/2013/04/15/death-of-a-revolutionary. Accessed 03/03/2015.

Fausto-Sterling, Anne. 1993. 'The five sexes: why male and female are not enough', *The Sciences* 33, pp. 20–4.

2000a. *Sexing the Body: Gender politics and the construction of sexuality*. New York: Basic Books.

2000b. 'The five sexes: revisited', *The Sciences*, July/August, pp. 18–23.

2003. 'The problem with sex/gender and nature/nurture', in S. J. Williams, L. Birke & G. A. Bendelow (eds.), *Debating Biology: Sociological reflections on health, medicine and society*, pp. 123–32. London and New York: Routledge.

Federici, Silvia. 1975. *Wages against Housework*. Bristol: Power of Women Collective and Falling Wall Press.

Federici, Silvia & Gago, Verónica. 2015. 'Witchtales: an interview with Silvia Federici', *Viewpoint Magazine*, 15 April. Available at: https://viewpointmag.com/2015/04/15/witchtales-an-interview-with-silvia-federici/. Accessed 17/04/2015.

Ferguson, Michaele. 2010. 'Choice feminism and the fear of politics', *Perspectives on Politics* 8(1), pp. 247–53.

Fineman, Martha. 1995. *The Neutered Mother, the Sexual Family and Other Twentieth Century Tragedies*. New York: Routledge.

Finlay, Barbara. 2006. *George W. Bush and the War on Women: Turning back the clock on progress*. London: Zed Books.

Finlayson, Lorna. 2014a. 'How to screw things with words', *Hypatia* 29(4), pp. 774–89.

   2014b. 'On mountains and molehills: problems, non-problems, and the ideology of ideology', in *Constellations: An international journal of critical and democratic theory* 22(1), pp. 135–146.

   2015. *The Political Is Political: Conformity and the illusion of dissent in contemporary political philosophy*. London: Rowman & Littlefield .

Firestone, Shulamith. 1971. *The Dialectic of Sex: The case for feminist revolution*. London: Cape.

Folbre, Nancy. 1994. *Who Pays for the Kids? Gender and the structures of constraint*. New York: Routledge.

Forna, Aminatta. 1992. 'Pornography and racism', in Catherine Itzin (ed.), *Pornography: Women , violence, and civil liberties*, pp. 102–13. New York: Oxford University Press.

Foucault, Michel. 1980. *The History of Sexuality*, vol. 1: *An Introduction*, trans. Robert Hurley. New York: Vintage.

   1985. *The History of Sexuality*, vol. 2: *The Use of Pleasure*. New York: Pantheon.

   1986. *The History of Sexuality*, vol. 3: *The Care of the Self*. New York: Pantheon.

Fox News. 2013. 'Military leaders lift ban on women in combat roles', 24 January. Available at: www.foxnews.com/politics/2013/01/24/panetta-opens-combat-roles-to-women/. Accessed 04/03/2015.

Frankfurt, Harry. 2005. *On Bullshit*. Princeton, NJ: Princeton University Press.

Freeman, Jo. 1976. 'Trashing: the dark side of sisterhood', *Ms.* magazine, April, pp. 49–51, 92–8. Available at: www.jofreeman.com/joreen/trashing.htm. Accessed 05/03/2015.

   1983. 'The building of the gilded cage', in Anne Koedt, Ellen Levine & Anita Rapone (eds.), *Radical Feminism*, pp. 127–50. New York: Quadrangle Books.

Friedan, Betty. 2013 [1963]. *The Feminine Mystique*. New York: W. W. Norton.

Frye, Marilyn. 1983. *The Politics of Reality*. Berkeley, CA: Crossing Press.

Geuss, Raymond. 2008. *Philosophy and Real Politics*. Princeton University Press.

2011. 'Raymond Geuss on freedom of speech at the occupation'. Available at: www.youtube.com/watch?v=xz6TVGyQ_FA. Accessed 03/03/2015.

Gilligan, Carol. 1982. *In a Different Voice: Psychological theory and women's development*. Cambridge, MA: Harvard University Press.

Godwin, William. 1986. *The Anarchist Writings of William Godwin*, ed. Peter H. Marshall. London: Freedom Press.

Goldberg, Michelle. 2014. 'What is a woman? The dispute between radical feminism and transgenderism', *The New Yorker*, 4 August. Available at: www.newyorker.com/magazine/2014/08/04/woman-2. Accessed 26/02/2015.

Goldman, Emma. 1897. 'Marriage', *The Firebrand*, 18 July.

1969 [1910]. *Anarchism and Other Essays*. New York: Dover.

2003. *A Documentary History of the American Years*, ed. Candace Falk. Berkeley, Los Angeles and London: University of California Press.

Goldman, Emma & Most, John. 2008/2009. 'Talking about anarchy', *Black Flag* 228, p. 28.

Guérin, Daniel (ed.). 1997. *No Gods, No Masters: An anthology of anarchism*, trans. Paul Sharkey. Oakland, CA, and Edinburgh: AK Press.

Hald, Gert *et al.* 2010. 'Pornography and attitudes supporting violence against women: revisiting the relationship in nonexperimental studies', *Aggressive Behaviour* 36(1), pp. 14–20.

Halwani, Raja. 2003. *Virtuous Liaisons*. Peru, IL: Open Court.

Hanisch, Carol. 1970. 'The personal is political', in Shulamith Firestone & Anne Koedt (eds.), *Notes from the Second Year: Women's liberation: Major writings of the radical feminists*, pp. 76–78. New York. Also available online at: www.carolhanisch.org/CHwritings/PIP.html. Accessed 03/03/2015.

Haraway, Donna. 2004. 'Ain't (Ar'n't) I a woman, and inappropriate/d others: the human in a post-humanist landscape', in *The Haraway Reader*, pp. 47–61. New York and London: Routledge.

Harding, Luke. 2004. 'The other prisoners', *The Guardian* online, 20 May. Available at: www.theguardian.com/world/2004/may/20/iraq.gender. Accessed 04/03/2015.

Harris, Paul. 2013. 'Women in combat: US military officially lifts ban on female soldiers', *The Guardian*, 25 January. Available at: www.theguardian.com/world/2013/jan/24/us-military-lifts-ban-women-combat. Accessed 04/03/2015.

Haslanger, Sally. 2005. 'What are we talking about? The semantics and politics of social kinds', *Hypatia* 20(4), pp. 10–26.

2012. 'Gender and race: (what) are they? (what) do we want them to be?', in *Resisting Reality*. New York: Oxford University Press.

Hennessy, Rosemary. 2003. 'Class', in Mary Eagleton (ed.), *A Concise Companion to Feminist Theory*, pp. 53–72. Malden, MA: Blackwell.

Hill Collins, Patricia. 1998. 'It's all in the family: intersections of gender, race, and nation', *Hypatia* 13(3), *Border Crossings: Multicultural and Postcolonial Feminist Challenges to Philosophy (Part 2)*, pp. 62–82.

2000. *Black Feminist Thought: Knowledge, consciousness, and the politics of empowerment* (2nd edition). New York: Routledge.

Hobbes, Thomas. 1985 [1641]. *Leviathan*. New York: Penguin Books.

Hochschild, Arlie. 1989. *The Second Shift: Working parents and the revolution at home*. New York: Viking Press.

hooks, bell. 1981. *Ain't I a Woman? Black women and feminism*. Cambridge, MA: South End Press.

2000a [1984]. *Feminist Theory: From margin to center*. Cambridge, MA: South End Press.

2000b. *Feminism Is for Everybody: Passionate politics*. Cambridge, MA: South End Press.

Horkheimer, Max. 1999 [1937]. 'Traditional and critical theory', in M. O'Connell (ed.), *Critical Theory: Selected essays*, pp. 188–243. New York: Continuum.

Hyde, H. Montgomery. 1964. *A History of Pornography*. London: Heinemann.

Ibn Qayyim al-Jawziyya. 1998. *Zad al-Ma'ad*. Beirut: Al-Risalah.

ISNA (Intersex Society of North America). 1993–2008. 'What is intersex?' Available at www.isna.org/faq/what_is_intersex. Accessed 22/02/15.

Itzin, Catherine (ed.). 1992. *Pornography: Women, violence, and civil liberties*. New York: Oxford University Press.

Jaggar, Alison. 1983. *Feminist Politics and Human Nature*. Lanham, MD: Rowman & Littlefield.

al-Jahez, Abu Uthman. 1964. *Rasa'il al-Jahiz*, ed. Abd al-Salam Harun. Cairo: Maktabat al-Khanji.

Jeffreys, Sheila. 2003. *Unpacking Queer Politics: A lesbian feminist perspective*. Cambridge: Polity.

2008. *The Industrial Vagina: The political economy of the global sex trade*. Abingdon: Taylor & Francis.

Jenkins, Katharine. Forthcoming. 'Amelioration and inclusion: gender identity and the concept of *woman*', *Ethics*.

Kanazawa, Satoshi & Perina, Kaja. 2009. 'Why do so many women experience the "imposter syndrome"?', *Psychology Today*, 13 December. Available at: www.psychologytoday.com/blog/the-scientific-fundamentalist/200912/why-do-so-many-women-experience-the-imposter-syndrome. Accessed 04/03/2015.

Kappeler, S. 1992. 'Pornography: the representation of power', in Catherine Itzin (ed.), *Pornography: Women, violence, and civil liberties*, pp. 88–101. New York: Oxford University Press.

Kavka, Misha. 2002. 'Feminism, ethics, and history, or what is the "post" in "post-feminism?' *Tulsa Studies in Women's Literature* 21(1), pp. 29–44.

Kempton, Sally. 1970. 'Cutting loose', *Esquire* 74, pp. 53–7.

Khan, Shahnaz. 2008. 'Afghan women: the limits of colonial rescue', in Robin L. Riley, Chandra Talpade Mohanty & Minnie Bruce Pratt (eds.), *Feminism and War: Confronting US imperialism*, pp. 161–78. London: Zed Books.

Kingston, Drew *et al.* 2009. 'The importance of individual differences in pornography use: theoretical perspectives and implications for treating sexual offenders', *Journal of Sexual Research* 46(2–3), pp. 216–232.

Kittay, Eva. 1999. *Love's Labor*. New York: Routledge.

Kornegger, Penny. 1975. 'Feminism: the anarchist connection'. Available at: http://theanarchistlibrary.org/library/peggy-kornegger-anarchism-the-feminist-connection.pdf. Accessed 03/03/2015.

Kropotkin, Peter. 1897. *Anarchist Morality*. Available at: www.marxists.org/reference/archive/kropotkin-peter/1897/morality.htm. Accessed 03/03/2015. Also published 1921 as *Anarchist Morality: sow seeds around you*. London: Freedom Press.

   1970. *Selected Writings on Anarchism and Revolution*, ed. Martin A. Miller. Cambridge, MA: MIT Press.

Langton, Rae. 1993. 'Speech acts and unspeakable acts', *Philosophy and Public Affairs* 22(4), pp. 293–330. Reprinted in *Sexual Solipsism*, Oxford University Press, 2009.

Leeds Revolutionary Feminist Group. 1981. 'Love your enemy? The debate between heterosexual feminism and political lesbianism'. London: Onlywomen Press.

Lenin, Vladimir. 1969 [1902]. *What Is to Be Done?* New York: International Publishers Co.

   1972 [1919].'Letter to Sylvia Pankhurst', in Lenin, *Collected Works*, vol. 29, 4th English edition, pp. 561–66. Moscow: Progress Publishers. Also available at: www.marxists.org/archive/lenin/works/1919/aug/28.htm#fw01. Accessed 03/03/2015.

Lerner, Sharon. 2001. 'What women want: feminists agonize over war in Afghanistan', *Village Voice*, 6 November.

Levy, Ariel. 2005. *Female Chauvinist Pigs: Women and the rise of raunch culture*. New York: Simon and Schuster.

Lovelace, Linda (with Grady, M). 1980. *Ordeal*. Seacaucus, NJ: Citadel Press.

Lukes, Steven. 1987. *Marxism and Morality*. Oxford: Oxford University Press.

Luscombe, Belinda. 2014. 'Why 25% of millennials will never get married'. *Time*, 24 September. Available at: http://time.com/3422624/report-millennials-marriage/. Accessed 02/03/2015.

MacKinnon, Catharine. 1979. *Sexual Harassment of Working Women: A case of sex discrimination*. New Haven, CT: Yale University Press.

1987. *Feminism Unmodified*. Cambridge, MA: Harvard University Press.

1989. *Toward a Feminist Theory of State*. Cambridge, MA: Harvard University Press.

1994. *Only Words*. London: HarperCollins. First published in the USA in 1993 by Harvard University Press.

2012. 'Preface' to Ishani Maitra & Mary Kate McGowan (eds.), *Speech and Harm*. Oxford University Press.

MAKERS. 2013. 'MAKING HISTORY: Catharine MacKinnon Works to Legally Define Sexual Harassment', video online at: www.makers.com/blog/making-history-catharine-mackinnon-works-legally-define-sexual-harassment. Accessed 01/03/2015.

Malamuth, N. M., Addison, T. & Koss, M. 2000. 'Pornography and sexual aggression: are there reliable effects and can we understand them?', *Annual Review of Sex Research* 11, pp. 26–91.

Malatesta, Errico. 1965. *Errico Malatesta: His life and ideas*, ed. Vernon Richards. London: Freedom Press.

1995. *The Anarchist Revolution*, ed. Vernon Richards. London: Freedom Press.

Malos, Ellen (ed.). 1975. *The Politics of Housework*. New York: The New Clarion Press.

Marcuse, Herbert. 1965. 'Repressive tolerance', in Robert Paul Wolff, Barrington Moore & Herbert Marcuse, *A Critique of Pure Tolerance*, pp. 85–123. Boston: Beacon Press.

1968. 'Postscript 1968', in *A Critique of Pure Tolerance*, paperback edition. Boston: Beacon Press.

Marx, Karl. 1873. 'Afterword to the Second German Edition'. Available at: www.marxists.org/archive/marx/works/1867-c1/p3.htm. Accessed 03/03/2015.

1875. *Critique of the Gotha Programme*. Available at: www.marxists.org/archive/marx/works/1875/gotha/. Accessed 03/03/2015.

1967 [1844] *Economic and Philosophic Manuscripts*, reprinted in L. D. Easton & K. H. Guddat (eds. and trans.), *Writings of the Young Marx on Philosophy and Society*. New York: Anchor Books.

Marx, Karl & Engels, Frederick. 1987 [1932]. *The German Ideology*. London: Lawrence & Wishart.

1998 [1848]. *The Communist Manifesto*. London: Verso.

McElroy, Damien. 2003. 'Home abortions soar in Iraq as unwanted pregnancies rise', *The Telegraph*, 26 October. Available at: www.telegraph.co.uk/news/worldnews/middleeast/iraq/1445160/Home-abortions-soar-in-Iraq-as-unwanted-pregnancies-rise.html. Accessed 04/03/2015.

McElroy, Wendy. 1995. *XXX: A woman's right to pornography*. New York: St Martin's Press.

Mies, M. & Shiva, Vandana. 2014. *Ecofeminism*. London: Zed Books.

Mikkola, Mari. 2012. 'Feminist perspectives on sex and gender', in Edward N. Zalta (ed.), *The Stanford Encyclopedia of Philosophy* (Fall 2012 edition). Available at: http://plato.stanford.edu/archives/fall2012/entries/feminism-gender/.

Mill, Harriet Taylor. 1998. *The Complete Works of Harriet Taylor Mill*, ed. Jo Ellen Jacobs. Bloomington: Indiana University Press.

Mill, John Stuart. 2006 [1869]. *On Liberty and the Subjection of Women*. London: Penguin.

Millbank, Lisa. 2011. 'The gender ternary: understanding transmisogyny', blogpost available at: https://radtransfem.wordpress.com/2011/12/12/genderternary-transmisogyny/. Accessed 27/02/15.

Millett, Kate. 1969. *Backlash*. University of Illinois Press.

Mills, Charles. 1998. *Blackness Visible: Essays on philosophy and race*. Ithaca, NY: Cornell University Press.

  2005. '"Ideal Theory" as ideology'. *Hypatia* 20(3), pp. 165–84.

Mohr, Richard D. 2005. *The Long Arc of Justice: Lesbian and gay marriage, equality, and rights*. New York: Columbia University Press.

Morgan, Robin (ed.). 1970. *Sisterhood Is Powerful*. New York: Random House.

  1971. *Goodbye to All That*. Pittsburgh, PA: KNOW Inc.

Morris, Steven. 2009. 'Ducks like water study "waste of £300,000 taxpayers' money"'. www.theguardian.com/science/2009/may/20/research-proves-ducks-like-water. Accessed 03/03/2015.

Morrison, Sarah. 2013. 'Special report: Intersex women speak out to protect the next generation', *The Independent*, 30 November. Available at: www.independent.co.uk/news/uk/home-news/special-report-intersex-women-speak-out-to-protect-the-next-generation-8974892.html. Accessed 24/02/15 .

Musallam, Basim. 1983. *Sex and Society in Islam*. Cambridge University Press.

Nadar, Carol. 2002. 'Women and children main casualties of war', *The Age*, 4 October. Available at: www.theage.com.au/articles/2002/10/03/1033538723853.html. Accessed 04/03/2015.

Nechayev, Sergey. 1869. 'The revolutionary catechism'. Available at: www.marxists.org/subject/anarchism/nechayev/catechism.htm. Accessed 03/03/2015.

Nicholson, L. 1994, 'Interpreting gender', *Signs* 20, pp. 79–105.

1998. 'Gender', in A. Jaggar & I. M. Young (eds.), *A Companion to Feminist Philosophy*, pp. 289–97. Malden, MA: Blackwell.

Nielson, S. 1988. 'Books bad for women: a feminist looks at censorship', in G. Chester and J. Dickey (eds.), *Feminism and Censorship: The current debate*, pp. 17–25. Bridport, Dorset: Prism.

Nochlin, Linda. 2007. *Courbet*. London: Thames & Hudson.

Okin, Susan Moller. 1989. *Gender, Justice and the Family*. New York: Basic Books.

1999. *Is Multiculturalism Bad for Women?* Princeton University Press.

Orwell, George. 2001. *Orwell in Spain*, ed. Peter Davison. London: Penguin.

Oshana, Marina. 2006. *Personal Autonomy in Society*. Aldershot: Ashgate.

Painter, Nell Irwin. 1996. *Sojourner Truth: A life, a symbol*. New York: W. W. Norton.

Palac, Lisa. 1995. 'How dirty pictures changed my life', in A. M. Stan (ed.), *Debating Sexual Correctness*, pp. 236–52. New York: Delta.

Phillips, Joshua. 2005. 'Unveiling Iraq's teenage prostitutes', *Salon.com*, 24 June. Available at www.salon.com/2005/06/24/prostitutes_4/. Accessed 04/03/2015.

Pisan, Christine de. *The Book of the City of Ladies*. Available at: http://history.hanover.edu/courses/excerpts/165pisan.html. Accessed 27/02/2015.

Porter, Eduardo. 2013. 'For American women, is it enough to lean in?', *New York Times*, 24 September.

Power, Nina. 2009. *One-Dimensional Woman*. Ropley, Hants: Zero Books.

Preves, Sharon. 2008. 'Intersex narratives: gender, medicine, and identity', in Abby L. Ferber (ed.), *Sex, Gender and Sexuality: The new basics (an anthology)*, pp. 32–42. New York: Barnes & Noble.

Puar, Jasbir. 2008. 'Feminists and queers in the service of empire', in Robin L. Riley, Chandra Talpade Mohanty & Minnie Bruce Pratt (eds.), *Feminism and War: Confronting US imperialism*, pp. 47–55. London: Zed Books.

Rajczi, Alex. 2008. 'A populist argument for same-sex marriage', *The Monist* 91(3–4), pp. 475–505.

Rawls, John. 2005 [1971]. *A Theory of Justice*. Cambridge, MA: Harvard University Press.

Raymond, Janice. 1979. *The transsexual empire: The making of the she-male*. Boston: Beacon Press.

1994. *The transsexual empire: The making of the she-male*. Re-issued with a new introduction on transgender. New York: Teachers College Press.

Rich, Adrienne. 1980. 'Compulsory heterosexuality and lesbian existence', *Signs* 5(4), pp. 631–60.

Riley, Robin L., Mohanty, Chandra Talpade & Pratt, Minnie Bruce. 2008. 'Introduction: feminism and US wars – mapping the ground', in Riley, Mohanty

& Pratt (eds.), *Feminism and War: Confronting US imperialism*, pp. 1–16. London: Zed Books.

Rocker, Rudolf. 1938. *Anarchosyndicalism*. London: Secker & Warburg.

2005. *The London Years*. Nottingham/Oakland, CA: Five Leaves Publications/AK Press.

Rosen, Michael. 1996. *On Voluntary Servitude: False consciousness and the theory of ideology*. Cambridge, MA: Harvard University Press.

Rossi, Alice. 1973. *The Feminist Papers: From Adams to de Beauvoir*. Lebanon, NH: Northeastern University Press.

Rubin, Gayle. 1993. 'Misguided, dangerous and wrong: an analysis of anti-pornography politics', in Alison Assiter & Avedon Carol (eds.), *Bad Girls and Dirty Pictures*, pp. 18–40. London: Pluto Press.

Russell, Diana. 1992. 'Pornography and rape: a causal model', in Catherine Itzin (ed.), *Pornography: Women, violence, and civil liberties*, pp. 310–49. New York: Oxford University Press.

1993. 'Introduction', in Diana Russell (ed.), *Making Violence Sexy: Feminist views on pornography*, pp.1–20. Buckingham: Open University Press.

Sandberg, Cheryl. 2013. *Lean in: Women, work, and the will to lead*. London: W. H. Allen.

Satz, Debra. 2013. 'Feminist perspectives on reproduction and the family', in Edward N. Zalta (ed.), *The Stanford Encyclopedia of Philosophy* (Winter 2013 edition), http://plato.stanford.edu/archives/win2013/entries/feminism-family/.

Saul, Jennifer Mather. 2003. *Feminism: Issues and arguments*. New York: Oxford University Press.

Sax, Leonard. 2002. 'How common is intersex? A response to Anne Fausto-Sterling', *Journal of Sex Research* 39(3), pp. 174–8.

Scales, Ann. 2000. 'Avoiding constitutional depression: bad attitudes and the fate of Butler', in Drucilla Cornell (ed.), *Feminism and Pornography*, pp. 318–44. New York: Oxford University Press.

Schluesser, Jennifer. 2013. 'A star philosopher falls, and a debate over sexism is set off', *New York Times*, 2 August. Available at: www.nytimes.com/2013/08/03/arts/colin-mcginn-philosopher-to-leave-his-post.html. Accessed 03/03/2015.

Schneir, Miriam. 1995. *Feminism*. London: Vintage.

1996. *Historical Feminism*. London: Vintage.

Schultz, V. 1998. 'Reconceptualizing sexual harassment', *Yale Law Journal* 107, pp. 1683–1805.

Scott, Joan W. 2010. *The Politics of the Veil*. Princeton University Press.

Segal, Lynne. 1990. 'Pornography and violence: what the "experts" really say', *Feminist Review* 36, pp. 29–41.

Shumway, Chris. 2004. 'Pattern emerges of sexual assault against women held by US forces', *New Standard News*, 6 June. Available at: http://newstandardnews.net/content/?action=show_item&itemid=478. Accessed 04/03/2015.

Sifferlin, Alexandra. 2014. 'Women are still doing most of the housework', *Time* magazine. Available at: http://time.com/2895235/men-housework-women/. Accessed 01/02/2015.

Sivard, Ruth. 1996. *World Military and Social Expenditures*. Leesburg, VA: WMSE Publications.

Solomon, Deborah. 2009. 'Fourth-wave feminism: questions for Jessica Valenti', *New York Times* magazine, 13 November. Available at: http://www.nytimes.com/2009/11/15/magazine/15fob-q4-t.html. Accessed 03/03/2015.

Spargo, Tasmin. 1999. *Foucault and Queer Theory*. New York: Totem Books.

Spector, Jessica. 2006. *Prostitution and Pornography*. Stanford University Press.

Spelman, Elizabeth. 1988. *Inessential Woman*. Boston: Beacon Press.

Staff and agencies. 2013. 'Gender pay gap stands at 15%'. *The Guardian*. Available at: www.theguardian.com/money/2013/nov/07/gender-pay-gap-official-figures-disparity. Accessed 21/02/15.

Stanley, Tim. 2013. 'The Pentagon allows women to fight on the front line: when did feminism become pro-war?' *The Telegraph* blog. Available at: http://blogs.telegraph.co.uk/news/timstanley/100199981/the-pentagon-allows-women-to-fight-on-the-front-line-when-did-feminism-become-pro-war/. Accessed 01/03/2015.

Stavri, Zoe. 2015. 'And they've replaced page 3 with something far worse', blog post at *Another Angry Woman*, 20 January. Available at https://stavvers.wordpress.com/2015/01/20/and-theyve-replaced-page-3-with-something-far-worse/. Accessed 01/03/2015.

Steinem, Gloria. 1984. *Outrageous Acts and Everyday Rebellions*. London: Fontana.

Stoljar, Natalie. 2000. 'The politics of identity and the metaphysics of diversity', in D. Dahlstrom (ed.), *Proceedings of the 20th World Congress of Philosophy*, 21–30. Bowling Green State University.

Stone, Alison. 2007. *An Introduction to Feminist Philosophy*. Cambridge: Polity Press.

Strossen, Nadine. 1996. *Defending Pornography: Free speech, sex and the fight for women's rights*. London: Abacus.

Stychin, Carl. 2005. 'Being gay', *Government and Opposition* 40, pp. 90–109.

Swain, Dan. 2012. *Alienation*. London: Bookmarks.

Sweet, Corinne. 1992. 'Pornography and addiction: a political issue', in Catherine Itzin (ed.), *Pornography: Women, violence, and civil liberties*, pp. 179–200. New York: Oxford University Press.

The Onion. 2003. 'Women now empowered by everything a woman does', 19 February. www.theonion.com/articles/women-now-empowered-by-everything-a-woman-does,1398/. Accessed 04/03/2015.

Thompson, Denise. 2001. *Radical Feminism Today*. London: Sage.

June 2003/February 2004. 'Introduction to refereed papers'. Blogpost available at: http://users.comcen.com.au/~deniset/brefpap/aintrorefpap.htm. Accessed 01/03/2015.

Tolstoy, Leo. 1900. 'On anarchy'. The Anarchist Library. Available at: http://theanarchistlibrary.org/library/leo-tolstoy-on-anarchy.pdf. Accessed 03/03/2015.

Valenti, Jessica. 2007. *Full-Frontal Feminism*. Berkeley, CA: Seal Press.

Vega, Vanessa & Malamuth, Neil. 2007. 'Predicting sexual aggression: the role of pornography in the context of general and specific factors', *Aggressive Behaviour* 33, pp. 104–17.

Viner, Katharine. 2002. 'Feminism as imperialism', *The Guardian*, 21 September. Available at: www.theguardian.com/world/2002/sep/21/gender.usa.

Vogel, Lise. 1995. *Woman Questions: Essays for a materialist feminism*. New York: Routledge.

Wajcman, Judy. 2004. *TechnoFeminism*. Cambridge: Polity Press.

Walker, Alice. 1990. 'Definition of womanist', in Gloria Anzaldúa (ed.), *Making Face, Making Soul: Haciendo Caras*. San Francisco: Aunt Lute Books.

Weaver, James. 1992. 'The social science and psychological research evidence: perceptual and behavioural consequences of exposure to pornography', in Catherine Itzin (ed.), *Pornography: Women, violence, and civil liberties*, pp. 284–309. New York: Oxford University Press.

Weitzman, Lenore. 1985. *The Divorce Revolution: The unexpected social and economic consequences for women and children in America*. New York: Free Press.

Wilchins, Riki. 2004. *Queer Theory, Gender Theory: An instant primer*. Los Angeles: Alyson.

Williams, Bernard (ed.). 1981. *Obscenity and Film Censorship: An abridgement of the Williams Report*. New York: Cambridge University Press.

Williams, Reginald. 2011. 'Same-sex marriage and equality', *Ethical Theory and Moral Practice*, 14(5), pp. 589–95.

Williams, Sally. 2009. 'My four mums', *The Guardian*, 4 July. Available at: www.theguardian.com/lifeandstyle/2009/jul/04/feminism-communes-children. Accessed 01/02/2015.

Willis, Ellen. 1981. *Beginning to See the Light: Pieces of a decade*. New York: Knopf.

Wilson, Charlotte. 2000 [1921]. *Anarchist Essays*, ed. Nicholas Walter. London: Freedom Press.

Wolff, Jonathan. 2003. *Why Read Marx Today?* Oxford University Press.

Wolff, R. P. 1970. *In Defense of Anarchism.* Harper & Row.

Wollstonecraft, Mary. 2004 [1792]. *A Vindication of the Rights of Women.* London: Penguin.

Young, Iris Marion. 1990. *Justice and the Politics of Difference.* Princeton University Press.

2005. *Throwing Like a Girl and Other Essays.* New York: Oxford University Press.

Zalesne, Deborah. 1999a. 'Sexual harassment law: has it gone too far, or has the media?', *Temple Political and Civil Rights Law Review* 8(2), pp. 351–76.

1999b. 'Workplace paranoia: media propaganda', *Women's International Net* 21 (May).

Zetkin, Clara. 1984 [1896]. 'Only in conjunction with the proletarian woman will socialism be victorious', pamphlet reprinted in Zetkin, *Selected Writings*, ed. Philip S. Foner, trans. Kai Schoenhals. New York: International Publishers.

Zillman, Dolf. 1989. 'Effects of prolonged consumption of pornography', in D. Zillman & J. Bryant (eds.), *Pornography: Research advances and policy considerations*, pp. 127–57. Hillsdale, NJ: Erlbaum.

Žižek, Slavoj. 2009. *Violence: Six sideways reflections.* London: Profile.

Index